IN MY FATHER'S SHADOW

A MEMOIR

~

Marcelle Mignault-Strong

© 2013 by Marcelle Mignault-Strong

All rights reserved

ISBN: 978-1495292828

ISBN: 1495292827

Printed in the United States of America

*To my son Bruce, and my daughter-in-law
Christina, and their children Severn and
Laurence-Archer, and to my daughters Michèle,
Dominique, and Claudia, and her daughters
Sophia, Michelle, and Jordan I dedicate this
memoir.*

CONTENTS

A letter to my family and to my friends

I want to take advantage of the publication of this book to express my gratitude to ma famille Québecoise for their support.

Many texts would have remained unwritten but for the help of cousine Louise Chaurette and her husband Phillipe Angrignon who gave me family photos, and newspaper clippings from 1937 describing the centennial celebration honoring our Patriots. Renée Chaurette inspired me to write the story of Uncle Achille's somersault in the church main aisle, by telling me the story with as much humor as Uncle Achille would have demonstrated, if he had been the teller. In the family tradition Jacqueline Chaurette-Paquin answered pages of questions and offered new knowledge into family lore. Pierrette Wooley, grand-daughter of Uncle Arthur and Aunt Marie-Louise Sauvé, wrote pages enlightening me about the family connection with the Mignault.

Without the help of Mireille Pagé, daughter of Dr. Pagé of Saint Benoit and Alice Mignault, Papa's oldest sister, and Mireille's husband, Paul Dufresne, the relation between Malvina Filiatrault, second wife of my great-grandfather the "Old Doctor Mignault" with Marie-Louise Sauvé, and my dear Grand- maman Alphonsine Rhéaume would have remained a mystery. It is now a novella resting in a file drawer, waiting to be resuscitated. To my new and wonderful friend Marie Rolland merci for the lovely surprise of her find regarding Uncle Jean Charbonneau, le poète, and for reading an early version of the manuscript and her suggestions.

The memories of my growing up in Saint-Eustache were reinforced when my friend Lise Pesant and her husband Claude Lethiec invited me to spend two weeks with them at their home in Saint-Eustache, situated near the house where I grew up, and facing the river I always loved. Lise shared with me her memories, and showed me postcards of Saint-Eustache, taken in the early nineteen hundreds, as a promotion for her grand fathers' hotel. I could then visualize the village into which my parents moved in 1926. On that same trip I had the pleasure of spending time with Laurent Calame, a friend of the tennis club period. Tennis was no more part of the conversation; however, we discovered a common liking in music: lieders and some great interpreters of the genre. But Laurent, an architect by trade also was interested in the preservation of our heritage. With him I visited Oka and its relics of the eighteen hundreds, and of course came back with a round of Oka Cheese. During the same trip, a stay at my dear friend Claudine Thibodeau not only brought many memories back but I was delighted to find in her a very productive writer who shares with the community her love of poetry inviting a new generation to embrace the craft.

I cannot forget our dear cousin, l'abbé Maurice Mignault, not only for his knowledge of the family genealogy of old, but keeper of more recent happenings. We could count on him and his brother Dr Gérard Mignault, sons of Uncle Gustave, a younger brother of Papa, to join the enlarged family Mignault when one of us had called it a day. I regret to have known so little about that wonderful family.

Without the guidance and talent of many writers from the Pacific Coast to the Gulf of Mexico my memoir would not have been published. In California, I joined two wonderful writing groups and still cherish a friendship with Judie Rae. I expect, mixed with news of her family and friends, to hear about some of her poems or short stories being published, while inciting me into sending mine to publishing houses.

In Florida, I joined The Florida South West Writers. I owe a debt of gratitude to its founder Ginnie Ward and to the members of the group: Luci Bailey, Beverly Miller, Barbara Peer, Diane Burt, Barbara Altenburg, Jesse Phillips and our dear Betty Kuyper, all of them bringing different shades of talent and experience. A special thank you to my friend Beverly Miller who, while keeping an eye on a sleeping patient, edited chapter after chapter of my story. I am indebted to Hana Whitfield for her invaluable help, thoroughness, and love of the craft, always protecting the "foreign voice" of the author even in an English tour de phrase. A special thanks to Ginnie Ward and Luci Bailey for reading the original manuscript we thought of as the finished product. However, since then, some thirty chapters were added; some of them part of the second tome to follow.

To my niece Louise, my nephews Jean, Raymond and Louis, I offer this story where you will meet the child Suzanne you have not known, but who already showed at a young age the qualities you admired in her as a mother. You may also discover a different grandfather than the one you knew and loved. The image you still carry in your memory is nonetheless true. He was a multi faceted man.

I cannot close this letter without acknowledging ma chère cousine France Mignault Labbé, who both gave me encouragement, but also many hours of pleasure reading her poetry or prose. To the other cousins and friends of my generation Lyse Mignault-Banville-Acard, and Jeannine Leblanc-Mignault and André Mignault and of a younger one, Louise Wooley and Geneviève Labbé who have been looking in old boxes to find photos and send their treasures: I love you all dearly. However, none of this would see the light of day as a book without the devotion of two friends dedicated to bringing this writer to put a final period and gave them the task of turning a manuscript into a book. Dear Lisa and Jesse Phillips, a heartfelt thank you.

Grand merci à Marie Rolland et cousin Serge Labrecque, son of Jacques and grandson of Aunt Berthe and Uncle Charlie, who for two weeks took me away from the heat of Florida to soak in a perfect Autumn Québecois, from the Laurentian Mountains where they live, to Saint-Eustache, and to a trip to Papa's hunting grounds, the Mountains of Oka and Saint-Joseph. Marie and Serge had ordered a perfect day and it appeared dress in red, ocher, and gold under a cloudless blue sky. In Montréal as in Saint-Eustache I had the immeasurable pleasure of spending time with family and friends I had not seen since 1997; a memory enriched by the photos taken by Serge.

I must acknowledge the contribution of my husband Don Strong, who after hearing me vocalize for decades, encouraged my new found "quieter talent" and typed my stories until he could no longer. At sixty five years old, I finally learned how to type, for at an early age I had decided on a singing career, and why on earth would I need to know how to type? ... Ah, the dreamer!

You may wonder how I can remember so much. The conversations around the dinner table when Aunt Berthe, Uncle Charlie and Grand-maman Rhéaume came to visit were lessons on how to build a repertoire of memories. I heard the same stories many times. And as the Mignault, the Sauvé, and the Rhéaume where joined through the old grandmother Mignault, I heard the same stories through a different point of view. My memories increased when as a child sitting at the kitchen table I watched Maman iron or cook while she told me stories about her youth. At the end of her life through the hours of keeping her company she answered my questions about events in her life I could not recall. She also revealed a secret she had kept to herself those many years, a secret the young Marcelle had known only partially as told in the chapter The Threat.

In my memoir each chapter has a truthful core from which I build the story. But, as the daughter of Louis "the great story teller" I have learned that stories are kept alive not only with memory but with the imagination of the story teller.

I hope you enjoy our collective project.

With all my affection,

Marcelle

CHAPTER ONE

LEAVING HOME

Saint-Eustache, 1936

Not long after he left, we prepared for our move away from Saint-Eustache, the only home I had ever known. Maman dried her tears, made phone calls to Montréal, found a boarding school for Suzanne, my older sister, and an apartment in the city. Every day she cleaned and scrubbed and washed and packed and served the meals on time, still drying the inopportune tear.

Harried, and carried on waves of events I could not understand as a five-year-old, and being told more than once to move out of the way, I left the tension and busyness of the household, and ran outdoors with my doll.

Once in my quiet world I watched the water recede from our lower terrace unveiling the cement wall that separates our property from La Rivière des Mille-Îles. I peered at the nascent green through the lawn's winter burn and roamed around in the field next door looking for spring flowers under the long dried grasses. If the sun shone bright and hot, I would stretch myself on the still damp ground to gaze at a canopy of new leaves bursting from their winter sleep; giant elms coiffed with feathery greens. There I would let my imagination carry me away to a land where mothers shed no tears and fathers were present at night to tell stories and lull their children to sleep.

Already eight years old, Suzanne, like me, did not know the reason for our father's absence, and why we had to leave our home and village. We heard whispers and snippets of conversation between Maman and her family, but her reticence at revealing the problems in her marriage must have left even the phone operator begging for more details. We knew our usually light-hearted mother cried a lot, that for over a month Papa had not been home for dinner, and that Tellie, our English setter, no longer waited for him at the front door. We pretended not to watch for his return. But I still did.

The only advantage to our father's absence was that every morning Suzanne and I no longer had to eat a horrible soft-boiled egg too too soft that slid up and down the throat until launched to its destination with a swallow of milk. When home, Papa had insisted we eat at least one each day, a must for good health.

The father of our days might have been an intransigent figure; however, the father who walked in our bedroom at bedtime wore a different cloak: the mantle of the poet, the beloved storyteller. I missed that special hour when one night he lay on my bed, the next on Suzanne's, and delighted us with his tales of old, his voice and gestures adding unforgettable pictures in our minds…but he was gone, and so were our moments of expectation and wonder. And later on so was Tellie, and we did not know where.

On the day we left for Montréal, I played outdoors as usual.

"Please, don't dirty your dress or your shoes," Maman admonished me. "And, do *not* go in the field."

So I stayed in the driveway pushing my doll's carriage up and down the incline to the street. Once, as I drew nearer to the house, I heard the phone.

3

Maybe it's Papa calling. Maybe he will say that it's all a big mistake, and that he's going to stay with us forever!

I grabbed my doll and ran into the house as fast as I could. But no, Maman was saying, "*Non,* Louis is gone, and we are leaving in an hour or so...*Merci,* Gabrielle...Yes, I also wish it were otherwise. Good-bye." When I heard Maman say Louis, my heart flipped. Nevertheless, even before it settled, I knew she had been talking to Papa's sister. I stood next to her hoping...not too sure for what.

She hung up the receiver and looked past me, her eyes brimming with tears. She went about scrubbing the sink that already sparkled, and telling my sister, "Suzanne, put this here, that in the other suitcase, please."

Neither of them paid attention to me. I felt as dejected as if she had spanked me, yet she had not even looked at me.

I rushed to my bedroom. On the way, the sight of two bags of discards on the floor between my parents' bedroom and ours intrigued me. I stopped. I had to inspect them. I sat my doll on the floor. In the first bag I found no treasures, only cigars and pipes, tobacco, rocks

4

and a stack of Natural History magazines. In the other, a creamy yellow colored material appeared. I pulled and pulled to see what it was: a suit, and underneath, more material of the same color, maybe a coat. I carried the jacket in one arm and dragged the bag to the kitchen.

"Maman Margot," I called. She liked us to use her first name, and when I wanted to make her especially happy, that is what I did. "Maman Margot," I repeated, "Why is the yellow suit in the trash bag? Can I keep it?"

"Put it back where you found it! Right now."

"But ..."

"Now."

The forbidding tone of her voice cut me off. I had visualized an Easter coat for Suzanne and one for me made from all that material. Reluctantly, I nudged the suit back in the bag; a sleeve hung limp over the side.

I picked up my doll sitting against the frame of my bedroom door, tucked her in my arms, walked in, and lay on the bed. I could not understand why Maman did not store the yellow outfit in the trunk with other discarded suits and dresses.

Every year, two or three discarded outfits started a

5

new life. Sometimes a dress lost its bodice and a skirt appeared. A round neckline saw a new day as a v-neck, a bow removed, piping added, buttons were upgraded; hems went up or down depending on the fashion of that year. Seams were taken in or let out, mostly the latter, except when the garment was for Maman who kept a slim figure. My aunts called the remade garments, *Version Number Two* or *Version Number Three*. Often they joked remembering one of the versions that did not quite meet their fashionable standards.

With nothing else to do I tried to remember some of Papa's stories, but like everything else around me, they became entangled: words that belonged to one story slid into the other, and characters got lost in unknown landscapes. So I stared at the cream and rose-striped wallpaper with its floral border and my eyes drifted to the ceiling light fixture that had been there since my last birthday.

The wood-hanging lamp was made in the shape of a little girl sitting on a swing; like a two-foot paper doll cutout. Uncle Charlie painted her to look like me, blonde hair and blue eyes, the same blue as her puffed-sleeve dress, and on her cheeks a permanent blush. Her arms stretched out to the cords, her tiny hands holding on tightly; on each side, under the seat, hung a light bulb in a milk glass globe.

That day I saw my precious lamp with the eyes of a rescuer. "Uncle Charlie made it for my birthday," I muttered, "and I won't leave it here!" I stood up on my bed and tried to grab it, but my arms did not reach. Frustrated, I thrust myself upward and instead landed on the hardwood floor with a thump and a scream. Maman rushed in, followed by Suzanne. They picked me up. Too proud to cry, I defiantly faced them and waited.

"Marcelle, what do you think you're doing?"

"I want to bring my little girl swing with me."

"You can't. I already told you."

"Why not? It's mine."

With patience, she told me yet again. It annoyed me because she kept telling me the same thing: "It will make a hole in the ceiling." I did not care. The thought that the renters would believe the little girl on the swing was theirs distressed me.

They can put up their own light. The sentence hung at the edge of my lips.

7

"Let's have lunch," Maman said, "and then we'll be ready to go." I jerked myself from her embrace and shouted, "I don't want to!"

Maman lost patience. She dragged me to the kitchen and sat me forcefully at the table. Humiliated, I refused to eat. With a quick swing of my legs, I wriggled out of the chair and ran back to my room. When Maman caught up with me, I was firmly hanging onto the window curtains facing the river, my river. With jaws as tight as my fists, I dared to say, "I'm staying here."

"Marcelle! Let go!" Maman tried to pry my fingers open. "That—is—enough!"

I knew I could not hold on much longer. In one last effort I shouted, "I'm staying with Papa." Maman's nerves snapped. Her hand hit the side of my head with a blow. My fingers lost their grip. I crumpled to the floor.

Maman and Suzanne knelt, their arms surrounding my shaking body, sobs lifting their chests in cadence with mine. Maman dried my face, kissed me and went back to the kitchen. Suzanne helped me up. Like a miniature mother, she held my hand. Her long, dark eyelashes kept her tears half-concealed. I saw them, but it was her smile that made me hold on to her hand. For the first time that day I felt safe.

From the kitchen, as if nothing had happened, Suzanne and I heard the familiar refrain, "Girls, the soup is getting cold." For a fleeting moment a feeling of normalcy returned. Even on this gloomy day of dislocation, a lukewarm meal would not do.

After lunch, Maman sent me to the living room to wait for Uncle Charlie who offered to drive us to Montréal. I did not mind being alone and away from Maman's, "Hurry, hurry!"

Walking by my bedroom, I saw my lamp from the corner of my eye. My stomach squeezed itself into a ball and I hurried to the dining room, which also served as a sitting area.

The afternoon sun shone through the French doors' sheer curtains, brightening the dark colors of my parents' comfortable chairs where they sat at night. Papa read *Le Devoir*, a nationalistic newspaper, and Maman, pencil and Larousse at hand, did the crossword puzzles and perused the theater and music critics. During the school year Suzanne and I joined them. We sat at the dining-room table to study and fill pages and pages of homework to satisfy our strict teachers. The library atmosphere of the room lifted when Papa turned on the radio for concerts to *French Radio Canada*, the only station he allowed.

Even through this upheaval, Maman kept everything tidy; our coats hung on the backs of three chairs, and in front of each, on the table, lay their respective hats and gloves one more sign of our imminent departure. I averted my eyes and kept on walking through the archway to the living room.

Instinctively, I climbed into my father's favorite chair. He liked to sit and smoke his pipe while enjoying the sunset through the large picture window. I often sat on his lap to watch with him, or listened to a story. On that moving day, the feeling of warmth and comfort from Papa's nearness had vanished. The lowered shades blocked the outdoors and my gaze rested on Grand-maman's old piano. The day before, Suzanne had washed its yellowed ivory keys and I dusted the nooks and crannies of all the carvings. With the lid closed it looked like a macabre monument.

I wondered if the renters had a little girl of my age. *Maybe, if they do, she will sit on the floor and hide under the keyboard between the pillars as I used to, and pretend they are the entrance to a mysterious castle.*

10

I could not explain why something in me wanted it to be so and why again, my stomach did not like the idea. Could it be that my heart inhabited the little girl sitting between the pillars of the castle, but my head saw only the intruder?

My eyes had moved away from the piano to the empty brown tiled fireplace and to the bookcases on each side still containing rows of cream and gold hardbacks. I could not tell if Maman had boxed my book, "La Fontaine's Fables." I chose not to move, adding my own punishment to the one inflicted by my parents.

"Marcelle where are you?"

I guessed my silence unnerved Maman. "I'm sitting in the living room, in Papa's chair."

"Please, stay there until your Uncle arrives."

"Alright, I will." Three words uttered with as little enthusiasm as possible, yet loud enough to be heard.

For the last time, I looked around the living room decorated mostly in shades of brown: the elm woodwork, the fireplace tiles, the gargoyles, and a hunting scene in a tall tapestry. My eyes stopped at the stained glass windows, an oasis of light and color on either side of the fireplace. Growing up it did not occur to me that only the front windows' sheer curtains distinguished it from a room in a gentleman's private club.

I heard wheels crunch on the loose pebbles in the driveway, and a door slam—Uncle Charlie's signature. Aunt Berthe, Maman's older sister who was Uncle Charlie's wife, would not come because we needed a lot of space in the car.

I loved Aunt Berthe. She had a kind smile and gentle manner, for a child a reassuring presence. If one had asked me which of the two I preferred, I could not say. She was like a gentle river, and he, like a wide lake bristling to the smallest breeze.

Unlike his wife who had had the advantage of good schooling, Uncle Charlie did not. When he moved with his family from the United States to the mostly French speaking Province de Québec, he abandoned his studies to help them in the running of their new venture—a farm. Outwardly proper, under the surface of respectability he tried to maintain, there lay a roughness that from time to time warped its veneer.

I heard Papa say more than once, "Charlie is like a tornado, loud and fast. He never sits still. It's not surprising Berthe is ill." But I thought not, he was too much fun to make anyone sick. To me he was perfect: joyful, energetic, ready to fix that which was broken or anything else looking out of kilter. And best of all, he had made a lamp with a swinging girl and a teeter totter with a sculpted horse's head at each end—their ears the prop Suzanne and I held onto while we swung. Indeed no one could have convinced me that Uncle Charlie was less than perfect.

Hearing the quick thump of his steps on the veranda, I struggled out of the deep chair and managed to reach the vestibule before he rang the bell and opened the outside door. I hugged him. He bent over and kissed the top of my head.

"Well, Blondie, where is everyone?"

The tap, tap sound of Maman's heels preceded her greeting.

"Here we are. Thanks for coming, Charlie."

"Oh, I was in the neighborhood."

Maman smiled. Montréal was at least twenty miles from Saint-Eustache, but she said nothing. Suzanne, waiting patiently at her side, ran into Uncle Charlie's opened arms.

"All right now, ladies. Enough kisses and hugs for a day. Let's get organized."

His instructions, like his steps, came quickly and without hesitation. Suzanne and I soon wore out our usefulness and were told to wait in the car while Uncle Charlie arranged the trunk space.

Maman went back and forth into the house, always for a last check. Each time she came to the car, I stared at the tiny streaks on her cheeks where tears had furrowed through rouge and powder. When she finally joined us, I saw no more streaks; only blotches where she must have patted her face with a handkerchief. She handed me my doll without saying a word. *Merci*, did not come close to my lips, and after she had turned around, I let my doll slip to the floor. Silent, Suzanne frowned.

The car, like a steel box of sealed secrets, enclosed us in silence until it shivered under the forceful closing of the trunk lid. In a second Uncle Charlie shouted: "All aboard! Here we go!"

I sat at the edge of the seat looking at what we were leaving. I saw a wedge of the river, then the tops of the giant elms spreading their branches over the roof of our

14

white stucco house. My last glance embraced the long rows of poplars lining the walkway. I slumped into my seat. Through the side window, I saw only sky and treetops, all going away and never coming back.

We turned onto my favorite street, rue Saint-Louis, its trees forming a harbor of shades and songs; few nests survived the snows and northern gales, but it was spring, and soon there would be new nests, birds singing and chirping; from each side of the street a greeting of branches, a rustling of leaves; the arching roof always in motion.

Below this unrolling wonder, I imagined and heard the daily tap-tapping of heels on pavement, the steely rumble of roller skates deftly jumping over the root-torn sidewalks, the clop-clopping of Monsieur Richer's two muscular horses laboring under the weight of an ice load, and the clop-clippety-clop of Monsieur Vannier's spirited horse pulling a harvest of fruit and vegetables; my village symphony. I could not yet fathom how much I would miss it all.

I sat straighter to embrace all I could see. I knew how the street would look once foliage and flowers covered the poverty of the little whitewashed houses, their gardens and crooked fences. But, for the time being,

15

geraniums, petunias and nasturtiums grew in aluminum cans, seedlings of hope on windowsills.

The wheels of the car hit the first wooden plank of the rickety bridge over the lazy Rivière du Chêne; Uncle Charlie slowed down. I sat on the edge of my seat, my doll abandoned on the floor. A few days before my father left, I stood on the bridge with him. He lifted me in his arms and together we watched ice crashing against the moving ice floats of our river. But, on the day we left, the ice was gone—and so was he.

We left the wobbly planks for smoother pavement. The presbytery, the church, the school, the manor house all wrapped in gray stone, went by one by one. It was the end of our village; there was nothing else to watch.

Maman at a picnic 1925

Papa, Maman, Suzanne, Marcelle
on Uncle Charlie's Teeter Totter

CHAPTER TWO

AND THIS IS MONTRÉAL!

As soon as we left Saint-Eustache, I picked up my doll from the floor. Wriggling into the corner of the seat, I held her tightly against me. My eyes refused to stay open, and an hour later I awoke to the bustling noises of the city.

After many turns and grumbles of annoyance from Uncle Charlie, who found fault with most drivers, he pulled into a driveway shaped like a half moon and stopped in front of a tall apartment building. Seeing the expanse of cement and stone, my chest tightened at the grayness of it all. I felt the same panic I had experienced when we left our home.

Uncle Charlie imitating a train conductor shouted, "Alright everybody! The train stops here. Ladies and gentlemen don't forget your luggage, your sandwiches, and your galoshes!"

Suzanne and I exploded in laughter. Even Maman's face broke into her beautiful smile. Uncle Charlie had once more lifted the gloom. How I loved him!

"All right," he went on, "Enough giggling for a day. Let's get to work. You too Blondie, grab a bag!"

"I will, Uncle Charlie. I will."

I tried. But I could not climb the first giant step. Still giggling, Suzanne pushed me from behind. Maman went in with us, turned on the few lights she could find, and then returned to the car to get more bags.

The strangeness of the new place prickled my curiosity and I went exploring. I peeked in the first door at the left of the entrance and my mouth dropped open.

"What sort of a kitchen is this?" I muttered. "I can't sit here and watch Maman bake or iron. There's just no room." Maman had always complained about our kitchen at home, but this one looked like a narrow passageway. Except for a wood icebox, everything else looked like the inside of a hospital: glossy white. My mouth dropped when I saw hanging from a wall a table, barely big enough to accommodate a butter plate and a doughnut hole.

Maman and Suzanne came in carrying boxes. "Please, Marcelle, move out of the way," Maman pleaded. They backed up and let me out.

I went to explore down the dark hallway. Behind me, I heard Suzanne laugh. I turned around to see why. She had tried to squeeze herself and a box past Maman and got stuck in the middle. I chuckled, and continued down the corridor, which for a moment of gaiety appeared less forbidding. I followed it to where it fanned out. A bare light bulb hung over a round table that showed signs of age and many owners, and tucked underneath, three chairs of the same vintage. At my left I opened a door to a large room furnished with two beds and two bureaus. *It must be Suzanne's and my bedroom.* I thought.

I crossed over the next threshold and faced a pitiful room with a narrow bed, a large, threatening armoire, and a small barred window. That was it. That was all there was to see.

I ran out of the room to the kitchen.

"Maman, Maman!" I called at the top of my voice, "Your bedroom is so tiny."

"*Non, non*, Marcelle, that's your room."

"But where will Suzanne sleep?"

"With me in my room until she goes to boarding school in the fall.

"But we always sleep in the same room…always!"

"I know. But you are a big girl now and you can have your own."

"Yes, but…

"Marcelle, it's enough! I am busy."

The slicing effect of her tone of voice sent me back marching along the hallway, head bowed, lip quivering, fighting tears, and making sure my Mary Jane's tapped on the bare wood floors. I rushed by Uncle Charlie, talking on the telephone, and stomped into the ugly little room. Going straight to the window, I put my face near the grimy pane, taking care not to touch it, and looked outside.

A tableau of misery revealed itself in shades of gray: a cemented yard between tall buildings, dusty blades of straggly grass growing through cracks, and at the end of the pavement an enclosure lined with trash cans against a low cement wall. On the other side, halved by the wall, I saw the upper body of men framed in garage doors.

22

Further still, like a backdrop to the pitiful décor, spindly trees like stilt-walkers stretched their emaciated tops toward a pewter sky.

I turned from the window and slumped onto the bed. I closed my eyes, trying to keep in my tears. In my child's mind I dramatized that never again would I see my river sparkling in the early morning and at night the moon drawing long corridors of orange shadows on its surface, that no longer would I see water lilies and birds swooping over its surface before the rain. No, from now on, I convinced myself I would see only cement outdoors, and bare light bulbs inside.

Feet squarely planted on the ground, elbows on my knees, fists pressed against my eyes, I willed myself to erase the gray tableau and replaced it with a picture from the past, still so near, my heart could feel it.

We are in Saint-Eustache. Papa lay next to me on my bed to tell us a nighttime story. Our bedroom is dark but for the hallway's bright light which projects the elongated shadows of our father's pantomime on one wall. Through his graceful movement and powerful hands, he describes a lake, a forest, a far horizon; I see the round body of a grouse, and then, a crane in flight, legs trailing, wings flapping, head and beak thrust forward.

23

I kept pressing hard against my eyes, but the picture faded away. Only shadows and specks of light remained. Instinctively, I knew that with my father gone and Suzanne leaving soon there would be no more storytelling, and to top it all, the narrow bed could not accommodate more than one person.

I sat, numb but for the warm tears streaming down my cheeks; I wiped my nose on my sleeve. Looking up, my heart skipped a beat. A large armoire loomed over me. I always feared things that might be hiding in closets and under beds, my imagination generously feeding my dread. Automatically I lifted my feet off the floor, but just as fast, I mustered enough courage to propel me off the bed and flee to the hallway.

"Uncle Charlie!" I shouted. "Please, please, take me with you."

He spun in my direction and hung up the phone.

"Take you where?"

"Please, I want to live with you and Aunt Berthe."

"Well, well. And where do you think you would sleep?"

"You could put two big chairs together. Remember when I was a little girl you used to make…"

24

"Well, now, I cannot believe that you would leave your mother all alone. You love your Maman, don't you? You don't want to make her cry."

I wanted to tell him she cried all the time anyway, but I had argued a lot that day and was rewarded with a swat on the head. What's more, I knew that as long as cousin Jacques lived with them, there would be no place for me to sleep.

Uncle Charlie cupped my face in his hands.

"I'll tell you what, Blondie," he said. "Maybe, just maybe, today we can make an exception. You're all coming for dinner tonight … and who knows, your Aunt Berthe might invite you to sleep over."

"If I stay with Maman, can I be your little girl anyway?"

"Marcelle, you'll always be my little girl."

Without another word, Uncle Charlie sealed his pledge with a kiss on my head and one on the tip of my nose.

"Now let me go and help your mother for a while, alright?"

I nodded.

"Dear me!" Uncle Charlie took a second look. "Your

face looks like an overflowing fountain. Let me fix that or we're going to have a flood." Uncle Charlie pulled out a clean handkerchief from his coat pocket and patted my eyes.

"That's better"

"It's alright, Uncle Charlie, you can go help Maman now," I managed to say in a Suzanne-like mature tone of voice.

"Well, thank you very much Mademoiselle Marcelle." Uncle Charlie bowed and pirouetted toward the kitchen.

Not knowing what to do, I sat at the table and lay my head on my arms.

Prompted no doubt by Uncle Charlie, Suzanne walked behind me softly and pinched my ribs. I screamed. Nerves pulsating too near the surface, we both laughed uncontrollably. Before I had recovered, she took my hand and asked to see my bedroom.

"What for?" I said, still shaking and not sure which, tears or laughter, would follow. "It's ugly and tiny. It has a dirty window full of bars on it, and..."

"I don't care, I want to see it."

"Alright, I reluctantly mumbled."

"Hmm...yes...hmm...I see." There was a long silence, and another mumbling. Finally, head askance she looked at me, and with that big sister reassuring look she declared emphatically, "I'm sure Maman will fix it up for you. I promise. You'll see. You *will* have a pretty bedroom. You know Maman always makes things look pretty."

I still had doubts, but that was not my only worry. "Suzanne, who will tell us stories?"

She sat down on the edge of the bed. "I never thought of that. Hmm...tell you what, when I'm here, I will."

"You know Papa's stories by heart?"

"Maybe not all of them, but you can help. When we can't remember, we'll make some up, just like Papa did. He never told the same story twice in the same way."

"But my bed is too small for both of us."
"Let's try. Come on. Lie down on the bed with me."

I squeezed next to the wall. We tried to fit shoulder to shoulder but Suzanne slipped off the edge.

"Slide down a bit," coaxed Suzanne. After more

27

adjustment we fitted snugly and without losing one more minute, she began to tell me the story of "The Golden Apple." Soon her voice reassured me, every word bringing me back to the safety of familiar landscapes.

CHAPTER THREE

RUE SAINT ANDRÉ A VILLEARY

Suzanne had not yet reached the end of Papa's story when a booming, "Well, well, well!" startled us. Uncle Charlie and Maman were ready to go. As one body, Suzanne and I rolled off the bed, drowsy but eager for Aunt Berthe's dinner.

Uncle, Aunt, and cousin Jacques, lived on rue Saint-André, a street lined with maple trees, and designed for two-family living. All the way up and down the street, dozens and dozens of spiral staircases, like unfurled steel ringlets, led to upper balconies and apartment entrances.

The sun was still warming the day when we arrived. Waiting for us, Aunt Berthe waved from the balcony. I rushed out and climbed up the stairs. When Aunt Berthe bent over to embrace and kiss me, I took advantage of her smiling face near mine to whisper in her ear, "Can I sleep with you tonight? It's alright with Uncle."

"Nothing could give me more joy," she said. "Jacques is singing in Québec tonight so we can use his bedroom." Then she turned and kissed Suzanne, and invited her for a visit later on. Even though I was their goddaughter, they treated us equally.

Aunt Berthe's invitation stripped away the remainder of my child's anxiety. Entering the house, the rich fragrance of oak furniture filled my nostrils. Half way down the corridor, the aromas of a pork roast in the oven and a freshly baked butter cake overcame the first. Sorrow could not squeeze itself into this welcoming-scent-filled apartment.

Once the hugs, and—let me hang up your coats—were over, Aunt Berthe convinced Maman that she needed no help, and to go sit in the living room and rest. One look at her younger sister's sad smile, sloping shoulders and dark circled eyes, told her as much as a long heart-to-heart talk. She knew, through previous conversations, that Maman still loved her unfaithful husband, and that leaving the house and village, home

30

for the last eleven years, heightened her grief.

Uncle Charlie served Maman a glass of his homemade wine and shared the evening paper with her. They sat in silence while Suzanne practiced softly at the piano. I followed my godmother to the kitchen. After all, from now until tomorrow morning, I was her little girl.

Aunt Berthe had already set the table for the evening meal, taking away the only useful thing I could have done. So I sat in Uncle Charlie's chair and watched her every move.

I loved the spaciousness of this room. Unlike our own in Saint-Eustache, here, all fitted nicely: no squeezing between table and sink or between stove and table, or more so, no protuberances of pantry and stairwell taking away valuable space.

The outside kitchen door displayed a glass panel at the top and wood at the bottom. On the same wall, a curtained window let in the morning sun, and between them hung a regulator clock. I could not read the Roman numerals, but its melodic chimes and the invariable ticking of the gold pendulum gave me as warm a sensation as the extra wool blanket Maman put on my bed, on a night when frost, between the double window panes, created sceneries etched in ice.

In addition to the usual kitchen equipment, a large gas stove and a small two-burner wood stove stood side by side. The latter, a relic of the past, provided a handy source of heat when the thermometer in the curtained window showed what everyone felt in his or her bones. Two cozy chairs completed the décor.

From time to time I sat in Aunt Berthe's dainty upholstered rattan chair, rocking while conversing with her or looking at books; however it did not satisfy the daydreamer adventuress or the treasure huntress in me.

Uncle Charlie's Craftsman's chair came close to fulfilling my expectations though it did not measure up to lying on the Persian carpet under the dining room table, or sitting under the clavier between the carved columns of the old piano; however I conceded that it provided a major attraction.

Lifting the giant armrests of uncle's chair with their cache of minor treasures always filled me with a sense of wonder. A wish and a wink transported me between two pirates' coffers unveiling, not a cache of gold, muskets or swords, but an array of pedestrian treasures: playing cards, pads, pencils, tin boxes full of rubber bands and thumbtacks, pennies and stamps, and, if in luck, a wondrous tin box filled with peppermints.

My explorations over, I sat quietly in his chair watching Aunt Berthe the same way I watched Maman in our kitchen in Saint-Eustache. The two sister's movements differed as much as their looks and temperaments. Aunt Berthe went about the kitchen and her cooking in an *andante tempo.* Consequently, her pots and pans kept their shapes, and through the years flat bottoms and fitted lids remained intact.

Maman, on the other hand, favored a *vivace tempo* and her pots and pans told a different story. Full of bumps and bruises, round bottoms shimmied on the stovetop and ill-fitting lids jingled their own tunes. Despite the disparity in tempo and the manner of handling their cookware, the two sisters possessed equal gifts in the cooking domain.

From time to time Uncle Charlie peeked into the kitchen, impatient to carve the roast. Before his fourth inquiry, Aunt Berthe called him in; it was done. Uncle Charlie began his presentation, a complete show for me—his gallery of one.

Armed with two long carving knives, gesturing like a

whooping crane attempting to take flight, he slid the blades against one another, and then tested them against his thumb. Finally, with a victorious, "Ah! Ha!" he declared himself ready and sent me to the living room to tell Maman and Suzanne that dinner would be served in two minutes.

I found Maman slouched in her chair, eyes closed, newspaper and pencil on the floor, the crossword puzzle barely begun. She looked so tired that I could not bring myself to wake her. I tiptoed toward Suzanne who, after exhausting her two piano piece repertoire, tentatively played the melodic lines from Cousin Jacques' *Italian Song Book*.

Hanging over the piano, his portrait showed a handsome young man in his late teens. He had inherited a quick wit as well as a quick temper from his father. When provoked they both easily boiled over. Looking at my cousin's picture, I saw only the softness and sensibility of his mother. Maman told me he had also inherited her lyrical voice, though beneath it simmered a passion, an undercurrent that kept the voice dynamic without losing its beauty.

I loved Jacques a whole lot, but I felt tongue-tied in his presence. His teasing always transformed my light complexion to the color of a ripe tomato. How I feared the embarrassment of blushing! The heat mounted from my throat, spread to my neck, ears and cheeks, until my whole head came to a boil, my coloring telling the whole world, this girl is terribly shy or guilty as sin.

While I scrutinized Jacque's portraits, I absent-mindedly put my hand on Suzanne's shoulder and startled a yelp out of her that was mother to one of my own, followed by a burst of laughter from both of us.

Maman awoke abruptly. "What's happening? What's happening?"

Between apologies, more giggles and explanations, we made our way to the kitchen. We did not linger at the table, as we were accustomed when visiting with them. Uncharacteristically, Maman did not correct us every minute, and left her plate half full, excusing herself for her lack of appetite.

Soon after dinner, Uncle Charlie drove Maman and Suzanne back to the apartment. At last, I was alone with my godmother.

Suzanne & Marcelle 1942

at Uncle Charlie & Aunt Berthe's home

CHAPTER FOUR

BONNE NUIT FLUTTERED AROUND MY EARS

For some years my dear godmother, Aunt Berthe, the aunt with a vocabulary of lovely words, and a slightly sad smile—like someone wanting to hide an emotional or physical pain in back of a serene façade—suffered from undiagnosed diabetes. She often slept on a chaise lounge so that, when sleep escaped her, she could get up without disturbing her husband. But in Jacques' absence, as on the special night of my stay, she used his room.

I undressed while Aunt Berthe partitioned the large bed Uncle Charlie and I would share. She arranged two pillows, end-to-end, in the center to stop me from kicking him while I slept. I jumped onto my side and she tucked me in, lovingly caressed my head, and kissed me goodnight. Imitating her, I asked if I could pat the curls at the back of her head. They were the prettiest, always in place and never looking stiff. With her permission I touched them. Under the softness of her hair I felt the backbones of invisible hairpins.

"How do you know where to put them all?" I asked.

"Oh, now it's easy, since your uncle made a harness that sits on my shoulders. With a mirror in front and one in the back, I can see what I am doing. I will show you tomorrow morning."

Drowsy, I received Aunt Berthe's last kiss. Her soft, *"bonne nuit,"* fluttered around my ears. She tiptoed out, leaving the door slightly ajar.

Soon I heard Uncle Charlie come through the front door, then, a whispering and rustling of newspaper pages, more doors opening and closing, and not long after the overpowering announcement of the toilet. It had a large tank suspended near the ceiling. When someone pulled the chain it flushed enthusiastically for a long time, twirling as if the whole Saint Lawrence River had burst into the bathroom. I stayed awake until its receding flow sounded as tame as a babbling brook. Safe and warm on my side of the partition, I fell asleep.

Nine hours later I awoke to the same sound of rushing water. This time a faint ray of sun peered in at the edges of the blind, and sparks of light animated a few bouquets of flowers on the patterned wall paper.

I followed the subtle sounds of Aunt Berthe preparing breakfast; the hushed opening and closing of the ice box, milk cascading from bottle to pitcher, corn flakes crackling from box to bowl, a tea kettle whistling, and water gushing into the tea pot. The noise of a jagged-edged bread knife on a crusty surface propelled me out of bed. By now I could not only hear breakfast, but smell and taste it as well. Too soon the morning ritual came to an end.

Ready for work, Uncle Charlie slid the newspaper into his overcoat pocket. Aunt Berthe helped me with my coat and hat, and kissed and hugged me, inviting me to come back soon. I would have loved to stay longer, but she explained that Maman would have to make a long trip by bus and tramways to pick me up, and with all the unpacking she had no time. Anyway, without them needing to say a word, I was sure I would be back: their unfailing love giving me that promise.

We followed Uncle Charlie to the veranda. He already stood half way down the stairs waiting.

"Come, come, Blondie. No time to lose."

I rushed down a few steps.

"*Non, Non, non*! The steps are too narrow there. Use the other side. Hang on to the railing. That's it! There you are."

Once on the sidewalk I ran to the car. Uncle Charlie opened the back door, and responded to my puzzled look.

"Let's keep the front seat for your grandmother, shall we?"

"Grand-maman is coming with us!" I could hardly contain my excitement. In my sorrow at leaving our home, family members, and friends in Saint-Eustache, I had forgotten that, by living in Montréal, we would be nearer other relatives we enjoyed visiting. But among all of them, Grand-maman, our only grandparent, held a special place in her three grandchildren's hearts. It did not matter that she could not afford to give us store-bought presents; Suzanne, Jacques and I loved her.

During his long and successful career Jacques never

failed, if he knew Grand-maman attended one of his concerts, to acknowledge and dedicate a song to her—always the same: *Les vieilles de notre pays,* the old ladies of our country, and always, she blushed and smiled.

With Grand-maman's visit in my thoughts, a new scenario unfolded. *Why not call on Maman's sister Irène? Papa didn't like her, but now it wouldn't matter, and she also could come to our apartment. Why not Maman's other sister, Flore, the one who lives in New York? I never met her. Maman keeps her picture in a drawer. I looked at it once. She does not look like her sisters, and Maman said, "Flore wouldn't want you to call her aunt." I cannot remember why. But I would like to meet her because Maman told me that Aunt Flore behaved like a movie star. To me, she did not look all blonde and frizzy like one, but dark and mysterious.*

I smiled, my vision extending to a larger picture of loving faces. Three more came into full color: our cousins Lise, France and André who lived on Boulevard Saint-Joseph. But best of all, in a few minutes, on that special day, Grand-maman would join us in the car.

My daydreaming in full flight, I did not feel the zigzagging of Uncle Charlie's erratic driving, nor was I disturbed by the monologues he addressed to slow or inept drivers. No, I was too busy envisioning the transformation that would take place in my bedroom when she made curtains for the window; and perhaps even a bedspread. *Certainly, Maman will paint the walls yellow. A pale yellow—yes, I will ask her.*

If, at that instant, Uncle Charlie had glanced at his niece in his rearview mirror, he would have seen yesterday's gloomy child transformed by hope—the invisible artist, who without a brush had painted a smile on a radiant face.

My only remembrance of the apartment in Montréal is the mental image of the first impression. It has not changed with the years. The large armoire with one of its doors ajar, the undersized bed, the barred window, the hallway and kitchen; time never erased their bareness and ugliness. I do not recall a transformation; however, there is no doubt in my reasoning mind that a change took place.

Despite her sorrow, Maman, the housekeeper who took pride in her lovely home, who adjusted with care the flow of a curtain or a drapery, who daily lined up the three living room shades, who served appetizing plates of well prepared food, who spent time arranging flowers, no,

Maman the perfectionist could not have breathed in the apartment's décor.

I can visualize my Grand-maman and my dear aunts pulling material out of trunks to fix this or that, and Aunt Irène perambulating the hill from her third floor apartment, rushing to Eaton's yard-goods department on Sainte-Catherine street to buy what the trunks were not providing. In my heart I know that is exactly what happened.

Flore circa 1921

Maman & Marcelle near Uncle Charlie's home

CHAPTER FIVE

A BITTER SWEET SEASON

Days became blustery; leaves dusty-green, droopy. Torn from their stems, they spun in the air and lay where they landed, underfoot, under wheels, washed into sewer drains.

June, July, and August 1936, were the first and longest summer months Suzanne and I had ever spent away from the unencumbered spaces and fresh river breezes of our village.

As fall drew near we welcomed Grand-maman, who stayed with us for a week to sew Suzanne's school uniforms and other fall and winter clothing. On that last week of August, she started a tradition that repeated itself every year until we had finished our studies.

I remember that year in Montréal. I see her sitting at the hallway table where she had installed her portable, black and gold Singer sewing machine, and asked Maman for brighter light. She sketched a pattern for Suzanne's boarding school uniform and pinned it onto yards of black material. She cut and basted with white thread. When Suzanne tried it on, every seam looked like the broken line of a highway on a dark rainy night.

Afterward, Suzanne sat next to Grand-maman, her youthful chatter accompanied by the whir of the sewing machine, the young and the old enveloped in the sizing odor of new material. The Singer's humming ran uninterrupted on the skirt's long seams, or spurted out a hasty refrain around armholes, collar, and sleeve edges.

Grand-maman must have found her granddaughter's nearness and babble distracting because she said, "Why don't you go outdoors and play with Marcelle? I will call you, when it's time to try on your dress again. Go, go, go," she insisted. "I promise I will call you."

Suzanne's face dropped a good inch. Instead of going outdoors, she ignored me and dragged her feet to the bedroom she shared with Maman. I shadowed and watched her.

As if following a daily ritual, she walked to the suitcase lying open on a chair. She removed the smooth-satin covered sachet Aunt Berthe had given her and gently held it against one cheek, then the other, inhaling its ripe perfume. You will smell like a rose all winter, Aunt Berthe had told her. Cautiously, because Maman had admonished her not to disturb the order, Suzanne slid the sachet back between neat piles of underwear; every garment tagged with her name written in India ink, even at the top of her long black cotton stockings.

I watched her stroke each pile of clothing she would take into her new world. She stood still for a while, sighed, and turning her face away from me, walked out of the bedroom. I could not tell if she was sad or afraid. I followed her to the kitchen.

Maman had carried a card table there, and squeezed it open between the stove and the wall. "There is good natural light in here," she said.

Maman had bought second-hand books from the boarding school. She erased pencil marks, taped torn pages and strengthened weak spines. To protect the cloth-bound books (catechism, math, and French grammar) she used brown grocery bags, and with care opened and ironed the creases. The softer homework books (composition, math and writing exercises) she covered with the thinner paper bags from the seldom-patronized dry cleaner. After measuring, cutting and covering the books, she opened her fountain pen and in her best handwriting wrote Suzanne's name.

Our fingers itched to touch the books. And we did. But in a voice that asked for no reply, Maman told us to go play outdoors.

"Take advantage of the sun. You will be cooped up in classrooms soon enough."

We left the musty smell of books, the sharp crunch of scissors on thick paper. We left the happy sound of Maman's busyness that buried her sighs for as long as her purposeful work lasted.

Half-heartedly, Suzanne and I went through the motions of play. Before long we sat on the front steps. I felt as ill at ease as I had the day we found out that Papa and Maman had separated. A few weeks later we left Saint-Eustache not knowing if we would ever see him again. And now, on days I could count on my fingers, my sister would be gone as well.

"Suzanne," I said, "Remember when I started kindergarten? That day you walked with me to school and Maman told you to hold my hand. Remember? But this year you won't be with me."

48

"Don't worry, Maman will go with you."

Shoulder to shoulder we sat, united in apprehension.

My big sister and I were seldom close, she often trying to shake away her pestering shadow, and I, two years and a few months younger, wanting a playmate every minute of the day.

"Suzanne, are you afraid?"

"Afraid of what?"

"Afraid of going all alone to a big school and staying there overnight."

"Oh… No."

To me it sounded like a big sister pretending.

"Will you take your doll to school?"

I can't. You know that."

"I forgot… Hmm…Maybe I can bring her with me when I visit you on Sundays."

Suzanne looked at me, smiled and gently removed a leaf from my hair.

"What a great idea," she said.

Maman & Marcelle
In Montreal

CHAPTER SIX

ONLY THE TWO OF US

Grand-maman had packed her sewing machine and returned to the one bedroom she rented in someone's house. She never talked or complained about her living arrangement. Being a child I assumed that all grandmothers lived similarly. Modest, despite her regal bearing, she accommodated her schedule and her life to the rhythm of the owners'. Her bedroom, always neat contained only the necessary: a bed, a sewing machine, and a straight back chair, a small table, a few books Aunt Irène provided and exchanged regularly and for reading them a well padded-high-back chair.

Through the years, in her different lodgings, and on top

of diverse shaped bureaus, I saw the same small jewelry box. She let me look inside this precious box, which she laid on the bed for me. One by one I removed all its contents: a few pairs of earrings, a pearl necklace nestled at the bottom of a padded pouch, a brooch decorated with garnet stones, hat pins: a white, a black, and a brown one; and four large mother-of-pearl hairpins to secure her chignon. In a separate compartment one piece attracted my fingers most of all: a small pocket watch.

I inspected the watch last, always. Two engraved, interlaced initials encircled in a delicate border decorated its gold convex cover. But for me the treasure rested inside, cradled in a bed of gold. The mechanism lay hidden under the watch face. On top, two hands, like thin threads of gold, circled every twelve hours without brushing away the delicate water color that only a fairy's fingers could have designed... a rose in bloom, and attached to it a bud, like a promise that more hours would bloom.

Who had given Grand-maman the watch? The husband who shared her life nineteen years and to whom she remained faithful her long ninety-six years of life? I never asked. She rarely spoke of herself, of her past.

Grand-maman had left as she had come—without fanfare. But the sound of the apartment changed. Gone was the familiar murmur of the sewing machine, gone the pleasing discourse between mother and daughter; gone the muffled modulation of their voices at night. For Suzanne and I, transplanted into new surroundings, the familiarity of the sounds had reassured us as much as if we had heard the song of the clock on the mantle of our home in Saint-Eustache, which sang its refrain every fifteen minutes, and was still singing it upon our awakening—the familiarity of our lives past.

When Suzanne and Grand-maman left, the apartment vested itself in a quasi silence; yet there was school for me, a new routine, new faces; and, as I recall many years later, the joyous expectation of weekends—joy taking roots on Saturday nights, and flowering on Sundays.

It all started late afternoon with a bath and a hair wash.

"A breeze," Maman said if I objected to her energetic rubbing. "With your short hair it takes a second." And a second was all I could take. I nipped any impulse to complain: too much pleasure awaited me to postpone it with jeremiads.

Dressed for the night, my Sunday clothes carefully

arranged on the back of my bedroom chair, I eagerly anticipated the familiar sentence Maman would utter, "Let's go prepare dinner."

While she readied the greatest treat in the world, I hurried to set the table in the hallway. The macabre looking corridor had lost its earlier forbidding look. Uncle Charlie had given the bare hanging light bulb a lift and a globe, and Maman had covered the table with an ecru linen cloth. A vase filled with branches of bright yellow and red maple leaves enriched the décor. After setting the table, I ran to the kitchen and watched Maman from the doorway, far enough to be out of her way yet near enough to see and savor in advance.

She was in the second phase of deep frying potatoes. They would come out of the bubbly volcano in thin strips, crisp, gold and irresistible. Three buttered buns lay face down on a cookie sheet in the oven while Maman turned over three boiled hot dogs in a frying pan until they were an even rich golden brown. She had decided that two each were too many; one did not quite satisfy our appetites, but one and a half seemed perfect.

At last the tray was ready. Maman poured an equal amount of Coke in each glass, salted the fries, added a dash of mustard to the buns, and, "Please, more relish on mine," I begged. We marched with our treats to the hall table.

We sat near each other, barely a kiss, an embrace away. After our first bite we looked at each other and winked; overcoming the barrier of age, an air of mischief crossing our faces.   Here we defied Papa's dictum forbidding hot dogs or Coke—an American abomination he always claimed would kill us. But he was gone, and anyway, Maman had once in a while broken the rule when in the past he went on hunting trips.

After dinner, Maman prepared the treat to take to Suzanne on Sunday: creamy, rich, chocolate fudge. I studied her every gesture, from mixing to stirring and beating, the last phase requiring an expert touch; one turn too few, the fudge would be too soft; one too many, the fudge too hard and grainy. Anxiously I watched as Maman poured the glossy wave of chocolate into a buttered pan. If the fudge neared perfection, I could scrape the pan in a few seconds. If not, Maman would start over and I would have to wait for my treat.

Most Saturdays she smiled.

CHAPTER SEVEN

SUZANNE AMONG FERNS AND STATUES

Sunday at last!

"Hurry Maman, we'll be late!"

The sentence froze in my throat. How often had I heard my father pronounce those words while he walked back and forth in the living room having nothing else to do but jiggle keys and change in his pocket waiting for his wife and two daughters. I knew how annoying it must have been for her, because every time it had happened, she muttered under her breath and her expression soured.

Up hours before her sleeping family to light the stove, prepare breakfast, wash and dry dishes, scrub the sink, peel and leave vegetables in cold water; she also dressed a roast so that shortly after our return from church we could sit down to a Sunday noon dinner. After all this, she readied herself and her daughters for Mass.

No, I would not repeat Papa's annoying sentence. Maybe she had not heard me. Why spoil a promising Sunday and add a darker shade to the still present shadow under her eyes.

Enthralled with the prospect of our Sunday outing it never occurred to me that Maman might not relish our travels as much as I did. Whatever her feelings were, and regardless of weather, after every Sunday Mass and a quick lunch, we walked to the first bus stop on our journey to Suzanne's boarding school at Côtes des Neiges, at the foot of Mont-Royal.

The transportation system evolved into my indoctrination to civility. I had to give up my place to pregnant ladies, tired ladies carrying many parcels, tired ladies with multiple children, anyone with an apparent physical disability, and old ladies and gentlemen alike, whether they looked exhausted or not. I thoroughly enjoyed this contest, and after a few trips I became adept at discerning which passenger might inherit my seat. While standing and holding onto Suzanne's doll, the challenge of keeping my balance during starts and stops made it twice as exciting.

When we reached her school and climbed the long staircase, I always disengaged my hand from Maman's and rushed to ring the doorbell. The sound, bouncing against walls and high ceilings, traveled unimpeded along endless corridors and found her, I was sure, wherever she was.

Of course, Suzanne never opened the heavy wooden door, but a nun whose appearance never failed to fascinate me. Swiftly my eyes embraced a costume that with the exception of basic black and white, long skirts, and yards of rosary beads hanging from the waist, differed from the habits worn by the sisters in our girl school in Saint-Eustache.

From the neck, halfway down their chest, Suzanne's nuns wore a stiff white bib shaped like a half moon; at its edge hung a shiny silver heart. A white cowl covered their heads and part of the forehead leaving eyebrows and chin bare. A large halo-shaped wimple, pleated like a fan, gave their faces a look of wonder and lightness, as if the veil hanging from the wimple could, at the slightest breeze, lift them up above the school in a Chagall dance.

Two generations of sisters greeted us: the young with a ready smile, a quick step, veil swaying to the inner pulse of her hopes and lofty ideals; the other, near retirement, sedate, ceremoniously old fashioned, barely hiding her annoyance at seeing parents whose periodic visits and departures transformed otherwise well-behaved children into sniffling, sobbing little misfits.

The doorkeeper might be different every week but the greetings never changed.

"Bonjour, Madame."

"Bonjour, ma soeur."

"Entrez je vous en prie. Who would you like to see?"

Though the nun always directed her question to Maman, I answered fast. "My sister Suzanne, if you please." I never doubted that everyone in the school knew her. I surprised Maman many times, conspiratorially mouthing our family name to the sisters, not wanting, I suppose, to spoil my joy and self-importance. The preliminaries over, the nun directed us to the parlor.

The parlors I entered in my student years shared the same austere look. They varied only in the size and number of potted ferns and statues. Without exception, straight-backed chairs like a row of Rocket dancers hugged the walls in perfect formation. Only the ferns' laciness softened the environment's white rigidity. A crucifix, and the picture of the founder of the community, hung on otherwise bare walls. More often than not, visitors averted their eyes from a statue of Jesus or Mary, its bleeding heart a painful reminder of the onlookers' presumed wickedness and the cause of such sorrow.

As for me, nothing could diminish my joyful expectation. During the week, alone with Maman, our life evolved so predictably that anything out of the ordinary became an event; a story to tell my sister the following Sunday.

The minute I saw her, with her turned-up nose and large green eyes speckled with gold, the same gold as the ringlets contouring her face, I forgot Maman's instruction to sit still and wait. I ran to Suzanne, kissed her, and thrust the doll into her arm. Together, hand in hand we walked toward Maman.

If I had a story to tell, I would barely give her time to sit and kiss Maman before it burst out, always prefaced by, "Guess what? Something *ex-tra-or-dinaire* happened!" I carefully enunciated à la Uncle Charlie.

"What?" It was all Suzanne could say without laughing out loud.

Unruffled by both Maman and Suzanne's amused smile I pursued my story.

One Sunday I announced, "Someone came to pick me up at school this week and it was not Maman."

"Papa?"

The word barely out of her mouth Suzanne and I looked at each other realizing her faux pas. I hesitated a second.

"*Non*, Jacques." I paused to make sure I had made an impression. "He came to pick me up at school, and he was silly," I added. "He said something to my pretty nun-teacher, and she blushed."

Maman interrupted, reminding us that a fine line existed between proper and improper behavior, and that our cousin Jacques had crossed that boundary. I was not so sure. There was something exciting about Uncle Charlie and Jacques tripping over the stiff proper line once in a while and doing it with such good humor.

By the end of the hour, the rows of straight back chairs were reshaped into small family circles where knees touched and hands clenched, separating only when the strident electric bell announced the end of the visit. Suddenly a tear, a sob, replaced the happy babble and traveled from group to group. One could hear a hopeful, "Be good," from parents, and an anxious, "Will you be back next Sunday?" from children.

I do not remember Suzanne ever being teary-eyed. On the contrary, a sister might ask her to guide a little one in despair to the recreation room. Maman and I watched her holding hands or putting her arm around the shoulder of a sobbing child, murmuring reassuring words. My eyes followed her until she turned the corner of a long corridor, taking with her a part of my joy and leaving me with the regret at not being the child with her arm around my shoulder.

On the Shore

S
U
Z
A
N
N
E

CHAPTER EIGHT

THE MISSING VOICE

I did not fully comprehend that I had lost more than a playmate, for Suzanne seldom spent time involved in games with me; no, what I missed without realizing it was the sound of her presence.

When I still lay in my crib and Suzanne a three year old, Papa had surnamed her *"Criquette,"* Little Cricket, because then, she often walked in the field adjacent to our house.

Dwarfed by long grasses and wild flowers, she could barely be seen but easily found by the sound of her chattering, while conversing animatedly with flowers and insects.

At nine years of age Suzanne had become the little old

lady who talked to herself and spoke with her doll. She had become Maman's bedroom companion who read aloud and laughed aloud—a distraction to Maman's weariness, a dish washing partner who brought singing back, and at times, a smile to Maman's lips.

The absence of Suzanne's animated chattering could not be filled by Maman's efforts at conversation with me. Like a fall garden shorn of its flowers, the rooms where we lived were strewn with holes of silence.

Suzanne at 8

In her Easter outfit

CHAPTER NINE

MISCHIEF IN THE AIR

Living alone with Maman, I wished for rainy days, when after school she brought a box filled with used greeting cards and decrepit children's books to the table, and handed me the little scissors shaped like a stork. We worked together cutting and pasting the pages of a scrapbook with flowers or winter scenes, or with characters from fables, creating new stories from the remnants of old ones. Once every page owned its story, and Maman deemed the result of our work acceptable, we gave our scrapbook away to children in hospitals.

On days when the rain stopped and clouds lifted, I knew I would hear, "Go outdoors, take advantage of the sun." But without Suzanne to play with me, it lost its appeal. *Anyway, what good was all that shine on cement?*

In Saint-Eustache if I awoke early, I joined Papa on the

upper terrace and stood with him looking at the river. "See," he would say," the sun loves the river, that's why he covers her with diamonds." But I learned on my own that by squinting, the myriads of diamonds blended into one, metamorphosing into yards and yards of gold lamé, and looking as splendid as the evening gown of my ample bosomed Aunt Irène.

Contemplating the river from the terrace, time and again I had fantasized about the old *curé* Lamoureux's summerhouse. Surrounded by trees and bushes, it sat on a small island facing our property. It looked as if a winged benefactor had dropped a seed that sprouted and grew into a house shaded and fanned by a canopy of tree leaves.

In winter the *curé's* summer home blanketed itself in a sea of white snow. But its unblemished, frosted landscape melted in spring, and as the waters came dangerously near the front steps, Maman always predicted, "The poor old man will crick-crack from arthritis." In early summer her concerns changed to invading pests. "Dear soul, she empathized, "mosquitoes must eat him alive."

In late fall, when leaves covered the ground, and branches turned black and cold with rain, I could have spied on the activities taking place on the island and watched human shapes scurry about. But by then, *le curé* was already tucked away in his gray stone presbytery, figuring out how to help the poor in his care, pay the bills to keep parishioners from shivering in church, and light up the crystal chandeliers during services. Inhabited or not, my imagination always peopled *le curé's* island; pirates and skulls and treasures abounded.

In the cemented landscape around the apartment building in Montréal, not a tree stood to shelter birds on their long journey. I saw them flying by in large groups. Bird weddings, my father called the flock flying away to warm weather. I could not tell if they came from Saint-Eustache or if they were on their way to join our robins and swallows on their migration. I greeted them all with my eyes and followed them until they became a dot in the sky.

I wondered if Suzanne could see them from one of the many windows of her boarding school. For a fleeting moment loneliness would fill my throat. I swallowed it in one gulp, drying my nose on my sweater sleeve. *If only I could fly away like the birds, and leave this cement yard.* But I could not. And, "that was that," as Maman always said. "Go outside while the sun shines."

One day, not a scrapbook day, I sat on the highest steps of the apartment's front entrance. I shivered, barely warmed by a white sun foretelling of cold and snow. If Suzanne had been sitting shoulder to shoulder with me, we each would have been warm, at least on one side. From my perch, a low fence partially blocked my view; the wheels of carriages and legs of people and horses disappeared. I only saw the tops of trolleys, wires, horses' heads and people's hats bobbing over the fence—a circus of missing parts—accompanied by sounds of screeching wheels and cling-clang of steel poles hitting rails. Leaving that unsatisfactory view I walked to the side of the building.

I dreaded my time alone in the yard with only my ball and jump rope. When Suzanne was there, we threw the ball at one another. She encouraged me with praise if I made a good catch, however refused to play if I dropped it too often, which happened more than I liked. Maman joined us sometimes so that Suzanne and I could take turns jumping, and then, the day smiled.

Left alone, I thirsted for excitement. Maman forbade me more than once from lifting the lids of trash cans where my instinct told me a treasure or two hid. It was the end of the month, and Maman had mentioned that probably a couple of families would be moving.

The moment she finished her sentence, a tempting thought took a comfortable seat in my mind: *they may discard some minor treasures. Tomorrow would be the day to peek under lids.*

I had one night left to plan my treasure hunt, and Suzanne was not around to tell me "you'll get in trouble!"

CHAPTER TEN

TREASURES IN FORBIDDING PLACES

The day had arrived, At least a dozen trashcans greeted me, lids tilted to one side like a jaunty berét offering a glance-but of what? I had to find out.

Armed with my ball and jump rope, I planned a strategy that I thought would deceive the best detective, my mother. I pretended total absorption in my play, and jump-roped around the yard.

Tired of postponing the moment, and without Suzanne reminding me that punishment might lurk around the corner, I dropped my rope on the ground and picked up the ball. Knowing that from the kitchen window Maman's eyes could not follow that far, I threw it in the direction of the castaways. Many throws fell short of my goal. Eventually, one landed at the foot of the wire fence. A big trashcan lay against it, the tilted top exposing an array of colors. I had to explore, and tuned out

Suzanne's voice.

Keeping a nervous eye on Maman's kitchen window, I walked around to the fence opening, then back to the other side until I found the can. I edged toward it. All at once a feeling of dread and glorious expectation battled for the front row of my imagination. I could not wait any longer. Embracing the glorious expectation I peeked under the lid.

Partially hidden among other trash I spotted the body of a concertina. I removed the lid and pulled out the miniature instrument. After discarding a wilted leaf of lettuce clinging in one pleat, the concertina looked almost new. I slid my hands under its handles. I squeezed and pulled trying to imitate an accordionist I had watched a summer ago at a church festival. Sounds came out, muffled at first, but as my enthusiasm increased, the volume, and my excitement grew.

I had to show my treasure to Maman. I stopped squeezing and pulling only to open the apartment building door. Once inside, I increased the tempo and pressure knowing that the sounds pouring from this musical treasure could not fail to please her. Contrary to my expectation, she greeted her strolling musician with a quizzical look and a disturbing question.

"Where on earth did you find that thing?"

"In the yard." My ears and cheeks started to burn.

"Where in the yard?"

I knew she saw the color in my face deepening. I could not lie—well maybe partially.

"By the trash cans," I mumbled.

Maman came nearer. Her eyes shifted from the instrument to my dress, then my shoes and finally the floor. I followed her gaze, seeing what she saw—bits and pieces of lettuce, carrots and tomatoes decorating the front of my dress, mingling with my shoelaces.

"Marcelle, you took this concertina from the trash can, yes?" Maman said while brushing away remnants of salad from my dress.

By then, my tomato-colored face gave me away completely. I could not even lie partially. I nodded and emitted a faint "*oui.*"

"It is filthy. Put it back right now!"

Heart-broken, dragging my feet, I walked out of the apartment to the yard. Still coaxing noise out of my find, I ceremoniously trudged back to the trashcan—a funeral procession of one—to the place of burial. Before laying my treasure to rest, with great energy I squeezed in and pulled out, over and over again, as the little concertina, old and wrinkled, poured out her Requiem.

Maman's tapping on the windowpane spoiled the melodic outpouring. I should not test fate. The ceremony had to end. I returned the concertina to its bed of lettuce, and gently closed the can. For once I appreciated Suzanne's absence and her big sister attitude. Still, I could hear her voice saying: "I told you not to do that!"

In my short life I had already learned that verbal arguments with my mother were not welcome; however, I could allow myself the privilege of protesting with body language. I squatted on the ground, my back against the fence and the partially hidden rubbish bins. I soon discovered that protesting alone lacked excitement, more so if no one watched the protester. After five long minutes sitting on cement, head bowed, knees up to my chin, arms circling legs, it dawned on me that I could find something better to do.

I untangled myself and looked around. At the corner of the enclosure, a few feet away from me, lay the ball I had thrown toward the trash bins. To play with it now would not substitute for the thrill of possessing the concertina, but it was better than the alternative. Resigned, I got up and walked toward the ball.

Bending to pick it up, my eyes scanned through the wire mesh. My heart somersaulted. I saw a scooter leaning against a post.

I dropped the ball on the ground and ran around to the opening of the trash compound. In seconds, my hands held the steering handle. After a quick inspection, I was certain that this new find might please Maman. I wheeled my new treasure out of the compound to the yard and stopped a few feet away from the kitchen window of our apartment. Waving back and forth with one hand, while holding onto the wobbly scooter with the other, I called "Maman, Maman Margot. Look, look, Maman!"

The window sash lifted. As soon as Maman's head appeared I shouted, "Look what I found Maman!" Silently she glared at my new treasure.

"Stay where you are. I will be right there."

The two minutes Maman took to join me seemed endless, and still, I had to wait longer for her verdict. Appraising my find, she took hold of the steering handles and carefully examined the scooter. She rolled it back and forth. The creaky sound echoed in my heart, but Maman seemed unperturbed.

"The scooter must have been left outdoors for a while," she said. Then she put one foot on the footboard. "It's solid."

"Do I keep it? Please, can I keep it?"

"Did you find it in the yard?"

Ah... If I answered yes, Maman would conclude that the scooter belonged to another child. If I said in the trash area, I might get in trouble. But I had to take a chance. "Not in the trash cans," I hurried to say. Even though I told the truth, the heat in my cheeks increased. I gestured toward the fence. "Against the fence," I mumbled.

"On this side of the fence?"

That was it! I had found the scooter in the forbidden area. Now, Maman would know.

"No, it was on-on-on the other side, against the fence." I made a large gesture to compensate for my stuttering. "But not in the trash cans," I declared with more authority. After all, I had only half disobeyed.

Maman looked at two imploring blue eyes in a landscape of red skin, and took pity. She shook the scooter one more time. I froze.

"Yes, I think it's alright."

Presto, my legs executed a jig of their own. Up and down I jumped and ran around Maman and my treasure, shouting, "It's mine, it's mine."

"Sh! Sh! Marcelle. You will disturb the tenants."

Out of breath, I finally settled against Maman, my arms around her waist. She bent over and kissed the top of my head. I looked up at her; she was smiling her beautiful smile of the good days.

Alas, my victory lasted only a short time, a very short time. After a successful tour of the parking lot under Maman's watchful eye, the scooter stayed in the apartment for three long days, my punishment for not quite obeying. On the second day, Uncle Charlie, equipped with his toolbox, paint and paintbrush, came to check its safety. He twisted a couple of screws and bolts, gave it a good shake, and said, "Let's go try it."

I watched Maman shake her head back and forth with an expression that said, "Charlie, you were not supposed to say that." I knew the language.

I waited. Uncle Charlie always found a way to solve such problems.

"Well, Margot. I wouldn't want to paint the foot rest and shine the hardware if it's not safe to use."

Maman did not smile. "Go ahead," was all she said.

I enjoyed showing my dear Uncle how well the scooter worked. I tried a sharp turn and his firm hand rescued me from falling. He strongly encouraged me to slow down until I mastered my new toy.

Ten minutes later it stood on sheets of newspaper while Uncle Charlie gave it a clean-up and a coat of bright red paint. Knowing my blemished record on obeying orders, he told me that if I put my foot on the footrest before the paint dried completely—two to three days—my foot would stick to it forever.

"Have you ever gone to bed with a scooter stuck to your foot, or climbed in a streetcar dragging one up the steps?" He looked stern, but I could not believe him; he joked and teased too often. Nevertheless, under the circumstances I knew I had better obey. My treasure was worth the excruciating wait. What's more, Sunday I could announce to Suzanne that we had a shiny red scooter, omitting the humiliating part of the story, however.

Marcelle 1935

CHAPTER ELEVEN

THREE GENERATIONS IN ONE PICTURE FRAME

Our Grand-maman,(Alphonsine Thifault Rhéaume), her sister in-law Marianna Rhéaume and her husband Jean Charbonneau, were the only three remaining relatives of the oldest generation in Maman's family.

Coming from a family of seven children, and with none of their own, great aunt Marianna and her husband welcomed their sister-in-law Alphonsine and her four daughters, our aunts Berthe, Irène, Flore, and our Maman Margot. They watched them grow, marry, and later, with the same warmth, embraced their nieces' children, Jacques, Suzanne and me.

I always knew that Papa had forbidden Maman to see her own aunt and uncle as well as her sister Irène, but I never knew why.

Now that we lived in Montréal without him, we could easily ignore his order. It also helped to assuage the guilt Maman felt when, living in Saint-Eustache, we had secretly visited them in the city and concealed the fact from Papa.

Worst for Maman had been the fear that Suzanne or I would unintentionally mention their names in Papa's presence. Too numerous to count were the occasions when Maman had interrupted us in the middle of a sentence, afraid that it could lead us to a point of no return. We had watched her inventing unrecognizable endings to our muddled narratives. We were too young to grasp the effects that Papa's questioning had on her well being. We did not connect the placing of her fist at the center of her breast to the tension and anxiety she experienced; only indigestion, we thought.

In our guileless childhood world, Suzanne and I saw no reason not to love every member of Maman's small family. We always looked forward to visiting them, especially Aunt Marianna and Uncle Jean who resided in Saint-Louis Square, a good walk away from our apartment.

Their property faced a park shaped by the symmetry of row houses and detached homes on three sides, and rue

Laval on the fourth. Their residence was lovely, a mansion to my young eyes. Like all row houses, it gained in depth and height what it lacked in width, and the high ceilings gave the illusion of enormous spaces.

The bay window in the dining room allowed a view of the park where, in summer, grass spread its green carpet, and shade trees invited families living within its outline to partake of its beauty and coolness. Mothers pushed carriages and stopped to admire other mothers' babies while bathing in the admiration of their own. Old men, a game of checkers between them, sat on benches freshly re-nailed, re-glued, painted a rich bottle green.

Through the front window Aunt Marianna and Uncle Jean saw the activities and watched the change of seasons. They did not, however, sit on the park benches or stroll under the shade trees; too many other activities kept them engaged.

At least four times a week, Aunt Marianna left the house early, on her way to the market. Carrying a large handbag, she slid its handles over her gloved right hand and held them secured in the crook of her arm. Some days, she stopped to visit a reluctant tenant, late with a payment, or maybe to check if a repair had been completed. Or sometimes she rode in a streetcar to inspect a house for sale.

Well versed in business, Aunt Marianna also loved the arts and was as agile with her hands, knitting, crocheting, and turning porcelain clay into flower shapes, as she was at turning a thoughtful compliment or fashioning a quick repartee.

A dreamer, Uncle Jean wrote poetry and prose, leaving business matters to his wife. Most of his devotion went to the publication of six volumes of his poetry and, with other writers, to the founding of *L'École littéraire de Montréal*. In 1922 "*l'Académie française* crowned his three-volume work titled: *Des influences française au Canada*.

While his wife attended to business or to the refilling of the pantry shelves, Uncle Jean dressed for the day. His hair and mustache had a touch of pomade, and a subtle scent of lotion followed him as he negotiated the long climb to his second floor studio. He kept his door closed, because to him the morning ritual was almost spiritual. He explained to Aunt Marianna that the process of opening the door to his inner sanctum, and then closing it, created a barrier between him and the unrefined world, and offered peace and space to think of exalted ideas and loftier purposes. Uncle Jean, I am sure, could not have offered such a pompous statement without a glint in his eyes acknowledging its overly stated preciosity. And that in turn, Aunt Marianna, with her usual quick wit, offered him a not so lofty repartee.

As I write this, I imagine him entering his studio. On his desk he rearranges pencils and pads, and restacks some sheets of paper. Actually, there is no need to straighten anything—he has done a thorough job of it the previous day before closing the door and joining his beloved Marianna. Nevertheless, he basks in the ritual. He makes himself comfortable in his desk chair, places a clean pad of paper in front of him, three well-sharpened pencils next to it, and one in his hand ready for inspiration's command.

Looking through the window, his gaze skims treetops, into the sky.

He closes his eyes.

At his altar, Uncle Jean waits for his muse.

CHAPTER TWELVE

CURIOS AND CHINOISERIES

What made our eyes sparkle at the thought of a visit to Carré Saint-Louis was not Aunt Marianna, and Uncle Jean's talents, though we mirrored Maman's respect for their accomplishments; no, it was their welcoming arms and the house itself, a wonder to the neophyte explorer.

At the entrance of their home an elegant carpeted staircase in a wide hallway led the eyes of the visitor to a wondrous second floor. Children with restless fingers did not belong there, Maman warned me. Uncle Jean's study, their bedroom, and to my regret the formal living room, topped the list of the "do not enter" areas.

On the few occasions Aunt Marianna invited Suzanne and me to join the adults at a special soirée, Maman reminded us, before entering the room, and while looking only at me, to stay at a distance from any fragile curios. From then on she watched my every move.

The moment I crossed the threshold I felt as if I had stepped into a bath of warm colors and rich tones. The light from the chandeliers gleamed over red mahogany, black ebony, and rosewood that framed the Louis XIV and Louis XV chairs and love seats. Heavy brocade draperies, velvet upholstery and thick Persian carpets mellowed the sound of our voices, and demanded the most elegant behavior from Suzanne and me.

How I ached to open the door of the gilded cabinet with its convex glass door. The gold key rested in its keyhole, such an invitation to hold and examine the music box, tiny pill and snuff boxes, and to caress the porcelain figurines. But I kept my hands to my side as instructed.

Near the cabinet a clock sitting on a gold shelf kindled my imagination. Like the mantel clock with the porcelain chinoiserie, it was mounted in a gilt-bronze case and embellished with a profusion of gilt c-scrolls and leaves. At the top, a small tree arched its branches over the sculptured figures of a young couple, one standing, the other sitting. The curved arm of the young lady, the man bowing over her, and a canopy of branches bending as if being moved by a breeze, all created an illusion of fluidity despite the heaviness of the gilded bronze.

How well I remember that night when walking toward Aunt Marianna, I wondered how I could persuade her to let me touch this marvel. Inspiration and words conspired, and to my delight, a sentence unfolded itself in a seamless flow.

"Aunt Marianna, may I dust all the leaves for you and the little people over the clock?" I always dusted in our home in Saint-Eustache, Maman told me that my fingers were just perfect to go in all the little nooks and crannies." I ran out of breath.

"*Mon chou*, this clock was broken years ago and we had difficulty repairing it. Since then, your uncle and I allow no one to touch it."

Aunt Marianna must have noticed my disappointment for she offered a compromise. "You see that stool in the corner? Can you pick it up and place it under the clock.

"Oh yes I can!"

"Please, go slowly and watch where you're going," pleaded Maman.

I slowed down just enough to avoid punishment. I picked up the stool, placed it under the clock, and Aunt Marianna helped me climb up on it. She put her arm around my shoulders to steady me and showed me where she and Uncle Jean had repaired the clock. I did not see any mended spots but had no doubt they were there.

"Do you speak to the little people while you dust the clock?"

"Oh, yes, indeed, they keep me company."

"And, did you ever find a tiny bird in the treetop?"

"No, I have not, but I am sure there must be one hiding from us under all those leaves."

"I thought so, too."

"You cannot have a courting couple without the songs of birds. Don't you agree?"

I nodded and smiled. She kissed the top of my head. It was time to get off my perch, leave the warmth of Aunt Marianna's arm, and go sit properly on a stiff settee next to Maman. When she found me too restless, she would suggest strongly that I go rest on the day bed set in a niche in the large hallway. Without fail, I accepted with grace because this cozy nook, all pillows and softness, enticed me anyway.

On each wall of the niche a sconce shed a discreet light on the faces of grandparents I had never known. The prints of the younger generation were clearer and the poses more relaxed. Pictures taken on Uncle Pierre's island reminded me of stories I often heard about a period in their lives when, during the summer, my mother and her three sisters joined aunts and uncles for a vacation of swimming and games. At night, Maman told me, they sang around bonfires.

I fell asleep surrounded by a gallery of ancestors who did not push me to speak, nor forbid me to touch or point fingers—a family whose gaiety, theatrical imagination, and passion for vocal music delighted me.

Marianna, Jean, ?
& Grand-Maman

Uncle Jean & Aunt Marianna's
In Le Carré Saint-Louis

CHAPTER THIRTEEN

A GOLD SPITOON AND A TALKING TUBE

None of our friends or other family members, with the exception of Aunt Marianna and Uncle Jean possessed a talking tube.

My imagination brimmed with ideas and I quivered with excitement thinking of the possibility of games with Suzanne, and maybe tricks played on her, freely offered to us by a system of communication existing between each of the three floors of their home. The long pipe with openings at each level became our favorite toy. Suzanne went on her own to the other floors and called me, while I stayed in the kitchen, ear glued to the opening, waiting impatiently for a flutter of breath followed by the muffled sound of her voice. Then came my turn to blow upward, signaling my readiness to talk and send some silly message. We never tired of the game.

Once in a while, the voice coming from the tube enticed me to join its owner on the third floor. I felt ambivalent about it being far away from the family even from the sound of their voices. Too many trunks and armoires spooked me, but Suzanne loved it showing an aggrandized attitude that said: I am in charge. There is nothing to fear.

"A great place for hide and seek," she insisted.

I agreed. But I thought it was too good because I could hide for an hour and never be found. I imagined being locked in a tiny closet or in a room full of dismembered furniture. Uncle and Aunt never threw away anything that they could use for repair—precious debris from the sixteenth and seventeenth centuries: two legged chairs, gaping desks, tarnished hardware, and tilted tables. The owner or their descendants may have even lost their heads to the guillotine. Had I known, I still would have climbed to this floor. I feared my fantasies, but my curiosity, and more so, the determination to impress my sister forced me to accept her challenges.

Despite the titillating experiences of the third floor and the grandeur of the second, I preferred the familiarity of the ground level. There we found Aunt Marianna and Uncle Jean day after day in the same cozy setting. Their actions, gestures and mannerisms, by sheer repetitiveness, are forever etched in my memory like a collage of superimposed images in a fixed décor.

The entrance of the elegant wide hallway offered three choices of venues to explore: climb to the second floor or turn right into a sitting area and dining room or, at the end of the hallway, enter into the kitchen.

Our own kitchen in Saint-Eustache, plus the one in our apartment, would have found ample space in Aunt Marianna's. What aromas could have filled its every corner if Maman had been in charge! In contrast, our aunts' many talents did not include gourmet cooking. It was the display of a dozen or more scissors hanging on three large hooks on the wall near the wood table, each one a different size and shape, that drew me to the kitchen. What riches!

At home, two pairs of scissors hid in Maman's sewing basket. She had another one for everything else from cutting paper to clipping fish fins. Oh, what intricate cut outs I could create by using Aunt Marianna's scissors! Birds with feathery wings and tails; butterflies, their markings hollowed like Maman's embroidered table cloth, each corner letting light through its intricate embroidery. Aunt Marianna had to be, without a doubt, the luckiest woman in the world, not only because of the scissors she owned, but also, because she never washed dishes.

"Non, non, non, Margot," she always told Maman. "Just a quick rinse, then we stack and turn off the lights. My cleaning woman will do the chores tomorrow morning as she does every day." I concluded it must have been the reason why my aunt never looked harassed or heaved sighs of relief when she joined Uncle Jean in the dining room for the evening.

Their dining room, larger than ours in Saint Eustache, also served two purposes: a formal dining area with its twelve place-setting table, a china cabinet and a sizeable buffet, and near the bay window an informal sitting space. It was there, that in late afternoon or after dinner, we sat with Aunt Marianna and Uncle Jean.

The routine did not vary much. Uncle Jean played Parcheesi and Chinese checkers with Suzanne and me, while Maman and Aunt Marianna compared their knitting and chatted quietly. Excusing themselves, they sometimes went to the kitchen and whispered. Usually Maman came back with moist eyes. If by chance our regards met she would offer me a pitiful smile, a smile that quickly vanished for lack of joy.

On certain nights Aunt Marianna turned the radio on for a concert. If a singer happened to perform, all activities stopped. Looks varied with the quality of the singer, and after the last notes, comments were generous. Frequently an opened box of Laura Secord chocolates kept Suzanne and me in the vicinity of the card table where temptation lay in full view. Once we exhausted our ration of two, we excused ourselves. With permission from Uncle, we left the adults for our favorite toy, the speaking tube.

The feeling of ease and warmth I sensed in Uncle Jean and Aunt Marianna's home emanated from their love and deep affection for one another. If a smidgeon of disagreement appeared, either one found an excuse to put a warm hand on the other's shoulder, or deposit a kiss on the head or the nape of the neck. Those gestures were as much a part of their lives as a porcelain flower she fashioned or a poem he created.

To this idyllic picture I must sound a discordant note. Maman said that Uncle Jean, the versifier, had a "dirty habit." In Saint-Eustache when I accompanied her to the general store, I had seen some men who had this same habit. They gathered at the back of the store among

99

barrels of flour, bags of sugar and crates of canned fruits and vegetables to discuss their crops and politics, their conversation sprinkled with jets of tobacco juice that did not always hit the intended spot.

Uncle Jean, a man so well groomed in his smoking jacket sitting with such poise in his high-back chair, a man who had mastered the rules of versification had the same "habit," but with a difference. This man, whose rhythm in poetry was in exact meter, had mastered the distance from mouth to copper spittoon with metric precision. In so many beats, between small explosions from his mouth, the projectile hit its target—plouff— smack in the center. The rim stayed spotless. Somehow Uncle Jean never lost his dignity, no matter how much Maman insisted that he still had "a very dirty habit."

My mother's strong dislike for tobacco juice projectile did nothing to diminish my enthusiasm for a visit to *Carré Saint-Louis* even though the talking tube lay silent since Suzanne's departure for boarding school. Then my explorations became limited to the periphery of Maman's vision—the sitting area in the dining room as far as the swinging door to the kitchen.

When becoming restless, I roamed the room and stood in front of the china cabinet. It resembled ours in Saint-

Eustache containing crystal, cut glass and lovely bonbonnières, however, at home I would find one usually filled with caramel or dark chocolate fudge.

There I stood fearing being caught if I dared open the glass door. Its narrow wood frame stuck to the cabinet, and when pulled, it trembled. Still, I faced a second step fraught with danger: lifting the lid of the cut glass jar, picking a desired piece of candy and putting the lid back on, all without a sound. Needing both hands to close the door, I put the candy in my mouth and proceeded in a push-and pull gesture-developed after many failures I used just enough pressure to hear a subdued click of the latch to avoid the wobbly door convulsing.

Aunt Marianna's empty bonbonnières did not attract me, but a set of china dishes in shades of gray, contoured like flounders, and a matching serving platter in the shape of an elongated fish kept me glued to the door. One day Aunt noticed my recurring fascination and joined me.

"Marcelle, at what are you always looking so intently?"

"The fish dishes, Aunt Marianna. Do you always use them on Fridays?"

"Oh, *non,* only when we have guests. Your Uncle

makes a delicious stuffed salmon and displays it on the long platter. Do you like salmon?"

"Oh, Yes, Aunt Marianna, I do," I hurried to say, though I was not sure.

"Well, good! We will invite you with your mother next."

"And Suzanne?"

"Of course, if she is not at boarding school."

"And you will use the fish plates?"

"Indeed we will."

Walking back together to the sitting area, Aunt Marianna put her arm around my shoulder. I cuddled next to her, my head against her upper round softness, my arms falling short of reaching around her corseted waist.

CHAPTER FOURTEEN

THE STUFFED SALMON THAT SWAM AWAY

True to her promise to invite me to one of Uncle Jean's special stuffed salmon dinners, Aunt Marianna also sent an invitation to Maman, Grand-maman, Aunt Berthe and Uncle Charlie.

Suzanne could not come. The Mother Superior of her boarding school would not allow it.

For the occasion I wore my best dress—actually a hand-me-down from Suzanne—one I looked at with jaundiced eyes since the first day she wore it: a red wine velvet dress with a bolero and Peter Pan collar. As usual, Maman parted my hair and bound it with a rubber band. To fashion a bow she took a ribbon twice the size of my black school ribbon. "See how well it matches the color of your dress." Maman delighted in her find and proceeded to make the biggest bow that ever sat on my head.

Uncle Charlie smiled when he saw me. "My, my, Blondie, you look like a butterfly. I will have to sit next to you in case you take flight. I am the only one quick enough to catch you."

I nodded in agreement; I could see a great game in the making. We winked at each other. I had practiced that whole week knowing Uncle Charlie would be there. But I knew I had not yet achieved the perfect secret wink, because the whole side of my face winked as well.

At the table, in front of each place setting, stood a small card held in a silver holder. By chance Uncle Charlie sat directly across from me. At home Suzanne and I never played games at the table at mealtime, and here, in this formal environment …well…with Uncle Charlie facing me, I felt an electrical charge floating back and forth across the table. With a palpable effort I concentrated on my Leek and Potato Soup; however, between it and the Stuffed Salmon my focus wavered, my restraint slackened; I glanced at Uncle Charlie. His face and upper body looked as rigid as a statue. He held his elbows against his ribs as if to thwart an imminent flight. The game was on.

I shook my head feeling my butterfly bow quiver. I fluttered my elbows and was well on my way to ascend, at which point I perceived, despite the adults' conversation, the electrical current, the quivering and fluttering, the ever-poised Aunt Berthe emit a soft *"Voyons donc* Charlie." Simultaneously, a deep restrained clearing of the throat from Maman forced me to fold my wings back to my side.

While I was busy playing butterfly, Uncle Jean disappeared into the kitchen. Aunt Marianna's helper removed the soup bowls, and brought in steaming serving dishes. She set a warm "flounder" plate in front of each of us. A sudden hush in the conversation followed her exit, and all eyes turned toward the swinging door. Uncle Jean made a grand entrance accompanied by a chorus of "ahs."

"Exquisite," Aunt Berthe said.

"Uncle Jean, you are an artist," added Maman.

Grand-maman smiled.

"Bravo," shouted Uncle Charlie. "A toast to the chef!"

Uncle Jean's broad smile lifted the corners of his mustache. His eyes sparkled with pleasure.

I tried to stand to have a better view. Maman pulled me down. I could see only the under-side of the platter, with parsley, like hanging ivy, precariously poised at the rim. Finally, Uncle Jean set the platter in front of his place. Now I could admire what everyone else had praised—a full-length salmon resting on a bed of ... Oh! No! It had a tail. And worse, it had a head, a gaping mouth and one sorrowful eye. I shivered. Instantly I closed my eyes to shut out the sight of that poor, poor fish. I willed my imagination to take me away, as far away as possible.

It is dusk. I am in Saint-Eustache on the golf course with Papa. We follow the brook where he usually gathers watercress. The water is limpid, moving around and over the rocks and caressing the sand without disturbing a grain. Papa lays his creel next to the water, lifts the lid and gently eases the salmon into the brook. Bay leaves and parsley float around and the slices of lemon change into scales. The fins flutter. Slowly, the body weaves itself into the soft current.

"Papa, where is the salmon going?"

"To our river."

His voice faded giving way to others engaged in civil conversation and to the restrained clinking of silverware on china dishes. Distinctly, Aunt Marianna's voice overcame all others and forced me out of my bucolic escapade.

"Tell me, Marcelle, what do you think of your Uncle Jean's salmon?"

What did I think? A quick push from Maman's elbow to urge me to say something brought forth a halfhearted response. "Oh ... yes, Aunt Marianna, it is very, very ..." Uncle Charlie's big word came to my mind. "Very *extra-or-ordinaire.*" Uncle Charlie winked at me, others giggled, and my already pink face turned a gleaming red...I could feel it. I stayed quiet for the rest of the meal, and swore to myself never, never to eat such a fish, not even when it came from a can where no shape of head, or tail, or sorrowful eye ever appeared.

CHAPTER FIFTEEN

CAN THIS BE A CHRISTMAS TREE

"Maman, where will the Christmas tree go?"

"On the table."

I looked at the table, then at the ceiling. It will go through the ceiling, I thought. In Saint-Eustache our Christmas tree was at least eight feet tall; no puny tree ever entered our house.

"This year we will do something different. I will need your help. We will make a surprise for Suzanne."

After leaving Saint-Eustache, Maman's sadness had increased, and more so since Suzanne's departure for boarding school; more deep sighs, more tears at night when she thought I slept, darker and deeper circles around her eyes. Yet, she pronounced the magic words,

"We will make a surprise!"

Never deterred by her sorrow, Maman, with childlike

joy, gave pleasure to others by celebrating holidays, birthdays or someone's achievement with humorous rhymed prose in their honor, or with culinary delights. For the first time I could help her prepare a surprise for my sister. Together we would decorate the apartment, cover its bareness, put a spark on its dullness.

As quick as a hello and a good-bye, Uncle Charlie brought an armful of pine branches and a red bucket full of rocks. "No time to stay any longer. I must rush to *Marché Bonsecours* before all the capons are sold. I need an extra big one for Blondie. She eats like a wolf." With a wink, a smile and a hug, Uncle Charlie went away, leaving behind a draft of cold air and warm feelings.

First, let's make our tree." She untied one bundle of pine branches, spread them on the table, and looked them over for the longest time. She untied another one, picked some branches and measured them with others. I sat and waited. She gave many hmm, hmm, in a variety of tones.

"Let's make ourselves a Christmas tree bouquet," she said finally.

The thought filled me with wonder, instantly replaced by another. *It won't be much of a bouquet and not much of a tree.*

"How many people do you think will have a Christmas tree bouquet on their dining-room table?"

"Only us," I said. Those two words barely out of my mouth were replaced by an interfering thought. *It's because they have a real tree standing proud and beautiful in their living room.* Yet, Maman looked so happy that I felt guilty, and, without much effort, surrendered to her enthusiasm and the joyous lilt of her voice.

One by one, she picked up the long branches and, holding them like gladioli, placed them in the center. She added more branches by height until it had the shape of a pyramid with its sides flaring out like an unpretentious pagoda. My resistance vanished. I admitted to myself that indeed, Maman had accomplished a small miracle.

"It practically looks like a tree," I said. "It really does!"

"Yes, I think it will be lovely."

"Can we decorate it tonight?"

"Yes, but first let's get the table and the floor cleaned up. Then, we'll slide a pad under the bucket."

Maman never received better help from me than on that night. Head, heart, feet and hands worked in perfect coordination. Astounding! Together we pushed the table against the corner walls, grunting and laughing at our pretense of hard labor. Maman went to the kitchen to fetch water. I liked hearing the water ripple on top and around the rocks, finding a crack, a spot to settle and go to work to keep our tree green.

Maman must have appreciated my work for she offered me the most thrilling job to do while she prepared dinner.

"Why don't you unwrap the ornaments and lay them on the table. Remember, most of them are fragile. Be careful. I'll call you when dinner is ready." I felt ten feet tall.

When we lived in Saint-Eustache it had been Papa who brought the Christmas tree in the living room, and he alone who decorated it. During that time Maman prepared *le réveillon de Noël*—the dinner after Midnight Mass. In the meantime Suzanne and I, tucked in our warm beds, dreamt wondrous dreams.

I took my job seriously as if Papa watched over me. I arranged the ornaments in groups: shiny balls, red cardinals and yellow canaries, houses—two inch squares of fairyland architecture and happy colors, and the cones Maman would fill with spicy fish candies. A gold star I had never seen before intrigued me. I rushed to the kitchen.

"Maman, I found a star!"

"You did?"

"Yes, it's so pretty! Where did you get it? It shines."

"An angel brought it."

I would have liked to believe it, but I knew better. *Maman must have made it while I was in school. And what's more...I had seen the shiny material before.* When Grand-maman or my aunts opened their treasure boxes of remnants, this same gold lamé always attracted my attention. Not wanting to spoil her surprise, I resisted telling her I knew the provenance of the star.

"Can I put the angel's star on the treetop?"

"Yes, it will be the first thing you do. You may have to climb on the table to reach the top,"

That day was improving by the minute. I failed to notice the night approaching until I heard Maman call.

We dined in the tiny kitchen sharing the wall table. Elbows and knees touched; we did not care. Eager to start our decorating, I did not try to postpone doing the dishes.

Less than an hour later I stood on a chair in front of our unadorned Christmas tree bouquet. Maman handed me the star. But I was not tall enough to reach the top. She helped me climb on the table. What fun!

"See, there is an opening on the back, you can slip the star over the top branch … that's it! Perfect. While you are there I will hand you the smaller ornaments."

After many directions as to the best spot for each one, I climbed down to the chair and heard the same, "A little bit to the right, hmm … not so much, this one higher." And on and on it went, with the same care to the lower branches. By then I was safely on the floor and losing some of my enthusiasm; my mother's exactitude diminishing my ardor.

At last, Maman slid our Christmas tree bouquet to the far end of the table in the corner, so that when the three of us sat for meals we would have enough space to eat and at the same time contemplate our creation.

"Let's look at our tree from the entrance," she said.

114

I ran as far as the door and looked back. The light from the ceiling shone over the tree. The star sparkled. My favorites, the colored glass houses, formed a miniature village of cottages in the forest, much like those in Perrault's fairytale book.

"I think we did a spectacular job."

The intruding voice had vanished. Spontaneously I hugged Maman. We giggled, happy with each other and our unique Christmas tree.

Maman turned around and opened the front door. The scent of a spring-like breeze enveloped us.

She looked at me as if overwhelmed by a sudden inspiration. "Let's go outdoors," she said.

My mouth dropped.

"Go, put on your coat and your boots," she added.

I ran to my bedroom. In the excitement I forgot my fear of the large, creaky armoire and its never closing doors. I dressed before Maman had time to help me. This was the most thrilling night I had ever known!

During the day, a heavy snowstorm had covered everything with a soft feathery blanket. Even the parking lot looked inviting. The cling clang sounds of the tramways were far apart and muffled. Couples went by, laughing and sliding. The stars lit up the early night. If Papa had been with us he would have stopped walking and told us to look at them. And, before resuming our walk, he would have said, "Take a deep breath; fill your lungs with pure air."

But Maman and I did not stop. We let ourselves bask in happiness, a joy in my mind projecting itself into the following day when Suzanne and I would play outdoors and make a snowman.

On the sidewalk, we mixed the imprints of our footsteps with those who trudged before us in the un-ploughed, ankle deep snow.

We were three nights away from Christmas Eve, and passersby greeted one another with *Joyeux Noël!* We walked a short distance. The exertion of lifting each foot out of six inches of snow, and the uncertainty of what the ground would be under the next footstep, icy or bumpy, made it less a leisure walk than I had foreseen. After a yawn or two from me, a couple of shivers, and an involuntary slip from Maman, our buoyancy waned.

"I think a cup of hot cocoa is calling us!" Maman said.

"I applauded while performing a pirouette, and like a top out of control landed in the snow bursting in laughter. A gentleman witnessing my indecorous dance offered me a hand and wished me, with his Merry Christmas, a set of healthy bones. "And you're going to need them, little lady, if you keep dancing on the ice like that." Maman thanked him for his help, and wished him equal good fortune.

We made our way home guarding our steps; spirits floating high in a realm seldom visited. Noël was near, and miracles did happen.

Marche Bonsecours

CHAPTER SIXTEEN

COMPANIONS IN MISERY

The sun had not yet replaced the moon when I awoke. I could not stay in bed. I tramped into Maman's bedroom wanting to wake her up, and announced, "It's time to go pick up Suzanne."

Maman mumbled, "Go back to bed, even the nuns are still asleep."

"I can't sleep anymore," said in a voice that would break any mother's heart.

"Oh, alright, come to bed with me." I climbed in her warm bed, a bribe that paid off. We both slept longer.

The trip to Suzanne's boarding school seemed endless. The return worse, and the impulse to say,

"We have a surprise for you," unbearable. The words pressed against each other in my mouth, trying to rush out. Once in a while, one escaped, and, in a flash, I had to invent a different sentence and push the secret word back. Suzanne seemed unaware of my predicament. In the streetcar, she quietly laid her head on Maman's shoulder, and let the tram cradle or bounce her at its whim.

Walking home from the last stop I jackrabbited in front of Maman and Suzanne wanting to hurry them along. To my dismay, my sister did not follow my lead; she and Maman plugged along in the snow. At long last we reached the apartment. Maman unlocked the door. Contrary to her habit of turning off the lights when we left the house, one of her many saving devices, she had left the ceiling light shining on the tree.

I held on to Suzanne's hand wanting no space between her joy and my mounting elation.

"How beautiful, how beautiful!" she kept repeating. She ran to the hall table with me hanging on her sleeve.

Giddy with excitement, I recounted pell-mell the events of Uncle Charlie's visit, and "You won't believe this, we went outdoors at night, late, and the stars were shining..." I had to stop a minute. Maman helped me remove layers of clothing. And then I took off my boots. Suzanne did the same, but on her own. Once we had finished, and put everything away, we sat at the table.

At last I could continue my recitation, but Suzanne laid

her head on the table resting it in the crook of her arm. Maman stroked her cheek and pushed away tendrils of hair, damp with perspiration.

"I think Suzanne needs a rest. Let's get you into bed, young lady." Without a word, she went with Maman. I followed, protesting the loss of my playmate. Turning around, Maman put a finger to her lips. "Later," she said.

I stood at the bedroom door and watched Maman tend to Suzanne. Unprepared for this turn of events and not knowing what to do, I stayed still, deflated.

An eternity later, Maman partially closed the door behind her and joined me.

"What's wrong with Suzanne?" I murmur.

"I'm not sure yet. She has a fever, but it's not a cold. I'm going to call Uncle Georges. He might still be in his office."

Uncle Georges, one of my father's brothers, was a heart and lung specialist. In looks and temperament he was unlike Papa. He had dark hair and dark eyes, a gregarious personality, and more curves than angles on his frame. I liked him.

Maman hung up the phone. "He will be here soon."

Everything came to a standstill. We sat at the table waiting for the doorbell to ring.

Uncle arrived with a reassuring smile on his face. He and Maman went into the bedroom. I tried to inch my way in but was told to stay in the hall. Maman came out a few minutes later, her forehead furrowed with worry.

"I have to call Aunt Berthe you will have to stay with them."

"But why?"

"Suzanne is sick"

"But..."

"Don't."

Her tone of voice froze any other words from popping out of my mouth.

Before long Maman came out of my room with a suitcase, and all the winter's paraphernalia I needed: my coat, snowcap, wool scarf, mittens and boots.

Bending over and smiling, Uncle Georges said, "Let me help you with your boots."

Recovered from my frozen state, I protested. "Why do

I have to go?"

"Suzanne has measles. We don't want you to catch it."

"But I don't mind. It's all right. It really is, Uncle Georges. I want to be here for Christmas."

"Just think," Maman said. "You will have two Christmases, one with Aunt Berthe and Uncle Charlie, and the other one when you come back home. Then the three of us will celebrate together."

All the turmoil, and all the words pouring from the adults made me numb. Maman gave me a hug. But our joy and the expectation of more festivities had vanished, buried deep under the snow that tomorrow the three of us would have shaped into a snowman.

I might as well have stayed home. Christmas Eve Uncle Charlie drove me back to our apartment. I had the same symptoms Suzanne had shown the previous day. Maman gave me her bed. "As long as you are both sick, you should keep each other company." It was fine with me. I did not want to go away in the first place. Suzanne and I smiled at each other, happy companions in misery.

Christmas Eve and Christmas day went by. I failed to

notice I had not heard church bells and sleigh bells at midnight; neither did I smell the rich aroma of ragout of pork or spices of home-made sausage, or seasonings of a golden turkey. I had not worried about Maman alone in my little bed, away from Papa and the home she had lovingly made. No, I was safe next to Suzanne, cared for by Maman. I slept soundly, fever and pills keeping me dull and drowsy.

Uncle Georges came back to check on us. He invited us to come visit him and Aunt Yvonne, his wife, as soon as we were well enough to go out. "You can skate and toboggan in the park," he added. That was enough to cure anyone; until then, however, it pasted broad smiles on our faces. I hoped it would be before Suzanne went back to boarding school so we could go together. The week following Epiphany she would leave us again.

Papa had come and left two parcels while we slept. I heard Maman say to Uncle Georges, "I'm sure that woman bought the presents, Louis never shops." Maman did not give them to us. I wished I had at least seen Papa. I knew he was afraid of illness, but we could have talked to him while he stood at the bedroom door...or maybe, he did just that, but as with Christmas the fever erased the memory.

When Uncle Georges tapped on my chest, I took advantage of his nearness to softly ask where Papa was at Christmas. He whispered in my ear, "In Saint-Eustache at your Aunt Gabrielle and Uncle Achille's home."

I wondered if he told stories to my cousins—our stories. Selfishly I hoped not, but I had a feeling he must have and my throat tightened.

CHAPTER SEVENTEEN

CHRISTMAS AND NEW-YEAR'S WENT BY

"Suzanne," I whispered, "Do you think Papa will come tomorrow morning to give us his blessing?"

"Maybe, Maman is cooking a lot."

"Do you want him to come?

"I don't know, do you?"

"Yes." I answered, although I was not sure. Maman had cried less and less since we started preparing for Christmas, and even started to sing. Suzanne and I could not figure out whether Maman would be happy or sad if Papa came to visit on New Years Day. Suzanne, in her nine years of acquired wisdom, thought that if Papa were to come he would probably leave again, and that would be terrible for Maman.

"She certainly would be twice as sad." She said.

New Year's morning arrived. Papa did not. And

Maman's song faded like a neglected memory. I guess she had hoped he would come. That New Year's Day would be the only one where my father disregarded the century-old French-Canadian tradition whereby on the first day of the year, the patriarch of each family blesses the members of his household. We pretended that all was well, and his name never passed our lips in front of Maman.

Like two rays of sun, Uncle Charlie and Aunt Berthe, both smiling, came by to visit, and neither said anything about Papa. Grunting, pretending exhaustion, Uncle Charlie showed us the large pot of chicken soup he carried.

"Here's your capon, Blondie. We melted it down in case you lost all your teeth."

I showed him how solid they were.

"Well, well, I guess I'll have to take the soup back home."

Suzanne and I protested for form, because we knew he would not.

"Charlie, let Suzanne and Marcelle rest," said Aunt Berthe peeking around his shoulders. "We will celebrate the three holidays all together next week. By then, you will feel much better. Your grandmother will be here and also Aunt Irène. Rest well." We smiled back. They left us and joined Maman. I could hear them whispering. Too feverish to make the effort to decipher what was being said, I let myself slide into slumber.

Maman busied herself all week. Day by day our fever diminished, and our faces regained their normal contours. We tried to persuade her, without success that we were well enough to get up. Maman, a firm believer in long convalescences, thwarted any escapade from bed we might contemplate, by joining us in coloring our books, playing games of Parchesi and Chinese checkers, and reading us stories.

One glorious morning, Suzanne and I, wrapped in our chenille robes, sat at the hall table with our smiling Maman. Christmas and New Year had past, but one holiday remained. The Christmas tree bouquet pouring forth its pine scent, and the ornaments shining under the ceiling's lighted globe, revived our excitement. At last we sat together, our expectations rising.

"When will we celebrate Epiphany Maman?"Suzanne asked. You can count the days on one hand," Maman said.

CHAPTER EIGHTEEN

THE THIRD HOLIDAY

Two days before Epiphany, Maman turned her miniature kitchen into a major culinary enterprise. The distinctive smell of ragout of pork, and meat balls spiced with clove and cinnamon, intermingled with the sweet fragrances of apple pie and maple syrup *tartelettes*.

Early morning, on the day of Epiphany (The three Kings) the aroma of a butter cake floated in the air. It was the French tradition to hide a pea and a bean in the batter. Maman had found a way to recognize where the two vegetables were, so that Suzanne and I usually received the propitious pieces. As soon as our teeth bit on the hard surface of the vegetables, we declared victory. Then Maman, the perpetrator of this deceit, deposited artfully decorated cardboard tiaras on our heads, and crowned us king and queen.

By afternoon, the buttery redolence of the Epiphany

cake had evaporated and replaced by the tantalizing scent of roasting capon. It teased our newfound appetites. Maman's happy busyness, and the return of her lovely soprano voice, announced the long awaited celebration.

The doorbell rang at four o'clock. A flurry of *Bonjour* and of *Bonne Année* crisscrossed in the air. Aunt Berthe and Uncle Charlie came in carrying a card table and chairs, followed by Aunt Irène with more chairs, and Grand-maman with presents.

"Stay in your room, girls, until the door is closed."

We heard the front door opening and closing, the swoosh of a car trunk, instructions and laughter. Finally they came in, with bags full of Christmas presents, and dropped them in the living room. We knew because, though our feet were in the bedroom, our heads and shoulders stretched toward the hallway.

We retreated quickly. Uncle Charlie brought the card table and two chairs into our room.

"We have to sit as far away from you as possible. We don't want your old germs attacking us."

I ran after him. "I will kiss you Uncle Charlie, I will kiss you." He was faster and hid himself behind the living-room door. I heard two voices at once: "*Voyons donc, Charlie,*" and, "Marcelle, go back to the bedroom," a family duet of sorts.

Quietly, Uncle Charlie tiptoed along the hallway, picked up the Christmas tree and took it to the ugly living room. He came back, still tiptoeing, and added a panel to the hall table. "Now, ladies," he whispered, "I will leave you and go read my newspaper."

In her most adult sound-alike-voice Suzanne asked, "*Le Devoir* or *La Presse* Uncle Charlie?"

"*La Presse.*"

We blew kisses at him. Pretending to be horrified, he put one hand over his mouth and nose and hurried away.

Aunt Irène and Grand-Maman did not hesitate to kiss us, and mention how well we looked. With a smile, Grand-Maman left us and hurried to see if Maman needed help. Aunt Irène stayed and looked over our coloring books, offering an equal amount of praises and criticism.

Most of the time, Aunt Irène sported a medium-sized good mood. She had no children, and did not suffer bad manners, foolishness or the stupidity of others. Men did not fare better, unless, of course, they were polite, intelligent, cultured, gifted with a sense of humor and talented in the arts. Her deceased husband lacked three of those elements.

At age forty-four, Aunt Irène had already been a widow for ten years and was financially independent. It gave her a certain air of authority, which coupled with strong opinions, antagonized my father. She disliked him just as much. We never saw her in our home, and Papa did not allow us to visit with her. Their shared dislike started before our parents' marriage, when Aunt Irène warned Maman that he was a lady's man, and at his age he probably would never change—a sentence the innocent young Margot had repeated to him.

When Aunt Irène left our bedroom, Suzanne and I followed her tiptoeing down the hallway. Maman saw us from the kitchen and we heard the too familiar, "Please, go back to your room, rest before dinner."

We dragged our feet back.

"Suzanne, did you see all the presents? Are they all for us?"

"Maybe for everybody. I don't know."

We wondered, and giggled, and imagined, and hoped that it would be such and such, or even better, something else. And, with all our wishing and wanting, dinner was ready.

Despite our young age, we usually enjoyed the period after a meal when adults reminisced. We did not realize then, that our family history registered in our souls. We lingered around the table not knowing that such moments, such sharing, such love could never again be stitched into so perfect a design. But for Suzanne and me, on that special night, joy, wrapped in colorful paper, shimmered at our fingertips. The adults reminiscing would postpone it all. Our fear, however, did not materialize. The scraping of chairs pushed away from the table brightened our outlook. The time for receiving presents was only minutes away.

During the time her sisters had put away the dinner's remnants Maman had straightened our bedroom; we were washed, combed and ready. Bright eyed, Suzanne and I sat up in our beds.

Everyone came in carrying presents. I clapped my hands in excitement. In all my life, I had never seen so many at once. I opened the first one. A doll? Not really. She had the face and body of an adult person and was dressed like a nurse. Her hand held a satchel. Puzzled and not thrilled, I kept a smile on my face, and said, *"Merci beaucoup."* Out of her box I watched Suzanne pull a doll, a little man, also carrying a doctor's satchel. That was not all; there was a horse at the bottom.

"Do you know who they are?" asked Aunt Irène.

"Docteur Thibodeau et garde Beauchamp?" I ventured.

"No. Think hard," said Maman.

The only doctor I knew who had horses was *Docteur Thibodeau.* I looked at Suzanne. She shrugged her shoulders.

"If the girls don't know should we still give them the other presents?" teased Aunt Irène.

"Oh, yes please," we begged, looking at the parcels she held.

Smiling, she handed them to us. "Be careful, it's fragile."

Suzanne and I gingerly unwrapped our boxes at the same time. In mine I found two five inch dolls dressed in white nightgowns, one decorated with a pink ribbon, the other a light green. I looked at Suzanne's. She had three identical dolls in the same white nightgowns with different colored ribbons. We looked at each other.

"*Les quintuplettes Dionne,*" we shouted in unison. Like the painted smiles of clowns, ours were stuck in awe as we opened a doll's wardrobe overflowing with knitted socks and sweaters of five different colors, and coats and dresses to match.

Suzanne, who had learned the basics of knitting, said. "I don't know how you can make things so small, Aunt Irène."

"With the patience of an angel," she answered. "Look at the work your Grand-maman did." She showed us the coats. They were lined. "Can you imagine how difficult it was for her to turn the little sleeves inside out? She did all of it by hand."

We lifted our arms toward them. They bent over to receive our hugs and kisses.

"Well, well, well, girls. I think that you have enough presents now. There is no more space on the beds. I think we'll have to wait until next week to give you the rest or… maybe not until your birthdays? Then we won't have to buy new presents!"

137

Aunt Berthe shook her head and smiled. "*Voyons donc*, Charlie, stop teasing the girls."

We hurried, and with Maman's aid we cleared enough space on our beds to receive Uncle Charlie's surprise.

Acting like *Père Noël,* he pulled two onions and two oranges out of a large red cloth bag. "There you are. You eat a raw onion and one orange, and you'll never have the measles again."

Like Aunt Berthe we shook our heads at him, and a chorus of "*Voyons donc,* Charlie," and laughter joined in protest.

"Well, well. I just want them to be healthy." Saying so, he pulled a bulb of garlic out of his pocket. There was one loud "Charlie!" and more laughter. Keeping his eyes on Suzanne and me, he rummaged around the bottom of the bag coming up with a tiny package, which he put at the end of the bed. A second, a third, and finally a fourth joined the first. I could tell they had been wrapped by Aunt Berthe they looked like individual pieces of art.

Suzanne and I watched our Santa closely. His hand was still in the bag and something protruded through the cloth. Grunting, as if pulling a boulder, inch by inch a wooden, homemade bed with foot and headboards appeared. We applauded. Uncle Charlie's act was over, and the bed was lovely. We opened the four parcels. Maman and Aunt Berthe had made a mattress, five pillows, two sheets, a blanket and a miniature quilt. Overwhelmed, Suzanne and I jumped out of bed to embrace everyone.

The adults left us to our world of make believe and went to the living room to exchange their presents. Mixed with the sounds of our own mothering, we heard Maman's steps in the kitchen. She was preparing the dessert. Somehow the Epiphany's crowns had lost their luster. We had more important things to do: put five babies to bed; find a home for the nurse, one for the doctor and a stable for the horse.

Our ears perked at Aunt Irène's laughter.

"I find bits and pieces of this dress of mine in the strangest places!" She had noticed the star. Suzanne and I glanced at one another, a smile of know-it-all on our faces. As we already knew, our own angel had rummaged in the shoebox and successfully transformed one more vestige of the gold lamé evening dress into the brightest star on top of a make-believe Christmas tree.

CHAPTER NINETEEN

PAPAS' THREAT

One day in the fourth week of January, Maman and I opened our front door to a cold, sunny afternoon. This time, no gale hurled around to snatch Maman's hat and send her running across tramway tracks in pursuit of her capricious wind-powered chapeau. Maman had accepted Uncle Georges' invitation, and Aunt Yvonne had confirmed it. She planned that I would go to the park and toboggan with their son, Jean.

Walking toward our destination, Maman smiled. Could it be she was anticipating the pleasure of being served, of dining and conversing with adults after being confined to the house for over three long weeks with two sick daughters? Or could it be that while she held my hand, a thought, not wanting to frighten reason, gently insinuated itself and displaced all others: he might be there. After all, it was at his brother's house that they had met so long ago.

Maman was eighteen then. She had large, brown eyes bright with life—and such a smile—a smile that opened wide on perfect teeth, ready to bite at a good word and release a quick repartee, a face expectant of love and adventure. He was thirty-two, tall, handsome and charming.

Maman smiled.

I was six years old and held on to her hand. She was my mother. Who else could she be but my mother watching my steps, answering my why's and why not's. She smiled. And I smiled simply because we were together on a pleasant outing.

We arrived one hour later, I, mummified in layer upon layer of wool, Maman with her hat still in place, tipped over the left eye. She looked best in those hats. But I preferred the spring and summer ones with the veils; they whispered of mysteries and secrets. On that special day she wrapped a green, ochre and yellow taffeta scarf under her collar, loosely looped in a laissez-faire bow that softly swayed on the front of an otherwise ordinary brown winter coat.

"Come in, you must be frozen."

Uncle Georges and Aunt Yvonne greeted us warmly. Aunt Yvonne, an imposing woman of towering height and personality, spoke with a well-controlled, powerful voice. Hatted with a horned helmet, she could have played the part of a Valkyrie. I shrank in her presence, but Uncle George's joviality helped me regain a couple of inches.

My cousin, Jean, relaxed and cheery, came in to say hello. He lived at home while studying for a degree in dentistry, and seemed delighted to have an excuse to leave the house.

"I have to breathe some fresh air. I've been cooped up studying all morning." He was ready to take me to the park. I did not know him well, but with his carefree attitude I could foresee a good time.

After a run and a mighty push from Jean we darted down the hill. We spilled more than once, barely missing a couple of trees, our screams and laughter intermingling. By the end of the hour, trudging up one more hill, I dragged behind Jean. He sat me on the toboggan and pulled me up the hill enough times to welcome the five o'clock apéritif and dinner call. As for

143

me, I decided that a big brother would be grand.

"Let's go in." Jean said. "We don't want to be late for dinner."

I knew if Aunt Yvonne said that dinner was served at a certain hour, we had better be on time and in the proper attire. I did not insist on staying longer.

Jean started walking, stopped, turned to face me, and said, "You know Marcelle, your name doesn't fit you."

I stopped. "Why not?"

"Hm." He shook his head; looked at me with a frown. *Non, non, non.* You are an Astrid. I went to Sweden and met the queen, and guess what her name was?"

"Astrid?" I mumbled.

"Yes, exactly. You are a pure Astrid."

I smiled, blushed, felt quite comfortable with this new name, I even visualized a crown on my head; I walked with great dignity to the apartment.

"Monsieur, Mesdames," said Jean as we entered the living room. "May I present to you Princess Astrid of Sweden."

As Jean had instructed me while we removed our outdoor clothing, I inclined my head slightly. Going along with our make-believe they stood up; I went around to each and shook hands. Uncle Georges was less proper. After greeting me with a cheery "Enchanted, Princess," he landed a gentle pat on my royal derrière, resulting in behind-the-hand chuckles from my subjects.

"Dinner is served, Madame."

I had forgotten the butler. Tonight he fitted perfectly with my new status. Going around the room, playing princess, I had paid little attention to Maman. At the dinner table I sat next to her and noticed that she kept her eyes riveted on her plate, joining the conversation only when asked a direct question. Before long she excused herself; a lull in the conversation ensued. Aunt Yvonne made a gesture to Uncle Georges. He got up and left the dining room.

I knew something was wrong, and asked permission to be excused.

"I think you had better finish your dinner first," said Aunt Yvonne.

Blushing, I whispered, "I need to go to the bathroom."

"Then, go ahead, dear."

I got up and went in the direction Maman had gone, down the hallway. I could hear Uncle Georges speaking. I followed the sound of his voice and heard Maman's sobbing. I stopped. I wanted to go in, but Uncle Georges' tone of voice prevented me.

"You have to stop crying, Margot. I tell you, if you don't you will lose the girls. Louis asked me…"

"*Hé, Princesse.*" Jean called. "Where are you?"

I wish I could have hidden somewhere, but he was too near already. I returned to the dining room. Forgotten were the trappings of my new title: the elongated neck, the jutted chin, the straight shoulders. I picked up my fork. With difficulty I swallowed a couple of bites. Aunt Yvonne must have taken pity on me; she rang the butler.

"I think Princess Astrid is saving space for Spanish cream," Jean said. I was not. A lump of fear took all the space in my throat; even the dish of chocolates did not tempt me.

Uncle Georges came back to the table. I looked at him.

"Your mother does not feel well. She will join us later."

I forced a smile and bowed my head looking at my dish of Spanish cream.

"Jean, I don't think that Marcelle has ever seen the lights and the skaters in the park," said Uncle Georges. "Why don't you take her out."

"Thank you, Papa.   One more minute, one more chocolate and I would have been caught between my chair and the table. Let's go, Astrid, my dear, the night is calling." He swallowed the rest of his wine in one gulp, which brought a frown to Aunt Yvonne forehead. Jean did not seem to notice. He excused himself, and I followed him.

It took my breath away. Ropes of Christmas lights lit the park. The skating rink, like a brook in the woods, meandered in no special pattern. Snow like blotches of white gouache lapped at tree trunks and branches sparkled.   From   the   speaker,   Strauss   waltzes accompanied the sliding and slicing of ice; skirts swayed, and my heart leaped, and twirled and embraced this gigantic Christmas card.

We watched. I held on to Jean's hand feeling safe. Nonetheless, like an inopportune guest, Maman's sorrow seeped through my joy.

147

"Jean."

"Yes."

"Jean, what does it mean?"

"What does what mean?"

"What Uncle Georges said."

"What did he say?"

"He said to Maman, if you don't stop crying you *will lose the girls.*"

"Where did you hear that?"

"Tonight, when Uncle Georges spoke to Maman in the bedroom…she was crying."

"You must have misunderstood. That's what happens when little girls listen at closed doors."

"*Non.* I know I heard it. And I don't want Maman to lose us. Where would we go?"

"It's impossible, Princess Astrid. My father would never say such a thing."

"Jean, my name is Marcelle." I was in no mood to play his game any longer.

"Alright, Marcelle, even if it were so, no one would let it happen. But I am sure you misunderstood. You have to stop snooping."

Embarrassed, but not persuaded that I was wrong, I looked at the ground.

Jean bowed deeply in front of me. "*Princesse* Marcelle, may I have this waltz? *S'il vous plaît princesse,* my toes are freezing. I have to dance, otherwise I shall become an ice statue."

His silliness broke through. I giggled. Jean picked me up in his arms and started dancing in the snow, pirouetting and singing with the music. It did not take too many pirouettes for him to lose his footing. Laughing madly, we landed in a heap in the soft snow.

As soon as we recovered, Jean said, "It must be time for another chocolate. Let's go before they eat them all." We ran hand in hand.

Our evening ended quickly. Maman, her eyes lined with red, valiantly smiled and made conversation. How well drilled women were in the art of propriety, and how well I already knew that smile, those empty words.

Uncle Georges drove us home.

As soon as we walked in the apartment, Maman said, "Let's get ready for bed. You must be tired, and I am exhausted."

We undressed, shedding the magic of the day, the foolish hope, the park, its lights, its waltzes. Bereft of their charms, Maman's hat and scarf rested on a shelf until the next outing.

We said our habitual I love you. She held me in her arms longer than usual, tucked me in bed, turned my light off and softly walked out, as if her quiet exit could put to rest the dread filling our minds.

I could not sleep.

Over and over I heard Uncle George's words,

"Margot, you have to stop crying. If you don't, you will lose the girls. Louis asked me..." How I wish I knew the rest of the sentence. I imagined sentences starting with, "Louis asked me... Louis asked me if I would take the girls, Louis asked me if I thought that Gabrielle would keep one of them, Louis asked me if I knew of an orphanage that would keep them both." Tears came to my eyes, pushed out by a heart filled with fear. I wanted to be with Maman.

I ran to her room.

As I expected, she was crying. I made my way to her bed and snuggled up to her. I patted her shoulder. "It's alright to cry, Maman Margot. I won't tell anybody, I promise. Not even Suzanne, not even Uncle Charlie, I promise. And I will never, never tell Papa."

Maman turned around and embraced me.

"I love you, Maman Margot," I whispered.

I kissed her salty cheeks. In the darkness I could not see her expression, but my heart perceived a smile.

Papa approximately 49 years old

CHAPTER TWENTY

PERRÔT ISLAND

Winter had gone: below zero weather, glacial winds, icicles—winter had been put away in cedar chests with woolens and furs. Ice patches broken into splinters under the impatient boots of a people starved for warmth, were now mere puddles; the sound of heels beating their cadence on bare side-walks—music.

Easter, on a warmer breeze, had visited us with its promise of a better life somewhere beyond billowy clouds and infinite stretches of blue serenity. On its journey it left us yellow ribbons and chocolate bunnies—paradise!

Summer showed up, and our life changed course.

Aunt Marianna arranged for us to stay at a friend's summer house the last week of June and the first of July. We had a week to prepare our escapade. Suzanne came home from boarding school that weekend to try on her summer clothes, as she had grown out of last year's. I inherited her dresses and was promised a new one.

153

Aunt Irène hurried to Eaton's on rue Sainte-Catherine, the shopper's paradise. She bought material and patterns, and Grand-Maman came to sew.

At night, from my bedroom, I could hear the continuing whirr of the sewing machine, the barely perceptible sound of the treadle's rocking motion and our two tailors' whispers.

"It's late, Maman let's go to bed."

"One more minute, Margot, I'm almost finished." The Singer's singsong slowed to a halt, and then more whispers.

Tired but expectant, we slept in that apartment where happiness, at times, painted a brighter scene; where, now and then, the shadow disappeared and joy radiated enchantment like a brave crocus on a new spring day.

We were ready for Uncle Charlie when he arrived to drive us to l'Île Perrot. What a great adventure!

As usual Uncle Charlie entertained us with his true or false knowledge of the towns we passed. We followed the Saint-Lawrence River, but did not always see it, and then a dash of wavy blue would appear through the wood clearings.

For a while the river narrowed and across it we could see the village of Chateauguay.

"There was a lot of fighting here over one hundred years ago," declared Uncle Charlie. "*Oui Mesdames*, we defeated *les Américains.* I know because I was there."

"Uncle Charlie, how old are you?" Suzanne asked.

"Well, well. You have been in school all year, you tell me."

Suzanne answered so fast I could not believe how clever she was.

"Uncle Charlie, you are at least one hundred and ten years old!"

His laughter filled the car.

"I have known for years," said Maman, "that your uncle must be Methuselah's age, he has so many tall tales to tell."

"Yes," I added, "and I can hear his knees crack."

"I will remember this, Blondie!"

I hid on the floor.

"Marcelle, no playing in the car, it's too dangerous, sit."

155

I simply could not understand adults.

Our chalet's architecture lacked originality: a square building with a screened-in veranda facing the lake, a second floor, for the most part unfinished, but still used when overnight guests overflowed the downstairs' capacity.

The summer nest, satisfying for guests and children, was less so for mothers who still had to cook, clean, wash, and if no father vacationed with them, watch diligently their children's swimming activities: indeed not a vacation. Nevertheless, all the home chores were accomplished in a pastoral décor. For Maman, any change of scenery might have been welcomed.

The lake was beautiful, but so large that for me it lacked coziness and mystery. I turned around and went to inspect the groves isolating the chalet on each side. I saw more pine trees and more cedars here than in Saint-Eustache and the oak trees had leaves as large as my father's hand. The ground was a mixture of sand, pine needles and plain old dirt, but the plusses were there—boulders—boulders to hide behind, to sit or stand on in order to watch the horizon for ships and rowboats bringing Jean Lafitte ashore.

"This is a good place to play pirates," I told Suzanne.

"Maybe," she said. Her voice projected no excitement, she was not a pirate person.

I stayed near her. I had yet to differentiate the look of our chalet from the others. I feared getting lost. I followed her to the edge of the water where she climbed on a huge boulder. I tried to follow her with much sliding back and grunting. Suzanne wore a look of resignation, but she helped me up. I squeezed next to her. I didn't know what to say and sighed. She looked at me. "Do you want to go back to Montréal when our two weeks are over? She asked.

I had not thought that far. "You?"

"Non. I wish I could go back to school."

I was dumbfounded. "Why would you want to go back to school in summer?"

"Because I have many friends there, and I can play the piano."

"But your friends have gone home, haven't they?"

"I suppose so."

"If you want, I can be your friend."

157

She didn't say anything.

"I will do everything you want me to do. I will even let you play with my scooter. I promise."

The word brought back to my mind the promise I had made Maman not to tell anyone if she cried. If only I could tell Suzanne what had happened that night, maybe she would think that I was more like one of her older friends; that I had important things to say, and we could both keep the secret. I had to think about this.

For five days, I played pirates mostly by myself and found a hiding place large enough to store a huge cache of treasure. Suzanne missed all that. She had her nose in a book—one of her end-of-the-school-year prizes. I let her read, but I wanted so much to talk with her.

So, with nothing better to do, I joined Maman in the kitchen. If she was busy writing a letter, I sat at the other end of the table and practiced my handwriting, or colored, or dressed paper dolls. I liked it best when Maman baked because then it was like being in Saint-Eustache again.

Through the kitchen window we saw trees and a sliver of the lake. A familiar scent of wood and water seeped through the screen door, a fragrant background to her cooking. I watched Maman's habitual gestures: mixing, stirring, whipping batter; her energy, her instructions. "You have to let the air in," she said as she intermittently added half a cup of milk and flour to the creamy, sugary mix, the color of pale egg yolk. "Not too much at one time, and always end with the flour," she reminded me, though I would never have the chance to try until after I married, but I had not forgotten her admonitions.

At night, we often sat on the porch and played games of Parcheesi, Chinese Checkers or Old Maid. Other evenings our chatter ceased when fog, like Sunday morning incense, floated over the shore. Thoughts, as nebulous as the conditions of her life, inevitably invaded her mind. As if a storm roared, she gathered her daughters, her only true possessions. Closing the door against an invading gloom, she turned the light on in the kitchen and fed the wood stove kindling and a small log. "It will chase the humidity," she insisted.

The warmth of the kitchen, a familiar announcer's voice on Radio Canada, and the music enshrined her in the safety of the known. Ignoring her newspaper, she joined her daughters in laughter and play, enclosing them in an invisible cocoon of normalcy, love, and protection.

159

CHAPTER TWENTY ONE

ONE CALL, MANY QUESTIONS

The first phone call we received after arriving at l'Île Perrôt came from Aunt Irène Mignault. To differentiate her from Maman's sister Irène, we called her by her full name or Aunt Irène-Alfred. Once we knew which one we were talking about she regained her surname without appendage.

Her husband, Uncle Alfred, Papa's youngest brother, had pursued studies in dentistry to please his father, however the minute his father died he cancelled his classes, although he already was in his last year of studies. His dream of being a musician had grown with him since his mother had taught him piano. In college he studied organ, and without thinking any further, unattached at the time, he embraced his new profession. Alas, the lingering depression of the twenties and thirties did not spare musicians. Music became a luxury.

Not long after making his decision he met Aunt Irène, a violinist. Still full of hopes Uncle Alfred proposed and married the beautiful musician. Years later, he confided that if he had met Aunt Irène earlier he would have finished his studies in dentistry. Nevertheless, they both were in love and both embraced a life that would ask from each to accept living sparingly. Uncle took a full time job as a church organist, and in his free time sold articles of worship necessary for the church services.

Aunt Irène with a growing family put her violin away and spent her free time making the clothes for her children and herself.

Once in a while, her youngest daughter France, recalled, "Maman took the violin down from the shelf. I watched her with the same intensity as if she had been opening a coffer full of precious stones. First she dusted the case, and then slowly flipped the latches and lifted the cover, smiling as if to say, "you are still here my old friend, I have not forgotten you;" the ritual becoming more precious as months of disuse went by. The removal of the bow from the blue velvet cover, and then the lifting of the violin from the case, the tactile embrace of musician and instrument like that of mother and child; the infant resting its head in the crook of his mother's neck, and responding to her touch."

"But with four children she had little time or energy to play the violin. She not only made all our clothes and her own," said France "but supervised our studies, and accompanied us to the library; plus, of course, doing the regular housework chores. No, through the years the violin slept untouched for longer and longer periods of time."

"One day," France said, "the empty shelf revealed a secret; Papa had traded the violin in exchange for a cello for my youngest brother André."

But what of Aunt Irène's longing? I wondered. How many times did she walk to the closet and rest her forehead on the door? What happened in her heart when she heard her son's feeble attempt on his first cello? As the years went by, I know that she took pride in André's accomplishments.

Aunt Irène's phone call to Maman lasted only two minutes. Conscious of cost, conversation was kept to a minimum. It mattered not who initiated the call. There existed an unspoken understanding that it was an emergency, or that some important information had to be communicated immediately.

We heard Maman say to Aunt Irène, "Yes, the girls will be so happy to see their cousins. No, it's no problem I assure you." She answered mostly, "Yes," and "No," and "Yes, I will try," and "Yes, we will see. Yes, thank you, Irène." When she hung up the phone, we heard a voice robbed of its natural lilt, saying, "Lyse and France will spend the weekend with us."

"Isn't André coming with them?" I wanted to know.

"No, he wouldn't like playing with four girls."

"But he might like playing pirate with me."

"Marcelle, it has been decided. Your Aunt Irène agrees with me." Maman walked toward the kitchen door, stopped but did not turn around. "By the way, your father will bring them over," she said, and walked out of the kitchen.

Suzanne and I looked at each other, befuddled. I needed someone to tell me if I should jump for joy, or be wary. I knew by the tilt of my sister's head and the wrinkles on her forehead that she was as puzzled as I.

"Let's go outside," she said.

We walked to the boulder near the beach. She helped me climb on top. We sat, at first silent, each pondering our own scenario.

"Do you think that Papa is coming to see if we can all be together again?" Suzanne said.

"Hmm, maybe, maybe he doesn't love that woman anymore. Or maybe she died." The last, an idea I particularly liked.

"I think Papa just wants to visit. Maman will be sad again."

Only a few minutes ago she had left the kitchen to go to her bedroom. That image superimposed itself on others I had already witnessed in my six years.

I stand at my parents' bedroom door in Saint-Eustache. My mother faces the window—always facing that window—as if her stare will conjure up her faithless husband. She cries. Timidly I go to her. Without looking at me, she folds me in her arms. We cry together.

Suzanne looked at me. "Why are you crying?"

Suzanne's question, like a key unlocking a box of sorrows, provokes a flood of tears.

"Maman can't- can't cry anymore."

"What?"

"Maman ... can't ... cry anymore."

"Why?"

"Because she will lose us."

"You make no sense. Why are you saying that?"

I waited before answering. The more I thought, the more I became persuaded that I had to reveal my secret to Suzanne before our father arrived. Knowing her, I was sure she would want to make him feel welcome, saying how much we had missed him. I feared that she would reveal that Maman, missing him so, had cried a lot.

"Marcelle, tell me, what were you saying?"

Still sniffling, I shed my guilt and told her what had happened that night at Uncle George's house. Suzanne listened without interrupting. She seemed to understand. But she appeared unimpressed by the recounting of my imaginary-tragic scenarios of what might happen if Papa took us away from Maman. Her solution was simple: we try to keep her from crying by always being very good. And if she still cries, then we keep it a secret from everybody.

"Let's go and see if she's alright." She said. She glanced at me with eyes raised toward heaven—a

166

wordless sign of annoyance…"There, blow your nose."

She handed me a clean, perfectly folded handkerchief. Mine had many uses, but none for the intended purpose. One might be used as a pad for an empty jar filled with wild flowers, another as a mat for treasures at the bottom of my pirate cache. My doll also enjoyed one on her head when we went out in the sun. After I was through blowing, Suzanne refused to take back the handkerchief.

"Keep it, and please, don't lose it. Come on, let's go." All said in a very annoying motherly tone.

We slid off our mount and walked back to the chalet.

Maman sat at the kitchen table. She did not look up. "You are just in time to help me decide on meals to prepare for the weekend," she said. "I need inspiration. We will go shopping after lunch."

"Alright," we shouted with enthusiasm as if Maman had offered us an outing to Parc Belmont, instead of having to help her carry bags of groceries from the store.

Irène Mongeau Mignault

Cousin André

Lyse,France,Uncle Alfred, André

Uncle Alfred

CHAPTER TWENTY TWO

THE VISITORS

Sunday afternoon we left the chalet at three-thirty and walked toward the train station.

Early that morning, the iceman, the milk man, and two farmers came by to sell their goods. We had already gone to the bakery to buy three loaves. To please all the children Maman purchased an Angel Food Cake and covered its top with a glossy, dark chocolate glaze that trickled on all sides to the plate and formed pools of chocolate on the unadorned china.

We walked and walked, finally turning the corner from the main street to the train station. We saw them coming in our direction, Lyse and France on each side of

Papa—France even holding his hand. My heart tightened. *Had he exchanged them for us? Were they his little girls now?*

Suzanne must have had no such thought, for she ran to greet them. But Maman and I remained at a distance. I could feel the grip of her hand squeezing my fingers.

The three girls approached us, chatting, while Maman and I waited, our feet glued to the pavement.

"P'tit Blond, aren't you going to come and kiss me?"

Maman disengaged her hand from mine. "Go, meet your father."

Papa smiled. I ran into his outstretched arms; he scooped me up. I buried my face in his neck. Like the sounds of nights near my river, his arms, his scent, his voice, his smile were home to me. He held me tightly while he walked. "My goodness, you weigh a ton!" I wished he would carry me all the way to the house like a precious parcel one holds despite aching arms; a thing so dear that one would not want, ever, to separate from it. But he put me down.

Blinded by my own feelings, I had forgotten Maman.

Back at the chalet, Suzanne, Lyse, France and I made

trip after trip up and down the narrow staircase bringing bedding to the attic, dropping this and that, laughing. What a picnic it was.

"Girls, when you are through making your beds, put on your bathing suits."

"Alright, Maman." "Alright, Aunt Margot," we replied in unison.

"Please, hang your dresses on the back of your chairs. Lyse, please, make sure they do."

"*Oui, ma tante* Margot," said Lyse. She took her role seriously. She was two years older than Suzanne. It was less of a picnic than I had foreseen, but if I complied I would be at the beach with Papa sooner than the others. Lyse helped me, and I was the first one downstairs. When I came to the porch I heard Papa say to Maman, "Let's discuss it tonight." He was smiling.

The lake's glacial water did not stop anyone from running in, except for me who stayed with minnows in a reassuring six inches of water. A frenzy of yelps and brrrrs disrupted the birds from their daily routine, and the splash of bodies momentarily interfered with the wave's orderly rhythm.

Papa's voice remained calm and firm. *"It's far enough,"* he told the three mermaids. He led me to deeper water trying to make me swim; however, he tired before I did, and decided it was time for a rest.

"Let's go sit on the beach a minute," he said.

I would have liked to stay in the water, but I followed him without fussing. I hoped that my good-girl attitude would entice Papa not to leave us again. I sat close to him, imitating his posture: straight back, knees up, arms around them.

"Suzanne, France, you are too far out, stay with Lyse." Papa kept his eyes on them.

I sat so near that I could feel the warmth of his body. I was quiet, yet a constant buzzing of unresolved thoughts kept me from basking in the joy of the moment.

"Lyse, it's far enough."

Questions that had taken root in my mind for months wanted to be answered. Without Maman near me, I feared I might make a mistake and say the wrong thing.

"Suzanne, stay with Lyse."

I was not supposed to know about Papa's other lady. I

would have loved to find out if she had died, or talk about what I had heard through the door at Uncle George's home, and ask him what followed after "Louis asked me."

"France, Suzanne, come and rest, you also Lyse."

No, without a doubt, if I brought up any of my questions, Papa would blame Maman for telling us, not knowing that my partial knowledge came from listening at doors or to phone conversations. And, even if I told him that I was guilty of snooping, he still would not believe me and accuse Maman.

I had to resign myself to speak of nothing else with Papa but little girl stuff.

At dinnertime we sat at the porch table. As in Saint-Eustache, Papa and Maman sat at each end of the table. But that night, we were two girls on each side, and we talked and laughed much more than when Suzanne and I were alone with our parents. Still, I watched my behavior. I knew what annoyed my father; too much laughter and I could be sent to my room for being hysterical. I remained quiet next to him, eating slowly, taking in small bites, watching my every gesture as if the rest of our lives depended on my perfection.

Papa did not speak much, but he looked relaxed and

did not chide us for our spirited chattering. When we finished our dinner, we heard him say in jest, "One less for the English!" As usual Suzanne and I giggled, joined, on this occasion, by France and Lyse. Maman smiled. She knew that the old saying had lost its political flavor, and now it simply meant: it was too good a meal to share with anyone else, least of all with an ancient enemy. An oblique way for Papa to complement Maman on a meal he particularly enjoyed, without having to do so directly.

He excused himself from the table and went outdoors to smoke his pipe.

As soon as I finished helping clear the table, and before anyone noticed, I joined Papa. He was walking back and forth in front of the chalet, smoking his pipe. I slid my hand in his and kept with the rhythm of his walk. Every now and then, when I raised my head to look at him, he smiled or simply winked at me.

"Do you like it here?" he asked me.

"Hmm, hmm." I nodded.

"Would you prefer to live in Saint-Eustache, or in Montréal?"

"In Saint-Eustache," I shouted. He put a finger to his

lips.

I pulled on the cuff of his shirt. "Are we going back home?" I whispered.

"I am not sure yet. I will talk to your mother again tonight. Can you keep this to yourself until tomorrow?"

"Yes," I said without a second thought, flattered by a secret shared with my father. But I carried so many secrets! Maman's crying secret, and the other I could not tell him: the visits to Aunt Marianna, Uncle Jean and Aunt Irène. And now Papa's secret I could not tell Maman, not even Suzanne or our cousins. Suddenly, I felt a surge of guilt, this predicament spoiling my joy.

We stood close, side-by-side. Papa took hold of my hand again. We walked in silence, stopping to look at the stars; the vastness of the lighted sky diminishing the importance of my secret.

The family Mignault, early 1900

Gustave, future high school teacher, organist, father of a large and wonderful family.

Gabrielle, mother of six children wife and secretary of Uncle Achille Chaurette, and organist.

Joseph, priest and science professor

Grandfather Pierre Zoël Mignault Md.

Georges, Md., at times our physician

Alfred, the future musician, father of Pierre, Lyse, France and André

Arthur, sadly, a very ill young man.

CHAPTER TWENTY THREE

PAPA'S STORY OF PÈRE LATOUR

Once we were ready for bed, we went out on the porch and gathered around Papa for storytelling time. Maman sat at the table with her Larousse Dictionary and her crossword puzzle as she used to do in Saint-Eustache. I guess that Suzanne would have felt like a baby in front of our cousins if she had outrun me to sit on Papa's lap, so I won the best seat. Unanimously, we voted on hearing the story of Père Latour.

"Once upon a time, when your Uncle Georges and I were about your age, we played a trick on poor Père Latour, and our father..."

"He was the grandfather of all of us, wasn't he?"

"Yes he was. As I was saying, father punished us

severely for our misdeeds."

"Yes you were!"

"Marcelle let Papa tell the story!"

I annoyed Suzanne but I loved the part of the story when Papa and Uncle Georges were punished. I ignored her. Replete with happiness I cuddled to Papa and closed my eyes.

"Now," said Papa "I want the four of you to close your eyes. All closed?"

I smiled.

"Yes Uncle Louis. Yes Papa"

"With your eyes still closed, imagine a kitchen with, at its center, a table large enough to seat fourteen people, and more if needed. You see that?"

"Hmm, hmm."

"Now, visualize a humongous stove, big enough for my mother's helper, Caroline, to cook a pot of soup, one of potatoes, one for a seasonal vegetable, one maybe for a chicken, beef and vegetable *bouilli* and in another separate container some soft foods for the baby. Of course, you must imagine fresh pies and bread staying warm on the stove shelf, and hot water simmering in a special stove compartment always at the ready for tea."

I saw it clearly in my mind because across the street from us, in Saint-Eustache, an old farmer and his wife had exactly the same big kitchen and stove; plus, if you opened a little sliding door on the back wall of the kitchen, a chicken or two would appear.

"Did you have chickens in the kitchen?" I had to ask.

"Sh... Marcelle."

I knew Suzanne would protest.

"*Non P'tit Blond*, we kept them in the barn. All right, keep your eyes closed. Now, I want you to see a long...long...long wood chest topped with a thick flowery pad. Next to it sat a bureau. A rocking chair provided my mother, or Caroline, a place to take turns feeding a baby or cradling an ailing child. This is where the story takes place."

"What was in the chest Uncle Louis?" asked France.

"Wood for the stove. It was also Père Latour's bed."

"And he slept on top of the wood." I blurted out.

"You know very well that he did not. *Please*," begged

181

Suzanne, "let Papa tell the story."

France and I looked at one another and instantly established a bond that in more than half a century never unraveled. And what pleasurable times we have had together!

"As I told you, there was a thick pad tied to the top of the chest, and it was on that pad that Père Latour slept. He kept the bed linen in the bureau next to it."

"During the cold season, the old man got up in the middle of the night and filled the stove with wood to keep the house warm. He then went back to bed until early morning. He always rose before anyone else. He again filled the stove so that when Caroline walked into the kitchen, it was ready for her cooking. Then, Père Latour went off to feed the chickens, milk the cow, and gather the eggs."

"On this particular night, my brother Georges and I hatched a scheme to tease the dear old man."

"After dinner, my father, your grandfather, usually retired to his office to read about current medical studies which might guide him in the curing of one of his patients. Meanwhile, my mother, who was the church organist, gathered the children in the living room for piano lessons and singing. Usually, at that point your grandfather, the church choir master, would join us."

"We know all that, Papa," I said. "Tell us what happened when you tickled Père Latour's feet."

"Are you ready?"

"Yes, yes, please, tell us."

"Alright then. On that evening, during dinner, my father was called to care for a sick patient. In accordance with our plan, Georges and I were extra helpful after the meal, taking the trash out, even bringing our own dishes to the sink. Dear Caroline gave us the biggest smile, but our two oldest sisters looked at us with suspicion. We put on our angelic faces. It was lost on them; they knew us *too* well. But, they were too busy to investigate the meaning behind such cherubic demeanors."

"In less than an hour, we figured, all the little ones would be asleep and the rest of the family would be in the living room. Caroline should be in her rocking chair, mending, and my mother at the piano leading the other children in singing, and, hopefully, Père Latour in his bed on top of the wood chest, would be sleeping soundly."

"But, it didn't happen that way!" I said. "Did it, Papa?"

"Marcelle!" Maman looked over her crossword puzzle and put a finger on her lips. I guess she did not understand that I wanted the story to last longer. I wiggled myself into a more comfortable position and listened.

"Well, it did happen like that to a point," replied Papa "That evening, it seemed to work as planned. The little ones were asleep, and in the living room Caroline bent over her mending. Mother sat at the piano with her back to the door we planned to use for an exit, and our siblings gathered around her. Everything foretold a successful outcome. Who could have predicted that disaster was about to strike?"

"Georges and I backed away slowly from the group. Quiet as mice, we opened the living-room door and in silence crossed the dining room to the kitchen door. Holding our breath, we pushed open the door that we had left slightly ajar and tiptoed over the creaky pine boards to the chest where the old man slept. Except for the distant singing, all was quiet as we knelt at the foot of the chest in preparation for the next step in our daring plan."

"To be honest with you, we were getting nervous about the whole venture. The chest, which during the day seemed to be an inoffensive piece of furniture, suddenly at nighttime looked like a coffin with a corpse on top of it. Adding to the spooky feeling we saw shadows of what we hoped were branches, and a pale, lifeless moon peeking at us through the window. Two unearthly big feet, attached to... we-knew-not-what, stared at us, sending a chill up our spines."

"Come, come Louis," whispered my brother Georges, pretending bravery. "It's only Père Latour's feet. Let's get on with it."

"From our pockets we took out a feather recently secured from our barn, and slowly, almost paralyzed with fear, lightly tickled the bare soles of the old man's feet. A jerky movement of the feet nearly scared me out of the kitchen. My knees shook, but since Père Latour had not risen and smacked us, we proceeded to the next phase of our plan, with less enthusiasm on my part, I must say. In our best soprano voices we attempted to imitate the voice of his dear departed wife: "Jooooooseph... Jooooooseph... Jooooseph...do you hear me?" Adding lots of woooooo...woooooo...woooooo.

"Suddenly, the old man's upper body rose in slow

185

motion like Frankenstein's monster returning from the dead. His face was hidden by a shadow, but in the light of the ghostly moon shining through the kitchen window, his white night-cap stood out and below that was a white nightgown from which two long white arms reached toward us."

"An eerie voice came from the disembodied space between the cap and the collar of the nightshirt."

"'Mariiiie is that you? Mariiiie, don't go away. Wait for me.'

"The white shape began swaying sideways and back and forth and before we could get up, there he was standing, reaching out to us with ghostly arms. Scared out of our wits, because it seemed to be a ghost and, even worse, because it might *not* be a ghost but Père Latour in the flesh, we got up and rushed to the other end of the kitchen to get the oversized table between whatever was chasing Georges and I."

"We managed to get out of the kitchen and into the dining room. We heard the floorboards creak, and the menacing sound of something growing close."

"'Stop, little ruffians,' he shouted! 'Stop, I am telling you, stop!'

"I turned around to see how near he was and found the real Père Latour close enough that I could see his nightcap slipping to one side, held only by one ear, his nightgown furiously flapping against his spindly legs and his arms moving like a windmill accentuating the threat directed toward us."

"I'll catch you, you little devils, and then we'll see."

"We pushed open the living room door and tried to close it behind us. The old man's arm held it open and our only choice was to keep on running across the room, and hopefully, out the other door. But we didn't get far because suddenly the pursued and the pursuer became aware that the living room was filled with shocked silence. First, I noticed Caroline who had dropped her mending basket in surprise; then, my mother and the family chorus were no longer singing but staring at us; and worst, my father came out of his office through the very door we needed for our exit. Alas, except for the two little ones, the whole family witnessed the results of our pranks and the distress of the dear old man."

"Père Latour, regaining his composure, readjusted his nightcap to a more seemly angle and apologized to my mother, Caroline and our sisters for showing himself in his nightgown, all the time trying to pull his gown below

187

his knees."

"Georges and I stood with heads bowed and knees shaking, waiting for the dressing down that was bound to follow this last escapade."

Suzanne and I particularly enjoyed this part of the story, which for a moment brought our dignified father closer to us.

"And, what happens next Papa?" We knew, but every time our father told the story, he had a way of putting a different twist to his yarn.

"Well," Papa went on, "First my mother reassured the old man that he had not offended her. Père Latour had removed his nightcap as my mother spoke to him. Then my father sternly took over and told us to apologize to Monsieur Latour, emphasizing the Monsieur. We did so promptly, hoping that perhaps it would be the end of it. No such luck!"

"'Père Latour, please return to your bed,' my father said with a great deal of courtesy in his voice, 'but, before you do, would you kindly put enough wood on the floor near the stove. I don't want Georges and Louis to disturb you during the night when they come to fill and stoke the wood in the stove. Oh, yes, include enough wood so that you can sleep in peace and gain the rest you lost tonight, so that tomorrow morning at five o'clock they may again fill the stove and make it ready for Caroline to be able to prepare breakfast.'

"'I beg your pardon doctor, but what about the animals? If I sleep too long they will be hungry.'

"'Oh don't worry, Georges and Louis will be happy to feed the animals, milk the cow, and gather the eggs after they stoke the stove tomorrow morning. Won't you boys? And in case I am not here, please show my two sons the work they will do in the barn until noontime. That is all for now. Good night Père Latour, and sleep well. Georges, Louis, follow Monsieur Latour. I expect *not* to have to remind you, ever again, to be courteous with everyone, but even more so with someone who lives with our family and is so kind to all of us. Go, now."

"Victorious, the old man bowed to the family with as much dignity as if he were wearing his Sunday suit. As he walked away, his nightgown flowed about him like a mantle of justice."

"And, this is the end of my story, and time for all of you to go to bed."

I gave Papa a hug and a kiss and many *merci's* and

buzzed his ear with a flow of chatter before Lyse, France and Suzanne could say their thank you. Then we kissed Maman goodnight. Like a schoolmistress she directed us, one by one, to the bathroom, and finally to the attic where she followed us to make sure all was in order. After the last embrace we heard her footsteps on the stairs.

Slowly our muffled chattering mingled with the sound of crickets and bullfrogs and the song of a night bird who, like us, could not retire from such a lovely night.

1
9
8
3

France and Marcelle

A lasting friendship

1995

CHAPTER TWENTY FOUR

AUNT IRÈNE'S DISCONTENT

Our vacation ended in a whirlwind, and before it was over we were moving back to Montréal to pack our belongings, and leave for Saint-Eustache. Caught in the excitement, I did not ask myself what would happen when we again live as a complete family.

Meals, baths, night sleep, naps—all were abbreviated. Maman permitted laughter but not silliness. Suzanne and I worked as a team; arguments not allowed.

Aunt Irène came to the apartment to help Maman pack. From the moment I greeted her at the door I could tell she was not happy about our departure for Saint-Eustache. She promptly joined Maman in the kitchen, leaving me behind. If Aunt Irène said good morning, how are you? I did not hear it.

"But her voice rose when she said, "He is going to win, isn't he?"

"I cannot refuse," Maman replied.

"Why, Margot. Why can't you? Do you really believe that Louis will ever be faithful?"

Suzanne and I stopped packing. She put a finger on her lips and walked to the bedroom doorway. I followed.

Maman did not answer. I wanted to run to the kitchen and hug her, but then they would have known that I was listening. Aunt Irène kept talking and talking.

"I don't know what he promised to make you change your mind," she said. "Do you honestly think that suddenly, by magic, he is a new person and that he can ever be faithful? Suppose for a moment that he is. You still would have to deal with his insane jealousy. Wouldn't you? That will not change. He was always envious of any friendship you had and denigrated every one of your friends. He questioned their morality; they were too masculine or too feminine. And of course, if you dared smile at any of their husbands he made a scene once you returned home. Margot, please, stop packing and listen to me!"

Suddenly it was so quiet that I dared not breathe. Suzanne turned around and looked at me, her lips quivered. I was afraid she would start crying, but she stood still and bit her lip.

"Have you forgotten," Aunt Irène continued, "that one time Louis locked you out of the house, when after visiting mother you arrived one hour late? He never answered the doorbell or your calls, and you had to walk to his sister's house and spend the night there..."

"I know, Irène, I know. That happened a long time ago."

Maman sounded tired. I wished Aunt Irène would stop.

"Yes, and you timed your whole life by his clock. You walked constantly on pins and needles; afraid to be late, afraid to displease him, afraid that the girls might say that they had visited members of your family—for goodness sake, Margot, you had to lie about seeing your own family. How could you live like that? How can you?"

Aunt Irène asks lots of questions, I thought, *but she never waits for an answer.*

"You have been tied in knots and miserable for most of

195

your married life. Is that what you want for the rest of it? Margot, I love you. I simply want you to be happy."

Maman must have been aware that we were listening, for a while we heard only the sound of dishes. But Aunt Irène was in no mood for muted conversation.

"Margot, please, speak to me."

Maman answered, but we still had to strain to hear. Holding our breath, and hoping that no board creaked, we tiptoed into the hallway.

"Irène, I had a year to think of my situation. I am not a widow and can never be divorced in the province, and the church doesn't allow it anywhere. You are well aware that despite the fact that I'm not in the wrong, the church puts the responsibility for a marriage, happy or not, on women's shoulders. As far as they are concerned my most important duty is to keep my husband happy and satisfied."

"Well, that's nothing new," said Aunt Irène.

"Separated from my husband I would have no place in society. You experienced a similar situation as a young widow. After your mourning was over, couples no longer welcomed you because the wives perceived you as a threat. Irène, I'm thirty-seven years old. It's a long life to live in a desolate apartment. What's more, I'll never have the money to better our conditi..."

"You could work, and you know very well that I would still keep on dressing you and the girls."

"Thank you Irène. I thought of working, but what of the girls? Who takes care of them? I don't want to be separated from them the way we were from Maman. ... plus ..." Maman stopped talking.

"Plus what?"

"I'm afraid that Louis would accuse me of neglect and try to take them away from me."

"He couldn't do that!"

"I have reason to believe that he would."

"Maman's secret," Suzanne whispered in my ear. But I knew there was a different twist to the secret—a secret that Maman might never reveal—not to anyone. How I wished Jean had not interrupted my listening at the door.

From the kitchen we heard a lot of whispering and nose-blowing. And then, as if nothing had been said, the noise of packing dishes resumed.

Soon afterward Aunt Irène left. We said our goodbyes. Her eyes brimmed with tears and her hugs were warmer than usual. There was hesitation in her leaving—a second embrace to Maman—a last look laden with regrets.

The door had barely closed when Maman said, "*Dieu merci,* your Aunt Flore lives far away. Let's hurry to finish our packing. Your Uncle Charlie will be here before seven o'clock tomorrow morning."

I was not sure what Maman meant about Aunt Flore.

"Maybe she would have chided Maman too," whispered Suzanne. We shrugged and returned to our chores, burdened by a knowledge too vast to comprehend, sadness hovering over us like a shadow we could not outrun.

Berthe, Irene, Flore
& Grand-Maman

Circa 1948

CHAPTER TWENTY FIVE

GOING HOME

Uncle Charlie arrived before seven o'clock. He looked subdued, an unusual state for him. He might have wondered how many more times he would have to move us. Papa had not replaced the car his friend had wrapped around a tree, twelve years past, and never would. When Uncle rang the doorbell, the apartment had already returned to its original drabness. We were ready to go.

A new July contemplated June's handiwork and basked in its beauty. Too sleepy to enjoy the landscape unrolling on each side of the car, Suzanne and I came to life only as we crossed over our river, La Rivière des Mille-Îles. Tranquil, she flowed under a blue sky: islands, bouquets of greenery dotting her course.

The car turned left onto rue Saint-Louis. I opened my

window to smell the Lilies of the Valley that covered the ground at the foot of le Manoir de Bellefeuille's stone fence. But their fragile white-bell-flowers had wilted and browned. Smiling at each other, Suzanne and I still inhaled an imaginary perfume.

Nothing had changed: the church with its canon ball wounds, the car hiccupping as it crossed over the rickety bridge and, my favorite part of rue Saint-Louis, the canopy of branches overhead. With each rotation of the wheels, one tableau at a time, like in each of Papa's stories, we entered into the familiar.

On our left, the little white washed houses, which at our departure a year ago in early spring had seemed abandoned by nature, were now framed in leafy green with vines of purple flowers growing on their flank. Leading to the front steps, petunias bloomed in pathways between newly painted white stones; nasturtiums—flower falls of orange and yellow—hung over window boxes. Hiding the gaping holes of poverty, wild roses grew over unmended fences.

A turn of the wheels to the left and rue Labrie, our street, unfolded her hills and curves in front of our eyes.

"Here we are Uncle Charlie, here we are!"

"Are you sure?"

The wheels squealed.

"Right here, Uncle Charlie!"

"Well, well, if you're sure..." he turned the wheels to the left into our driveway. I applauded.

As soon as the engine died, Suzanne and I jumped out of the car. Before I could rush up the stairs to the veranda, she put her arm across my chest. "Sh... you will scare the robin," she said.

I had forgotten she visited us every spring. On my toes I wobbled up the veranda's three steps and walked to the door before turning around to look at the nest. From her perch, a small platform between two columns, the robin looked at us. We greeted each other in silence.

Once Maman unlocked the front door I rushed past her with a peremptory "*Excuse-moi*, Maman," and ran to my bedroom. The little girl was still on her swing.

"What's that big smile all about, Blondie?" Uncle Charlie asked while putting our suitcases on Suzanne's bed.

"Look, the little girl is still there!"

"Did you expect she'd fly away?"

"No, not really, but..."

"Well, well, I see that everything's just the same; except you're a bigger girl now than you were when you left. How old are you?"

I showed six fingers and added one more, "very, very soon." I said.

"My, you're old! Your Maman is lucky. She'll have a good helper now."

That was not what being seven meant to me at all. I changed the subject.

"Uncle Charlie, will you come with me to look at the river?"

"I wish I could, but I have to go to work. Let me say good-bye to your Maman and Suzanne. Then we'll go out together. I'll watch you run down the hill, alright?"

Uncle Charlie waited for me while I descended the crooked cement stairs and ran across the terrace to the wall. I turned around; he was still there. We waved at each other.

I climbed the wall on the side facing the river. Legs

dangling, I embraced at once all that my eyes could see: to my left, the long bridge we had crossed barely thirty minutes ago; in front of me *le curé's* island; and at its back—like an immense stage scenery—another island, so vast that it seemed without end or beginning. It was called Île Jésus, and ran parallel to Montréal Island, that at its origin had been called Ville Marie by the founders, who were men of faith. It followed that they would name the smaller island Jesus Island.

Below my feet, the bulrush anchored in mud vibrated with life. In the past, stirrings of wings, jumping frogs, water skitters and all other manner of flying, leaping or crawling creatures had made the walk to our rowboat a frightening experience. The thought made me shiver.

"Marcelle, come put your clothes away, please."

"*Oui*, Maman." I swung my legs around.

"Please be careful."

She feared my falling off that eight-foot wall more than anything. Every spring, as the river lapped at its feet and kept on climbing, Maman's fear rose in unison. She could not erase from her mind the picture of a four-year-old Marcelle walking on the wall while the water neared the top. She had run down the hill and spoken calmly, to avoid frightening me. A sudden move on my part could have been fatal for both of us; she did not swim. After retrieving me from the wall, Maman had lost her composure: I received a good spanking.

At six years of age, seven soon, I still ignored her concern.

"Maman, the lilacs are all dead."

"*Non, non,* only the flowers. Tomorrow morning, you can help me cut them and next spring we will have beautiful lilacs again. I still have lots to do before your father comes home. Please, hurry, and stay away from that wall!"

We had arrived so early that Maman had time to call Monsieur Richer to deliver ice; Monsieur Comtois, milk, butter and cream; and Monsieur Trépanier, meat and groceries. Before nine o'clock, two blocks of ice cooled the icebox, and by lunch, the staples lined the pantry shelves. Left-over soup from yesterday's Montréal kitchen, too good to throw away, simmered on the stove.

Suzanne and I put away our summer dresses in our closet and folded the rest in the bureau we shared. When we were through with our chores Maman sent us to the bakery to buy the most precious item, a warm loaf of bread, but not before reminding me, "Marcelle do *not* break a piece off on the way home, unless you want to go without lunch."

"I won't, Maman, I promise I won't."

What had seemed, barely a year ago a chore, now became, on the day of our return home, a pleasure. During our stay in Montréal, Suzanne and I never went anywhere on our own. Giddy with excitement, we left the house in a flash. We ran down the hill stopping only a second to look at the shady brook meandering at the foot of an enormous oak tree. That area bristled with possibilities! I saw, I was quite sure, the perfect place for pirate games. I made a note in my mind…explore when alone.

We climbed the opposite hill under a penetrating noontime sun, and gratefully entered the shade of elms and maples arching over rue Saint-Louis. The doorbell, the two bakers' greetings, the strong scent of yeast, the black oven doors opened to a treasure of golden loaves; a blissful sensation.

We walked back home accompanied by the sound of the church bells tolling the noon prayer, the *Angelus.*

The chiming bells, the blight of the sidewalks, the

rickety bridge, the warm bread under Suzanne's arm, the robin sitting on her nest, all were part of the unvarnished beauty of our lives.

TWENTY SIX

GLYCERIN, PEROXIDE, EGGS AND TEA

Papa's visit to l'Île Perrôt eased his return. Like a well-oiled machine our days regained a smoothness that made it difficult to think it had ever been otherwise. Maman still rose before anyone to start the fire in the kitchen wood stove. Once done, she made herself beautiful, and only then woke our father.

Tucked in bed, I relished the familiarity of sounds: the rattling of stove lids, crunching of newspapers, scraping of kindling and wood through the opening of the wood stove, and the final rattling of lids, all for our father's two soft-boiled eggs and cup of tea.

From the minute Maman woke, all was done in an exquisitely choreographed dance. It started and ended

209

at a specific time so that Papa would have a leisurely walk to the train station and be at the office by eight-thirty. Like castanets, the frenzied tap tapping of her heels on the linoleum floor reflected the limited space and time in which she worked. Between two protuberant walls—one hiding the pantry and the ice-box, the other the stairwell to the cellar—five doors, a six-burner stove, a table and four chairs, sink and cupboards, there was no place for grand waltzing. No, three steps to the right, three steps to the left and Maman always stood where she needed to be.

Adjacent to one of our bedroom walls was the bathroom. Papa's soft whistling coated the kitchen's activities with a fluid grace interrupted only when he nicked himself shaving. We knew he would appear at the breakfast table with a tiny square of toilet paper stuck to the cut with resin gathered from the big pine tree on the lower terrace.

Before dressing, he engaged in one more routine: gargling with a mixture of glycerin and peroxide vocalized in a variety of tones, at times choking on the revolting concoction. After clearing his throat with faucet water, he was ready to dress and face the next two hurdles. First, hitching the suspenders he wore under his shirt to his pants, and then, fastening the starched collar to the back of his shirt: both exercises in contortion. As he battled in vain, he mumbled three words in quick succession—followed by a plea "Margot, I need help!"

The minute Papa left the bathroom; Suzanne and I started our morning ritual. Maman helped us, so we would be presentable to kiss our father and wish him *une bonne journée* before he reached the front door. Then the day was ours, and two full months of summer vacation, two magical words opening before us vistas of swimming, bicycling and playing with our friends.

CHAPTER TWENTY SEVEN

UNCLE ACHILLE'S GENUFLECTION

One week had passed since our return. The time had come for Maman to call all her friends. She stood near the wood phone box, receiver in hand, her voice rising and falling. Once in a while, cascading giggles and bursts of laughter filled the house; Maman was home.

After letting her sister-in-law, our Aunt Gabrielle, know that we had arrived; Suzanne and I went to visit our cousins. The walk was familiar. In rue Saint-Louis we recognized every home, garden, fence, and the slants and peaks of the root-torn sidewalks. We exchanged greetings along the way: a flow of *bonjour*, a shower of *comment allez-vous?*

Suzanne hurried me. We walked a mere hundred feet to the church, which faced the main street, rue Saint-Eustache, and crossed over. Suzanne held my hand, a gesture I found unnecessary and humiliating; I was practically seven years old. Once over, I pulled my hand away and ran ahead. A small smile of victory flirted on my lips as I waited for her.

Aunt Gabrielle and Uncle Achille's home faced the Paquin's general store, and was only a few minutes' walk to the varied amenities offered on the main street: from money exchanging to contract making, to food stores, to another general store, and a pharmacy. Two hotels furnished a goodly number of patients for the cures of the doctors Grignon, Corriveau and Thibodeau. Compared to the quietness of our street, our cousins' bustled with activities all day long.

Three years had passed since our cousin's family had lost its youngest child. It had been a painful loss. The three year old Hubert who loved to play with small bottles had climbed on a stool and reached in a closet finding the smallest and most tempting bottle. He swallowed its content; Aunt Gabrielle's heart medicine. By the time doctor Thibodeau arrived it was too late. It is a tribute to aunt's strength of character that in a household of five children, she remained a stable presence: the disciplinarian, the consoler, the teacher, the promoter of the arts, uncle's secretary, and like her mother, a long time ago, and now two of her brothers and a sister, she was the church organist.

Suzanne rang the front doorbell. Aunt Gabrielle greeted us with kisses and a warm, *"Entrez, entrez. Oh, my, look at you, how you have grown!"*

She was Papa's sister, seven years younger than he, and like him a blue-eyed blond, reserved and dignified, but with none of his phobias. She had a sweet smile but she never seemed to be as joyous as Maman, or as sad. I did not recall ever seeing her cry.

"Suzanne! Marcelle!" The hallway resounded with our names. Jacqueline, Renée and Louise embraced us: three sisters, between two and three years apart, with different features, eyes and hair coloring ranging from a soft hazelnut to a strong coffee bean, and differing personalities.

"Alright girls, why don't you go play outdoors or sit on the veranda? Your father has clients in the office, and I have to work." Aunt turned toward Jacqueline, the eldest. "If you could help me I would appreciate it; there are two contracts to edit."

Jacqueline's face lost its spark; however, she did not fuss and followed her mother to her office. Renée, Louise, Suzanne and I walked out to the front porch. Chatting and watching the modest bustle of the main

215

street from our comfortable rocking chairs, was an experience Suzanne and I always enjoyed. The general store facing us was partly responsible for the activities of the area. The store itself had no specific features, but the Paquin's house, attached to one of its sides, attracted my eyes like a powerful magnet. The body of the house was narrow, but had depth and unusual height. Its dark stone structure, wide staircase, large front window, and high Victorian front piece gave it a mysterious look.

"What did you do in Montréal?" asked Louise. She sat at the edge of her chair as if expecting a thrilling story from us. "Did you like it?"

Suzanne spoke about her time at the boarding school. Then I recounted important features of our visits to Uncle Jean and Aunt Marianna. "But we cannot tell Papa," I said. They did not ask why; they knew by listening to their parents, as Suzanne and I did, that Papa had forbidden us to visit with some of Maman's family.

"And what's happening here?" Suzanne asked.

Renée stood up. I envied her looks, dark and fiery. If I had inherited them, I would have modeled myself after the ladies in Papa's Geographic Magazines. I would have wrapped my body in vivid colors, worn extravagant hairpieces and strands of colorful jewelry.

But the year was 1937 in the conservative Province de Québec. In a class-conscious pre-World-War-Two society, the five of us, our families and a few others in the village, exemplified an upper class standing. If we had lived in a city like Montréal, most of us would have been lower on the social ladder by a half to a whole step, depending on name recognition or fortune.

In summer, our mothers wrapped us in soft yellows, blues, pinks and greens with matching bows in our hair. We hibernated in dark greens, browns, navy blue and black wools, and felt hats. In all seasons they fed us the "do's" and "do not's" of The Young Ladies Good Manners Manual, and of course "little Jesus will punish you" if we ventured outside those boundaries. Obediently we regurgitated mouthfuls of "if you please" and "thank you," and in adult company kept our voices down.

Indeed, we were well brought up young ladies.

"What's happening now?" Suzanne insisted.

Unlike me, my sister lived in the now. Renée turned toward the street and its activities, and with an encompassing gesture, said,

217

"What you see, *Mesdames et Messieur*s, is what is, and was, and will be for *all* eternity."

Suzanne and Louise burst into laughter. As quickly, Louise put her hand over her mouth. Aunt Gabrielle's head appeared in the doorway, a finger to her lips. Suzanne pinched her smile.

Maybe over the past year their lives had not been too exciting, I thought. So, I blurted out snippets of what had thrilled me. "I went skating with Cousin Jean in the park, and there was music, and I walked in the snow with Maman at nighttime, and we…"

"I heard that ten times already," said Suzanne.

"I know, but it was extraor-or…"

"Extraordinaire," she said with condescendence.

No one talked. I wanted to disappear.

Louise bent toward me and touched my arm. "I tell you, Marcelle, weeks before last Christmas we made holiday cards. I painted lots of winter scenes, and drew little houses on top of hills, and pine trees with blotches of snow on their branches…" she stopped. "But skating with cousin Jean must have been so exciting, and walking at nighttime in the snow with Aunt Margot…Oh, I wish I'd been with you." She smiled at me.

" It was lovely," I whispered, nodding and blushing. It was a word Maman would have used, and for the occasion it gave credence to Louise's endorsement of my experience.

"Maman insists," said Renée, "that the three of us take every art class and every music lesson the school offers. Apparently, our parents can only afford to send Henri and Jean-Pierre to college."She sighed, shook her head, raised her right hand and with the little finger curved, as if holding a fragile Limoges cup, she said, "but refined we shall be..."

"Better than having to study Greek and Latin," Louise interrupted. "I saw Jean-Pierre's books!".

"What's that I hear? Louise is learning Greek?" Jacqueline had joined us.

"No, we were talking about entertainment, like painting, playing the piano and watching the activities in the street. Louise thought it was better than studying Greek," said Renée with her usual dash of sarcasm.

"Studying Greek might not be such a bad idea." replied Jacqueline, "We could all read the original texts of the plays we see at our brother's college."

Jacqueline sat down. Silence. A chuckle, another. "Papa entertained us this morning," she said, chuckling even more.

I could never imagine Uncle Achille making jokes. I visualized him as an Indian chief, serious and thoughtful; not the one who declared war, but the wise man who said, "Let us consider..." He bore a strong oval face and square jaw, the cheekbones not yet chiseled by time, though worries visiting him too often left shadows under his dark, pensive eyes... No, after all, he could not be an Indian chief, because, under his nose almost to the corners of his upper lip, like a Mayan pyramid, grew a mustache. It was as black as the hair over his well-shaped dome.

Renée and Louise chortled.

"What happened?" Suzanne begged.

"You know how Papa is always so preoccupied by business or the village's problems," said Renée, "that his mind never seems to be where his feet are."

"Yes, I noticed." Suzanne agreed. "I'm never sure Uncle Achille sees me when I happen to meet him in the street."

"Well, listen to this," Renée said. "Before noon, Papa walked to the post office, and came rushing back in the house, shouting, 'Gabrielle, Gabrielle, my car has been stolen!' But Maman knows him well. 'Achille' she asked, 'didn't you walk to the post office?' There was a long silence. Papa lifted his hand as if he were about to make a statement; however, without a word he turned around, went to the garage, came back into the house through his own office door, and did not show up until lunch time."

"Did you tease him?"

"No, Maman told us not to. But I know that when Jean-Pierre and Henri are back from college, and when we tell them, they will."

"Hmm, Hmm," Renée cleared her throat. "Should I tell Suzanne and Marcelle about Sunday at church?"

"Yes, yes, do," said Louise, jumping out of her chair.

With the assured posture of a seasoned storyteller, Renée signaled Louise to sit down. Standing against the railing, she began.

"Papa always goes to High Mass arriving at church not one minute too early. When he's alone, it's his habit to invite someone standing in the back to go sit with him in our pew. Last Sunday he did it again. So there he goes, serious as a monk, down the aisle with his guest following. As the priest makes his entrance, Papa doubles his steps and trots forward, the man right on his heels. At our pew, Papa stops dead in his tracks, genuflects, sending the poor man plunging over him."

Forgetting Aunt Gabrielle, Suzanne and I roared. I could see Uncle Achille, always so serious, the Notary and Mayor of the village, on his knees, and a stranger flying over him.

"Both end up on their knees in the main aisle, their prayer books in mid air, pictures of saints and relatives' obituaries, falling on the waxed floor and sliding all the way to the foot of the communion balustrade."

Louise's cheeks bulged with restrained laughter, tears in her eyes.

"That's not all, that's not all," Renée said. "They get up in a flash, each grabbing his prayer book, picking up any picture he can reach. Avoiding all eye contact, they walk to their pew and sit like two altar boys waiting for punishment.

After awhile, Papa regains his composure and opens his prayer book to follow the text of the Mass. His eyes fall on the obituary picture of an old lady." Renée chuckled. "He does a double take. Staring back at him, looking as surprised to see a stranger, as he is to see

222

her, is this ugly, ugly old woman. He shoves her picture in the back of his book, overwhelmed by a mounting fit of laughter. He dare not glance at his guest; it could be contagious. Trying to chase away the face of the old bonneted, deceased woman, he closes his book, puts it out of sight in his coat pocket, and for the rest of the Mass, our dear father concentrates mightily on reciting the rosary. Never in his life did he concentrate as intensely or recite as many Ave Maria."

Once our chortling had died down, I asked if Uncle Achille had blushed.

"I don't know," said Renée, "but Papa was so embarrassed that he and his companion sat until the whole congregation had left the church. While they waited, they looked at the pictures in their individual prayer books, and returned each other's pictures to the proper pages of the proper book."

"When did he tell you about this?" I asked.

"After dessert, just as we were about to leave the table, he raised his hand, a sign that a statement was on the way…or again, maybe not, because sometimes he teases us and simply says 'Oh! I forgot,' and walks away from the table, but not this time. 'Guess what happened?' he said. And now it has become the story du jour. I'm sure that by the time our brothers arrive for their vacation, he will already have embellished it."

Church facing Main Street

Uncle Achille teasing a grandson, Aunt Gabrielle

225

The Lahaie general store and house where Uncle Joseph
died in 1949 and Aunt Irene in 1957

Part of Saint-Eustache Main Street

CHAPTER TWENTY EIGHT

A MONTH OF TOO MANY DAYS

The page on Maman's calendar proclaimed in large letters, for everyone to see, the words, JULY 1937. On the last square she had written my name in red letters. That day would be a day as no other; of that I was certain. Twenty-four long days and night separated me from the thirty-first, and all that happiness.

Surely being a well-behaved seven-year-old would encourage respect from adults, and without a doubt Suzanne would accept me as an equal, though I chose to ignore that since April she became a year older; and nine years old is quite old. My impatience grew, when I thought that on my birthday I would receive my first communion; the nuns had promised that it would be the most memorable event of my life.

In the meantime Maman anchored me in the present

by making me memorize the required prayers and catechism. I learned with some trepidation that I would have to confess my sins to the priest before he allowed me to receive communion. For a full three weeks I would have to dig deep inside to find my faults; gratuitously, Maman helped me in that regard. She recited a list of my shortcomings, and I added to them by being offended, and of course, surly.

But, one day, an ordinary day until then, as if by magic, one knock at the door transformed my summer.

"Marcelle, come here!"

This was not the voice that called, "Come here make your bed" or, "Come here pick this up." No, it was a happy, "Come here," a sort of, "Come here and lick the fudge pan," a call that pulled me toward Maman.

"Marcelle, this is Bernard."

A little boy, half-in-half-out the screen door, greeted me with a big smile and a soft, *"Bonjour."*

"Bernard and his family are here for the summer," said Maman.

"Our house is the last one at the end of the street. Do you want to play?"

I smiled and nodded, and followed my new friend, my first friend, to the end of the street.

Bernard had golden-brown hair and a freckled face. His full name was Bernard Baron, a princely name I thought. But he was a regular boy who liked to take his wagon and ride up and down the hills, and work in his father's tool shed. I saw that he was very clever at making little boats, though I found out later that when caught in a ripple, many tipped over. While I watched him trying to make his boats sea-worthy, I hinted that I might have found a place that could be a pirate landing.

"Where?" Bernard dropped his tools and looked at me.

"At the bottom of the hill," I said, at the brook."

"Mum," shouted Bernard; to his Irish mother. "We're going down the hill."

I had found a soul mate. Without waiting for an answer, we ran down the street to the little bridge.

"There it is." I pointed to the thicket of bushes and giant oak trees. In the background, through the crisscross of branches and leaves, we saw the river filling every space in blue, like a church stained glass window.

Bernard looked around. I could tell he was impressed. His eyes scrunched up against the sun, focusing on one particular area.

"There! That branch is perfect for spying on the river."

"Let's try to climb on it," I said.

Try as we might, we could not reach it.

"Let's go to my house," said Bernard. "We have a small ladder."

With his mother's permission we loaded it into his wagon. Bernard pulled and I followed at the rear making sure that our step-up to spying did not fall off.

The step stool stood uneasily on a terrain fertile with roots and soft spots of decayed leaves. Bernard propped up the sloping leg by sliding under it debris of all sorts. Without flinching he dug in the squishy ground with his bare hands. I gladly watched delighted not to have to do the same thus avoiding the encounter of squirmy little creatures.

It worked. We finally sat on that sturdy branch.

Bernard had picked the perfect spot. We could spy on the river without being seen.

The following day we scrutinized the horizon through a cardboard telescope Bernard had made. No matter which end we looked through, we saw not one ship. Nevertheless, our imagination peopled the few rowboats and their crews with the proper accoutrements and enough viciousness to frighten us down our spying tree and send us fleeing to the safety of our quiet street. No pirate worth his salt would dare walk on a concrete road.

Pierrette Wooley 1937 Granddaughter of Uncle
Arthur & Aunt Marie- Louise Sauve´

Pierrette Wooley & Marcelle 1994   A lasting friendship

CHAPTER TWENTY NINE

THE SENATOR, THE COBBLER, AND A SHOCKING SONG

Sandwiched between catechism, dusting, drying dishes and pirate spying, I floated intermittently between heaven, with side trips to the fantastic, and back down to earth. Maman contributed to this balance by introducing one more item: the visiting hour.

One favorite was to Aunt Marie-Louise and Uncle Arthur Sauvé. Because of their age they reminded me of Uncle Jean and Aunt Marianna.

"Actually they are your father's cousins," said Maman. "We called them Aunt and Uncle because they are of an older generation. Your father and Aunt Marie-Louise are first cousins; what's more, they are double cousins.

"What's that?" asked Suzanne.

So Maman told us. A brother and a sister Mignault

had married a sister and a brother Lachaine. Suzanne said, "Hmm, hmm," as if she understood. As for me, I did not try to understand. I liked them the way they were.

Uncle and Aunt Sauvé and their four children had moved to Saint Eustache in 1923, a few years before Papa and Maman built their house. Maman was close in age and temperament to their eldest daughter, Mercédès, with whom she had developed a friendship years before she met Papa, a friendship that continued through their mature years.

We seldom visited anyone as a family. Papa never accompanied us to Maman's even to the few whose company he allowed. But neither did he travel with us to Montréal, when in January we visited members of his family. If it had not been for Maman, Suzanne and I would have had few contacts with any of them.

On vacation, or Saturday afternoons, on his way to the post office, Papa sometimes stopped for a chat with his sister, Aunt Gabrielle, and her family. At other times he called on Aunt Marie-Louise who fondly called him, "my cousin the aristocrat." Ten years older than he, she remembered events and family members who had passed away before they had taken shape in his memory. More than blood, her joyful, unaffected nature, and a shared heritage of place and time made each visiting hour a cherished occasion.

Growing up, most Sundays I had seen Uncle and Aunt Sauvé at church or Uncle alone, at funerals. He always sat in the center of the church. Every time the congregation stood up he turned his body slightly to the right or to the left, and seemed to greet everyone as if it were his home. Having been a politician for years, I figured he knew everybody. Whenever I caught his eye, we exchanged a wink.

The year I attended kindergarten, many a day, on my way home from school, I had spotted him sitting on a wobbly straight chair in the doorway of the cobbler's little house. Was he waiting for a pair of shoes to be repaired, or just chatting with Monsieur Lapierre? *The Senator and the Cobbler, The Princess and the Pea, The Fox and the Crow,* not all fairy tales. My Uncle Arthur was real. When I saw him there, I slowed my pace hoping to attract his attention. On lucky days I did, and as we waved to each other it never failed to hoist my spirit and feet into a skipping mood.

Since we were back in Saint Eustache our visits would resume and maybe Suzanne and I might be invited again to a New Year's feast, like the one we attended when I

235

was five years old.

There were thirty to thirty five Mignault and Sauvé husbands and wives around the main table: the oldest two or three children of each family sat at a separate table at the end of the dining room. I was the youngest, and may not have said much, but I will never forget the sights and sounds of the festivities.

Two ladies of the village Madame Mondou and Mademoiselle Lanthier had helped Aunt-Marie-Louise prepare the feast and were there the night of the party to serve. I had never seen such a humongous turkey, or a table that stretched forever and did not collapse.

At the end of the meal, I remember sitting on the stairs with cousin Pierrette, Uncle and Aunt Sauvé's granddaughter, and my cousin's two or three times removed. Well we were not removed at all, we sat near one another listening and watching. When the meal was over, Uncle Georges got up and offered thanks humorously. Raised glasses followed and compliments abounded and then he announced that the mayor of Saint-Eustache, the very distinguished notary Achille Chaurette would deliver a speech in honor of our hosts.

Uncle Achille stood, cleared his throat, and lifted his

right hand to announce he was about to start. Like a magistrate in front of a court he slowly unrolled a scroll. Unlike anyone I knew, he delivered a funny speech written in rhymes and exact meters. His solemn expression, which contrasted with the hilarious text, brought about gales of laughter. Still, serious as a pope, Uncle Achille sat down. Then Uncle Georges announced that no evening would be complete without a song from Marie-Louise. Everyone applauded.

I looked at cousin Pierrette who winked at me. "It will be funny," she whispered.

Aunt Marie-Louise got up and bowed deeply. In a deep contralto voice, she started. ... "I have seen on the 25th of January, on the ice, a great ram that sautéed onions with snow balls in the ear of a pigeon and on the back of a jack-rabbit."

I was horrified. She went on and on, one silly verse after another. How could the wife of a senator, who had traveled with him to Europe and Egypt, dined with King Farouk, Prime Ministers and Presidents, be suddenly brought down to the level of a commoner! I could not understand and felt mortified.

I must have told my concern to Maman, because

afterward I saw them in a different light. They were real people. A life of politics, pomp and extravagant circumstances had not changed their nature. They were caring, intelligent, unpretentious people.

Now that Maman had reinstated the visiting hour, we were on our way to their home.

I had a feeling we would be kissed and hugged and fussed over, as we had by everyone we visited since our return. After the "How are you? How wonderful to see you," and "Please come and sit," we would go to the enclosed porch with all its windows overlooking la Rivière du Chênes.

As usual I would pay attention to the conversation in the unlikely event I would be asked a question. Then after a while I would sit further back in my cushioned rattan chair and, by and by, settle into a lovely torpor, cradled by the rise and fall of voices and enveloped in the familiar scent of Aunt Marie-Louise's perfume, my favorite scent of Coty *Muguet des Bois*.

CHAPTER THIRTY

A STATEMENT OF MILD WICKEDNESS

Despite my preoccupation with daily activities, excursions with Bernard near the brook, and visits to friends and family, Maman managed to feed me a generous diet of catechism and soul searching, so on the eve of my birthday I felt secure and ready to answer the priest's questions.

Together, we walked to the presbytery. This was not a leisured walk with time to smell flowers growing over fences.

"Please, Marcelle, stop dragging," Maman kept on repeating. "*L'abbé* Jolie is expecting us at two o'clock. Let's not make him wait."

Maman held on to my hand as if afraid I might take flight. I felt like it, but I knew that it would be useless to try to escape because she always chased after me.

When I did something wrong at home and knew that a spanking was at hand, I ran to the dining room. With Maman in pursuit, we went round and round the table. Out of breath she always said, "Stop Marcelle! It will be worse if you don't!" I had no choice but to do so; however, by that time, usually I had reached the "It will be worse" stage, which meant a spanking. Foolishly, I always tried the run-away; but not today. I did not want to add one more sin to my list.

When we arrived at the presbytery, my stomach rolled in a nauseous little ball. Maman rang the doorbell and *l'abbé* Jolie himself greeted us.

"Come in, come in. Let's go in my office, please follow me."

Like most adults trying to make children feel at ease he failed until I answered his first question and heard him say, "Excellent!" Only then did I regain my footing and my smile. Alas, he asked me only two more questions. I could not show off the vast knowledge that Maman had hammered into my head for one whole month.

When it came time for *l'abbé* Jolie to hear my confession, Maman excused herself and went to sit on the veranda.

I would have preferred to confess to the new priest who did not know me, and like everybody else go to confession in the dark cubbyhole in the chapel. Suzanne had told me, "He just opens a little window and doesn't look at you." Later on, if I met the new priest in the street, he would not recognize me or think, "There is the girl who disobeys a lot, is too curious, and is surly when corrected."

As usual Maman had organized everything, and I had to comply. Kneeling in front of *l'abbé* Jolie I started. The words came out of my mouth in a whisper; my sins stuck in my throat like pulled taffy in teeth. One by one I stretched them out, until unglued from their inner sanctum, I mumbled a poor little statement of mild wickedness.

CHAPTER THIRTY ONE

JULY 31, 1937

Purified by confession, two days earlier, I greeted my special day with eagerness. Papa did not have to jiggle his keys in his pockets to urge me to hurry. I joined him in the living room ahead of Maman and Suzanne.

"Let's go wait outside," he said.

"Papa, do you remember your first communion?"

"I am not sure I do. It seems to me that we attended church a great deal of the time and it was such a long time ago."

"You were in church most of the time?"

"No, but too often for my taste."

"If you remembered your first communion, you would remember if you had a party, wouldn't you?"

"I suppose I would, but I cannot recall." Smiling, Papa looked at me, "Why are you so interested?"

"Oh, I just wanted to know." I was on my way to receive communion and already a lie hung on my tongue. "I wanted to know if I'll have a party," I said bravely, not used to this self-correcting.

"I guess you'll have to wait and see." Papa bent over and looked at me. I saw a glint of tease in his eyes. "With that large brimmed hat of yours, I feel I have to fold myself in two to see your face."

I knew he wanted to do something to my hat. He had fiddled with it before: sideways, backward, forward it went. But Maman, the Hat-Queen, always set it back at the angle fashion dictated.

"Who made your new dress?"

"Grand-maman." I blushed just thinking that if Aunt Irène had made it, I would have had to lie; even today.

For the occasion Grand-maman had made especially for me, not a repaired hand-me-down, but a brand new white dress with pleats on each side and a lovely sailor collar. The hat, also white, was decorated with a navy blue ribbon matching the collar trim. I would have liked a real first communion dress made of organza with more bounce and frills, but Maman was not a frill person. "No, classic lines are never out of style," she explained, adding her usual, "and more practical."

I did not experience ecstasy as the nuns had predicted. I suppose that only a month of part-time soul searching did not qualify me for a state of levitation or rapture. Nevertheless, my little self-correcting propelled me into a loftier space.

I had seen no preparation for a party, but I still hoped, because Maman, the master surprise maker, could not resist such an occasion. Confident, I followed in Papa's quick steps, my new Mary Janes jumping deftly over the root-torn sidewalks. We were on our way home, I wished with all my heart, to a party.

Uncle Charlie's car rested in the driveway: a good sign. I hurried to the front door. Aunt Berthe, Grand-maman, and Uncle Charlie greeted us. Suzanne's friends Francine and Lucille, and Louise, our cousin, popped up from behind doors and sofa, screaming, "*Joyeux Anniversaire!*" Hiding in a corner my friend, Bernard, looked ill at ease in his Sunday pants and white shirt. We were both more in our element spying on pirates than socializing at a party, though I had dreamt

245

about this one for a long time.

"Alright children, it is game time—musical chairs, everybody outdoors!" Uncle Charlie took charge. We ran out the front door and followed him. He had already carried five chairs onto the lower terrace, but the Victrola was still sitting on the sidewalk in back of the house. . Uncle Charlie tried to convince Papa that it should be on the lower terrace. Papa disagreed.

"The sound will carry far enough if we leave it right here," he said.

Early that morning before Suzanne and I woke up, with Maman's help, Papa had lifted the one hundred pound, four feet tall music-maker and carried it out of the house and down the backstairs to where it sat, and should stay, as far as he was concerned.

But Uncle Charlie did not give up easily. "It's too far from here to the lower terrace. The children won't hear a thing over their screaming."

Reluctantly, Papa conceded.

Watched by six amused children, the old Victrola came down—*cahin, caha*—carried by two puffing men, one of whom probably wished that he had not insisted and the other that he had not given in. Fifteen minutes later, the gramophone sat proudly with nature on a bed of green grass. Papa hurried back up the steps, avoiding any more involvement with his brother-in-law until the time came to reverse the process and carry the music-maker back up two flights of stairs.

Uncle Charlie wiped his forehead, cranked the machine and sounded a victorious, "Are you ready?"

We watched him lower the needle onto the record. We started walking slowly, vying for a chair to sit on. The music stopped. We laughed and screamed, ran and landed in piles on the same chairs, scrambling to find an empty one. It went on and on until only Louise and Bernard were left, one chair standing between them. They looked like cat and mouse running round and round. Bernard, whose shyness had evaporated, won the first game.

Uncle Charlie started and stopped the music, and cranked the old Victrola leading us into more rounds. He was having as much fun as we, and seemed to regret our exodus when Maman called us for lunch.

On our way to the porch, we passed by Papa who had been turning the handle of the ice-cream maker while

Uncle Charlie cranked the Victrola. Done with their chores, they hurried away to their comfortable chairs on the front veranda, while Aunt Berthe and Grand-maman put the last touch to the table's decoration. Maman greeted her band of hungry gigglers with a bright smile, embracing me tenderly as I went by.

The party ended with my favorite butter cake topped with maple frosting and as much vanilla ice cream as we wanted.

One shade at a time the sun had fallen into darkness. Tomorrow the down-to-earth routine of daily life would resume; however my euphoric mind blotted out such a pedestrian thought.

CHAPTER THIRTY TWO

THE END OF SUMMER

August, like a soft-footed intruder, slid into the night while my heart still dreamed of an endless July thirty-first.

It was the last month of summer. All of a sudden children felt they had to hurry—play with relentless energy and splash in the river's cool water. After dinner our cousin Henri organized games at the corner of Saint-Eustache Street and First Avenue where our cousin's house stood.

Bronzed by a month of outdoor living, Henri, the third child in Uncle Achille and Aunt Gabrielle's family, looked Persian with his dark eyes, strong broad nose and black curly hair. I loved his smile, his rolling laughter and warm personality. We followed him without hesitation.

Louise, Renée, and some of their friends joined us. Henri divided us into camps, drew maps on the ground, and had serious consultations about the best hiding places.   We agreed and disagreed, laughed and whispered; birds could not hear their last songs of the day for all the rumblings under their nests.

When night took over the streets, time had come to go in and play cards. Sometimes our older cousins, Jean-Pierre and Jacqueline, joined us at the large kitchen table. We played the card game *Coeur,* and later on *Bataille,* the latter sprinkled with laughter and screams leaving us hoarse and limp.

On Sunday evenings, more pleasure awaited us. The "Molson Beer Company," in a grateful mood for the large quantity of beer the two taverns of our village sold during the hot summer months, offered us free movies in the boys' schoolyard. Carrying our folding stool, Suzanne and I walked twenty minutes to the center of the village, stopping on our way to meet with our cousins.

No French equivalent to the likes of the Three Stooges, Laurel and Hardy or the Marx Brothers existed in French movies, The Americans originals were fed to us with French subtitles, which did not keep any of them from looking less stupid or throwing fewer pies in each other's faces, or those of unfortunate passersby.

At the end of our evenings watching movies or playing

games with our cousins, Maman met with us at their house, and later we walked home together.

One by one the days of August had leaped out of the calendar page. Time had run out. The river rafts and rowboats were tied to the shore. Fall sales at Eaton's and its French counterpart, *Dupuis & Frères,* advertised the coming of winter and the protection their fur coats would provide.

Grand-maman arrived. The following day she removed the cover of the sewing machine, and carefully, oiled the nooks and crannies. After she rubbed every surface to make sure no oil had dripped. During this time Maman made trips to the attic to retrieve winter clothes smelling of mothballs, and promptly aired on the clothesline. Grand maman used an old piece of sheet to test the smoothness of the machine's mechanism. Once the moth ball perfume had evaporated, Grand maman, and Maman opened up and cleaned the seams of old garments ready for an upgrade. To my annoyance I always inherited Suzanne's old uniform or winter coat. A tuck here a pinch there and Maman handed a pretense new coat.

My father ignored our sewing activities, except to remind us not to drop pins and needles on the floor, for the benefit of Tellie's paws. At this season of the year, his passion lay mainly in the briskness of the air: yellow leaves, crab apples, grouse and woodcock; time had come to exercise Tellie's legs for the hunting season.

The gardens brought forth their last crops. Golden corn glistening with butter and sprinkled with salt garnished our plates. Papa liked his overripe. We liked ours crisp and juicy. Grand-maman sliced hers in a dish, buttered and sprinkled with salt and pepper. In the kitchen, barely audible from the summer porch, drops fell into an earthenware bowl. Maman had filled a cheesecloth bag with sugary boiled crab apples. It hung from a pantry knob and imperceptibly, one drop at a time, the bowl filled with golden red syrup: apple jelly.

I knew summer had truly come to an end when Bernard left for Montréal.

"I will be back next summer," he assured me, and gave me his best little boat. I had nothing to give him, nothing new, nothing a boy like Bernard would enjoy. I went to my bank and took two nickels out of my meager Christmas savings and gave them to him.

"You can buy yourself two ice-cream cones," I said. We had no conversation in our repertoire for such an occasion. Awkwardly we said goodbye to each other.

"See you next summer," he said. I think I repeated the same. And he left.

Trees would lose their leaves and burgeon anew; snow would cover the ground for months, then melt; rivers swell and recede; crocus, tulips, and narcissus bloom before Bernard would come knocking at our door once more.

Without the consent of children, September breezed in and installed itself in the village. Our male cousins and their friends were off to college; our school uniforms and books ready.

Grand-maman had finished her work, and after a day or two of rest returned to Montréal. She gifted her granddaughters with a small paper bag filled with round, white and red striped peppermints. Maman gave us one a day after making us swallow a revolting teaspoon of cod liver oil. This prevention would protect us all winter long, she assured us, and spare us from colds and other calamities; we never found out if it prevented the latter; it did not, however, stop colds and fever and coughing and sore throats.

I found it rather enjoyable to have Maman to myself

when cod liver oil had failed the test, especially when the fever was over and I could sit in bed. Then, together, we colored in my coloring books. When I became tired she fluffed my pillows, made me lie down, and read me stories.

Since Papa had rejoined our household, every night after work he returned to us. On weekends he went for walks with Tellie on the deserted golf course or across the farmlands. At night, through his wonderful story telling, Suzanne and I were transported anew to his world of nature and fairytales.

But the reality of our lives had a different flavor. Our parents no longer smiled at each other, and when, on rare occasions, Papa allowed himself to let down his stern mask, it felt like a menacing cloud had lifted and let in the sun. Why this sudden transformation? We did not know. Afterward, Maman always commented to Suzanne and me, "Your father can be so charming when he wants." We heard that sentence more than once, and each time the sound of regret colored her voice.

Papa had refused to choose between her and his mistress. And even though Maman was back in the fold, he played the part of the offended. He demonstrated no signs of affection toward her, offered her no presents on her birthdays or at Christmas. The bouquets of flowers, the boxes of candies were of the past. Instead, he offered a frown, a constant reminder that she could lose her daughters.

Under her eyes, dark circles returned. But she did not cry, or stand at her bedroom window, or ask me to call her Maman Margot.

CHAPTER THIRTY THREE

PAPA, MONSIEUR BINETTE AND SALLY

"Monsieur Binette, could you pick my husband up at eight o'clock tomorrow morning *Non, non.* This is not his week vacation, only one day."

Papa watched Maman as she waited for Monsieur Binette's answer.

"What is he...?"

Maman put a finger to her lips. "Yes, Monsieur Binette. Yes, he is ready. Can you pick him up tomorrow?" Maman smiled. "Wonderful. Thank you. Good bye."

"What was that all about?" asked Papa.

"Not much. He wondered if you were in a tizzy for having waited five days, since the hunting season already started Monday."

"That man has a gift for blabbing saying nothing."

Maman turned around, lifted her eyes in her unspoken, "there he goes again" monologue, and went back to doing her chores.

During the season, Monsieur Binette, part-time butcher, part-time taxi driver, was indispensable to my father. His spontaneous, good-humored nature accommodated itself well to short drives from the village to the railroad station, while he visited with his daily passengers. Abbreviated sentences and quick repartees were part of the twenty-five cent drive.

Papa's ride took Monsieur Binette ten miles away from his regular route, to *Montagne Saint-Joseph* or *La-Pointe-aux-Anglais,* where hunting grounds abounded with ducks, grouse and woodcock. For Papa, the introvert, and his chauffeur, the extrovert, it was a tug of war: one resisting conversation, the other struggling to pull sentences out of his taciturn passenger, urging him on with a burst of words which hung in the air like uninvited whiffs of sulphur. But together, every weekend during the hunting season, the unmatched pair went in the same direction, remaining miles apart inside the cab's confinement.

When Papa left the house, a weight lifted from our shoulders. Even on a cloudy day, no shadow could darken our moods.

Despite the strict rules Maman imposed upon herself and us so that our father could find no fault in her as a wife and mother, she had a childlike quality, a joy that bubbled.

"Let's make a surprise! A charade—an operetta! Let's write the lyrics in rhymes using songs we know!" And with her we created, laughed, and sang.

We could be ourselves twice during the year: eight days during the summer when Papa spent a week at Uncle George's lake, and eight days during the hunting season. Those days were around the corner. For eight days we would not hear criticism about Maman's friends, the government of our Prime Minister, Monsieur Duplessis, women who wore lipstick, the Masons, the nouveau riche, women who wore winter boots adorned with fur around the ankles, the English Royalty, and soon to join the fold, Charles de Gaulle, but presently, most of all—the Irish.

Papa transferred the animosity he felt toward his Irish boss—a man who blamed others for his failures—to

Sally, who, with her husband, committed the unforgivable sin of building a house next to ours.

Through the dining room's French doors Papa surveyed the construction, every brick a weight on his soul. He suffered when painters applied Irish green paint to the wood trim, and suffered increasingly when a black iron fence butted against our cedar hedge. When the fence was painted a lovely Irish green, he had an apoplectic fit. The fence dried quickly in the warm Indian summer sun, the green no longer shining bright, but more subdued; however, it still sang, "Danny Boy."

Once in a while, trying not to antagonize him, Maman agreed with him about one of his pet peeves: the paint color "Yes," she would say, "the green is a bit green. Nevertheless, it is a lovely house and can only enhance the value of ours. Don't you think?"

He seldom answered. Maybe a grunt, usually a negative repartee, as: "they ruined the cedar hedge," or "that house will block the sun in the dining room." Maman could have contradicted him in both cases, but it was easier and less frustrating to simply let it go.

As days passed, Papa's complaints diminished until... Oh, he would never forget, that while peacefully enjoying a particularly fine Sunday supper, he saw, from the corner of his right eye, something move through the cedar hedge across Sally's green painted fence. It was dusk and he could not quite make out what he saw. Or maybe, he did not believe what he saw. He promptly dabbed his mustache, placed his napkin next to his bread plate, and excused himself from the table. Tellie, our English setter, followed him outdoors.

Maman, Suzanne and I stood up, turned off the kitchen light, and saw, through the branches, a superb Irish setter. Suzanne and I glanced at each other and giggled.

"Stop girls! If your father hears us, he will send you to bed and blame me."

We suppressed our laughter and watched Sally's Irish setter come to the fence to meet Tellie. Knowing nothing about the colors or ethnicity of their respective clans they greeted each other, sniffing through the prickly barrier. They woofed a couple of times in their universal tongue, wagged their tails, lifted their legs, again and again, and with their territories well delineated, walked toward their respective homes barking once more for good measure.

Papa came in. His face, five minutes ago healthy and tanned, had turned ashen. He sat down, snapped his napkin and put it back on his lap.

"Is everything alright?" asked Maman innocently.

Suzanne and I bit our lips and kept our giggles in.

"That woman…that woman bought an Irish setter! Can you believe it?"

"That's why we heard some barking," said Maman. She looked at Tellie sitting quietly next to Papa. "I hope that your new neighbor is as good as you." Tellie wagged her tail.

Suzanne cackled, and tried to cover it up by clearing her throat.

"Drink some milk," suggested Papa.

Suzanne obeyed, but it was the wrong suggestion. Under the pressure of a mounting fit of laughter, the milk squirted out of her mouth. Seeing the jet land on the table, I roared.

"Both of you go to your room! And stay there until you are through with your hysterical laughter."

We heard Maman's feeble, "But Louis, they are only children."

"Don't take their defense. I don't need a bunch of hysterical women in my house."

We heard Papa's chair scrape the linoleum floor and the whine of the dining room swinging door. Maman stayed in the kitchen. Sobered, Suzanne and I sat on our respective beds.

In our joy of being home we had forgotten about Papa's phobias. Sally would not go away. But, each night at story time, he was the father every child wanted. Affectionate, serene, creative; we could even laugh when alone with him. The minute he entered our bedroom, a curtain was drawn that separated us from a reality we were only too happy to forget. When he finished his story he tucked us in and kissed our foreheads. And peacefully, sleep embraced us.

It would be another week before Papa went on his eight-day vacation and forgot about Sally. In the meantime, one more black mark was added to her name. It was the following Sunday, at sundown. Papa sat in his favorite chair facing the large picture window, watching a spectacular sunset across fields as far as the far end of Saint-Eustache.

From the corner of his left eye, he saw Sally's husband

carry an Irish-green trashcan, followed by their Irish setter, and Sally, herself, arms overflowing with small parcels. The husband put the trashcan down at the edge of the street. Relieving his wife of her load of well-wrapped trash parcels he deposited them, one by one, in front of and to the sides of the green can, as so many little presents at the foot of a Christmas tree.

"That woman is crazy! Margot! Take a look at that!"

Maman hurried to the living room, wiping her hands on her apron, joining Papa near the window.

"What is it, Louis?"

"That woman is crazy, I tell you. Look, look."

At a glance Maman saw the Irish couple in the joint harmonious pursuit of trash removal with implements matching their home décor. She turned her head slightly away from my father. If he had not been so mesmerized by our neighbor's trash and Irish Green, he would have been irked to a higher degree by Maman's smile, which had a desperate look, one that appears on the face of a church-attendant when trying to restrain a mounting fit of laughter.

"There is one thing to say about our neighbors," she

said in a voice squeezed by constricting muscles. She cleared her voice, regained control, and said amiably, "They are extremely tidy, aren't they. If every property in Saint-Eustache was as well kept as theirs, who knows, we could become a resort for excessively clean people."

"Hmm."

Maman lifted her eyes, shrugged ever so slightly, turned on her heels and exited to the kitchen.

Papa returned to his chair still seeing green. Like a regret, a remnant of pale rose glided toward the end of the day, and with it Papa's missed ecstasy.

CHAPTER THIRTY FOUR

THE VILLAGE WAS AFLUTTER

As if perchance spring, instead of fall had arrived, the village's atmosphere had lifted. Suzanne and I heard increased sounds of activities. Now and then, mixed in with hammering and sawing, a shout rose above the noise. "How's it going?" "You're going to finish on time?"

We found the answer to this surge of energy from Cousin Louise. Her father, Uncle Achille, was traveling through the county, she told us, to promote a big celebration commemorating the one-hundredth anniversary of the Patriot's Revolt. Louise's answer left me mildly interested, however, Suzanne bubbled with excitement. She pelted Louise with more questions than our cousin could answer.

Papa had no idea about the celebration. He never seemed interested in the affairs of the village except when something went wrong. But, he knew who the Patriots were. Papa said, "Le Père Latour told us that when he was a little boy he saw a battle between the Patriots and the Red Coats.

That got my attention. "What's the Red Coats?"

"It was a British army led by Colborne. The soldiers wore red jackets."

"What color jacket did the Patriot soldiers wear? "

"Marcelle, we don't even know who the Patriots are." Suzanne said wearing her Mother Superior look.

"First of all, the Patriot was a political party, like the Liberal or the Conservative." Papa said.

"Was Uncle Arthur a Patriot when he was younger?" Suzanne's eyebrow went up to her hairline.

"*Non, non*, and he is a conservative and so is your cousin Paul. Do you want to know more about the Patriots?"

"Yes, please," said Suzanne before I could say "No, thank you very much."

"The party became so fed up..." Papa hesitated. "It's a little complicated because it is something that fermented for many years. The citizens felt that the government ignored their demands for justice. Papineau, the chief of the party traveled to England to present his complaints and demands to the Colonial Office, alas, unsuccessfully. Bitter, he came back to Québec and started giving speeches explaining the demands of the party and the lack of cooperation from the local and overseas governments. He was a powerful speaker, they say he had a silver tongue."

"He had a silver tongue!"

Marcelle," Suzanne shouted as if I had committed a crime.

"When it is said of someone that they have a silver tongue it means that the person is a great speaker," explained Papa.

"So what happened?"

"After hearing him, many people thought they should revolt. Little groups of militia men formed, and when the speeches became more and more inflammatory, a group under Doctor Chênier decided it was time to be totally committed; they would form an army, and be ready to fight."

"That's why we're having a big party to celebrate, one hundred years later!" I said delighted with my knowledge.

"Yes, and no," said Papa. " We are celebrating courage, not victory. They lost. They lost the battle. Yet, by and by they won the respect of their compatriots and impressed the Colonial Office into treating the Canadians more equitably..."

I must have looked lost. Papa put his hand on my shoulders and said "equitably means with justice. For example, not taking land without the assent of all branches of our government and not over taxing the products we bought from them: rhum, wine, tea, cloth..."

"They fought because tea..."

"It was much more than that. A few years before the revolt there was an election and the other parties tried to stop the people they knew would vote for the Patriot party. Yet, the more they tried to stop them, the more people came, even if they had to wait in lines for a full day. When people revolt, P'tit Blond, it is never because of one thing."

I nodded as if I understood, and smiled. "Merci Papa, can I go and play now?"

"Yes, you have been very patient."

Suzanne stayed still. I ran out in case she asked another question and I would have to listen some more.

The Saturday following our lesson about the Patriots, Suzanne and I went to visit with our cousins hoping to find more details about the fun part of it. Suzanne objected to my presence and walked fast pretending she did not know me. The last hundred feet or so I ran and met her at the front door.

Suzanne charmed Aunt Gabrielle, into answering two questions about the patriots that Papa's answers had not satisfied, but "no more." Aunt Gabrielle said, "I have so much to do, you will have to excuse me. Monsieur Groulx will be here to rehearse, and so will Annette Dubois."

"You will play the piano at the reception?"I asked

"Yes, I will accompany some of the singers"

"Will Maman sing?"

"Not this time, Marcelle. Now, why don't you and Suzanne find Louise. She must be upstairs. I have to practice until they come."

I would have liked to see how Monsieur Groulx looks without his raccoon coat. I bet he would not appear so frightening and powerful. I knew I would hear Annette Dubois through the walls and ceiling, because Papa said, she has enough voice to raise the roof of the church! But her voice is not only powerful, it is lovely and warm, and that, Maman said, is the most important part.

Louise waited for us at the top of the stairs. Even before we reached her room she said, "I know why Aunt Margot won't sing. Uncle Louis won't let her."

"How do you know that?" Suzanne said

"I heard my mother tell my father."

"I don't understand why."

My father just said, "I'm not surprised, Louis is too jealous, he will never let Margot sing in front of a crowd."

That is all Louise heard, but she knew other things about the celebration. She told us that after the parade, Uncle Arthur and Cousin Paul and other important people would be speaking.

"Why will they all speak?"

Suzanne's eyes went up to the ceiling again. "Don't you know, Uncle Arthur is a senator and that's what he does, he makes speeches"

"Yes, that's right", said Louise, and Cousin Paul is a congressman and that's what he does."

I did not open my mouth again. But Louise and Suzanne's chattering continued. "After the parade and the speeches, Papa and Maman and a small group of notables, important people, will have dinner at Hotel

Bellevue."

When Louise said *notables,* she said it as if she had just heard Uncle Achille say it. I think she was using it for the first time. Louise didn't cut hers in two as I do with extraordinaire, but she said *important* after, maybe in case we didn't know what notables meant. Well, now I know what it means and if I could remember Papa's word equi...something, then next time I would have important things to say.

Suzanne and Louise kept on talking, but this time about school. I left them. I went looking for Cousin Jacqueline in the art room. Sometimes, one of my cousins works on a large canvas coloring with oil paint, or embosses on pewter, or paints flowers on delicate china dishes. My three cousins also play the piano. I was very impressed by Renée, who at last year's end-of-school ceremony had played a piano piece full of big chords and fast runs. Her fingers never hit a wrong note.

I knocked at the door of the art room, a long narrow room as tiny as our kitchen in Montréal. Jacqueline greeted me with a smile. At school, as part of her music studies, she taught the lower grades to read music. She stood in front of the blackboard where notes were drawn on the lines of a staff, the notes looking like birds on a row of electrical wires. I felt proud having my own cousin teaching us. But, she said she dreaded standing in front of a class even of the little ones. I think she was as shy as I. I sat and watched her paint; no talk, no questions, no answers, but once in a while we exchanged a smile.

Louise, Jacqueline & Renée celebrating Christmas 1994

Promenade

Paul-Sauvé

275

CHAPTER THIRTY FIVE

THE TENTH OF OCTOBER 1937

When the grand day arrived, Suzanne knew a great deal of facts about the Patriots of Saint-Eustache and of the many other villages in the County who revolted against the unjust rules of the British Colonial Office. The French population was not the only one involved. Many English-Canadians were also vocal in their grievances though few took arms against their own. Regardless of their smaller part in the revolt they were severely punished; the government fearing that if the movement grew, Canada would become the Ireland of North America. I heard Papa say that.

Suzanne told me about all the gruesome things that had happened, and that the poor Patriots who fought used mostly old French muskets and pitch forks and the like to defend themselves. They counted on their own being killed so that others could use the muskets of the fallen. But her telling me about farmers and their families being killed, and barns and houses burned and the animals screaming gave me nightmares. That horror story tempered my joy; the celebration lost its appeal.

Sunday the Tenth of October Maman, Papa, Suzanne and I walked among a throng of excited villagers still dressed in their church outfits. From our terrace, looking across the river, we had seen cars on the bridge standing still, bumper to bumper. Reaching the top of our street we met with the crowd filling the sidewalks and the street. Papa wondered where all the cars on the bridge would find a place to park. We greeted familiar faces, and automatically Papa raised his hat and sat it back on his head. It took us ten minutes more than usual to walk to Aunt Gabrielle's house.

All the family, minus Uncle Achille, stood on the veranda. How lucky we were to have a place to watch the parade and not be trampled.

"Achille is attending a luncheon given for the dignitaries." Aunt Gabrielle told us. "I'm sure they are finished now, but he must be checking that everyone is at his post. For the past six months he barely takes time to eat. It's one meeting after the other. Would you believe it, the office is busier than ever. I will be delighted when this is all over."

With a tease in his eyes Papa said, "People can be so

inconsiderate. How dare they insist on marrying, contract in hand, or dying with a will in due form, while Monsieur the Notary, Prefect of the County, Mayor of Saint-Eustache, President of today's Patriotic celebration is traveling on his white horse by mount and by vale."

Everyone laughed at Papa's tease but Aunt Gabrielle only smiled.

"I worry about his health, Louis. Achille is devoted to our community and people take advantage. For the past year, as president of the festivities he has been steeped in promoting the celebration and of course mending egos..." Aunt Gabrielle's voice trailed like a sigh. Of course Papa might not have thought that on top of running a household, making sure her five children were well educated and brought up, fed and well dressed, while she played the organ at church and helped with the office work, indeed I am sure that Papa did not realized that his sister might appreciate her husbands' presence and help, and may not have relished her brother's repartee.

"I think the parade's coming this way," shouted Jean-Pierre who ran back and forth to the corner of the street. It's coming out of Uncle Arthur's street."

"Please calm down Jean-Pierre," said Aunt Gabrielle,

279

in a soft voice. The parade will go up rue Ferré to the plateau and come down in front of the Manoir Globensky, pass in front of our house, then go to the college where your father will unveil the monument dedicated to Chênier."

"That's all?"

"*Non, Non*, the boys' chorus will sing, and the names of the patriots who died in the battle will be called. Then they will come back our way to rue Jean-Olivier Chênier where a huge tent has been erected and where the notables will give their speeches."

"I wonder why they started in Uncle Arthur's street." said Maman. "It's such a small street."

"Because the house is built on the site of Doctor Chênier's property," said Aunt Gabrielle.

"I didn't know that. Was there anything left of the Chênier's home?"

"Gracious, no. Colborne ordered to set fire to most of the houses in the village. I heard that at least eighty percent of the village went up in flames. They pillaged and destroyed the church from the inside. Nothing was left except the front wall that still stands as a reminder of the tragedy. The village was not enough. They went on a rampage in the farming areas, killing and burning."

"Maman, where's the parade going?" shouted Henri from the other end of the veranda. "It's not coming this way!"

With one finger Aunt Gabrielle gestured to Henri to come to her side. "I told Jean-Pierre two minutes ago," said Aunt Gabrielle. "Please ask him. And please, *do not shout*"

I left Maman's side and went with Henri where Jean-Pierre, and my other cousins and Suzanne had gathered. Henri resigned himself to the wait and called me to stand in front of him near the railing. "If you stay in back you will see nothing. While we wait, let's watch the people. We may see someone we know."

Both sidewalks were filled and try as I might I could not see anyone I knew. People came from all around the county and Montréal. This was a celebration for every French-Canadian.

Eventually, we heard a band playing and then men on horses dressed like the Patriots, with wool caps, three quarter length wool coats cinched at the waist by *une ceinture flèchées,* (an arrow patterned woven belt) went by, followed by a band playing patriotic music. And then the first allegorical float appeared. It depicted a house La maison Saint-Germain of Saint Denis sur Richelieu.

u

"The Patriots won a battle there, in Saint-Denis." Henri told me. "Did you know that the grandson of Doctor Nelson who led the Patriots in Saint-Denis, is here now? He will recite a poem when the monument of Doctor Chênier is unveiled."

"Will you be going?"

"Oh, yes, my father is doing the unveiling. Look, more people carrying flags. Watch, watch, another float is coming."

More people with more flags went by and a band followed them.

The second float showed a workshop where patriots forged arms. And one more group paraded holding its flags, another band played O Carillon, Henri and I sang at the top of our lungs. No one could hear us over the trumpets and the trombones.

The third float showed *Le Bivouac*, an outdoor camp, in front of the church. Some pretended cleaning their muskets but others shot in the air for real.

When Henri saw me jump, he told me the soldiers were firing blanks. I did not like it anymore than if they had shot cartouches. So far the parade left me unimpressed. I appreciated the marching bands, but the floats...I guess they were for adults. The fourth one represented the words of the brave Forget, I cannot recall the words but I know that three Patriots by that name died with Doctor Chênier. I wondered if Madame Forget had lost three sons or a husband and two sons. It must have been a terribly sad house. I hope the red Coats did not burn her house.

The fifth float showed the death of Doctor Chênier at the foot of the church. Not the real church, one made of wood and painted gray.

Henri said to me, "The Red Coats had set the church on fire, so the few Patriots left jumped out of the steeple and were killed."

More flags and people and another band went by, and then we saw the next float coming around the bend.

"That one represents the murder of young Marineau." said Henri.

I stood up on my toes. I saw a little boy standing in front of the door to his house. He had nothing in his hands, no musket, nothing. When I saw Red Coats ready to shoot him I squeezed myself by Henri and made my way to the front door. As I went in, I heard the shots. I closed the door behind me, ran into the living room and sat on the floor with my back to the piano. I pulled an encyclopedia book out of the rack and started looking at pictures. After the parade, Maman found me there slumped over, sound asleep, nose in the encyclopedia; knowledge not improved.

We said good bye and thank you to Aunt Gabrielle and our cousins, and left. Papa held my hand, but in the melee we lost Maman and Suzanne. When we reached our street we waited alone, away from the crowd, and finally we saw them.

"Ouff! I'm exhausted" said Maman.

"Papa, are we going to the concert and the fireworks?" asked Suzanne.

"Yes, Papa. The whole village and the church will be lit." I said. "It will be so beautiful. People are coming all the way from Montréal to sing or play the piano, and even Aunt Gabrielle will accompany Monsieur Groulx and Annette Dubois."

"It will be under a tent that has enough space to fit in three thousand people," said Suzanne

"This is too dangerous," said Papa. One person screams and there is a stampede, or the electricity goes out, somebody lights a match and the whole place is engulfed in flames."

"But Papa, at least we could go and see the church

and the village illuminated. And we could stay outdoors near the tent and still hear the music. Jacqueline is singing in a chorus of one hundred singers, one hundred, can you imagine that! She told me how beautiful it sounds." said Suzanne.

"Absolutely not," said Papa. "I told you why, two minutes ago."

"But Louise invited me to go with them." said Suzanne.

"That's enough girls." said Maman. "Your father is leaving tomorrow for his hunting trip. Monsieur Binette will be at the house early to pick him up."

Without Maman's help we knew our efforts were useless. The conversation had died with our hopes for an evening as no other had been in our lives.

Our knowledge about the impetus behind the rebellion, the role of the clergy and of our political leaders remained sketchy for years. Nevertheless, since I saw the parade in 1937, a new crop of historians have discovered in private collections, journals and documents, the true history of the period. New books have been written, and a comprehensive history of our past, like a replenished river after the ice melts, is renewed and unfolding for a population whose motto is still, *Je me souviens!* I remember.

Parade of the Patriots

CHAPTER THIRTY SIX

INTERLUDE

Papa left early in the morning for his long awaited vacation. He whistled under his breath, stopping only long enough to kiss Suzanne and me, and whisper into our ears, "Be good girls."

In two minutes Papa and Tellie were gone; gone for eight days.

For a few more weeks the village would display a shimmering of red, orange and gold and every subtle shade in between. We shivered in the mornings, relaxed during warm afternoons, and shivered again at night. Hunting was in the air.

The week of Papa's vacation, Maman and the smell of

warm, crusty rolls or other confections greeted us when we came home from school. On days when she left the house to visit friends, she hid the key under the doormat. Suzanne and I liked that. It made us feel grown up. She always left a note saying where to find our snack, and, "I will be back around five." We knew she had already prepared dinner and that in no time it would be ready to serve.

Before the end of the week Maman's friends, six of whom were regular bridge partners, and other ladies at whose homes she had been a guest during the year, were invited to a cocktail party. The cocktail itself, a mixture of gin and red wine, was kept on ice for a day and served from a decanter. It looked tempting, tasted innocently fruity, and offered an unexpected punch to the gentle ladies.

On that special occasion, Suzanne and I came in quietly through the back door and went to our bedroom where our best dresses hung on the closet door.

I knew all the guests. Still, I abhor having to walk into the living room and stare at a sea of faces and hats, dresses and smiles, all the while hearing the noise of chatter and laughter. Suzanne and I had to kiss most of those ladies, answer all their questions, and never forget to say, *Oui, Madame, Non, Madame, Merci, Madame*, if one happened to remark on our looks or good manners, knowing all the time that a blush would color my face in different shades of red and show my embarrassment. Oh, I dreaded it so!

I could smile and be polite, but cleverness did not come easily. Too afraid to say the wrong thing when asked a question, I held on to Maman's hand and she helped me out, as she did when Papa questioned me. She usually jumped in and finished my sentence afraid that my answer could lead toward disaster. Suzanne, however, was left on her own with the ladies, being all the things Maman wanted her to be.

Since Papa left, the days sped by. Maman's party had been a success. We had already eaten our forbidden meal of hot dogs and French fries and drank our Coca-Cola, feeling deliciously naughty.

The afternoons remained warm. Maman took advantage of the lovely weather to go to Montréal and visit Uncle Jean, Aunt Marianna and Aunt Irène. "Don't tell your father," she reminded us.

Saturday arrived. As if to announce that our week was over, rain fell in sheets. At times, gusts of wind tore away twigs and leaves with their stems. They were framed in our windowpanes, good-bye cards of the season.

Maman lit the oil furnace and the kitchen wood stove. The warmth, scent and crackling of wood made us forget that it was a damp, miserable day. Actually, cleaning on Saturday mornings became easier when the weather made us grateful to be indoors.

I had the best job. I dusted all the furniture's legs, though it was with trepidation that I approached the radio; so many wires lay on the floor. I feared that I would be blown to smithereens if I touched one of them. But I relished sitting under the clavier of Grand-maman's piano. The massive carved legs became the majestic columns at the entrance of an enchanted castle. The atmosphere and climate changed when I sat under the dining-room table. There, my imagination took flight. I was in the desert under a tent where exotic people waved palm leaves while others graciously waited on me.

"Marcelle, you're dusting in the air. You'll see the dust better if you keep your eyes open." I was brought back to a Persian carpet that was not flying, or resting on sand, but lay on a prosaic, immovable surface of hard wood floors.

That Saturday, Maman persisted.

"Hurry, Marcelle, I don't want the cleaning to drag on until after lunch. You and Suzanne have to finish your homework before dinner."

"When is Papa arriving?" I asked.

Around dinner time I imagine, or maybe earlier. This is not a day for hunting."

"Are we having *une perdrix au chou*?"

"Oh, no. It would take too much time to clean and dress the grouse; unless your father arrives early."

I loved the sautéed grouse smothered in roasted onions and cabbage. "What are...?"

"Marcelle, that's enough, no more chatting. Every time you say a word or think of one, your dusting rag is suspended in the air. I see lots of legs that need dusting."

By four o'clock the cleaning was over and our homework finished. The time had come to get ready for Papa's arrival. We washed, changed our clothes and Maman brushed our hair and tied ribbons to match the color of our dresses.

Suzanne helped in the kitchen and I sat at the piano to practice my scale, the only one I knew after four lessons. I remembered where to start. The first note of the scale, the Do, was right in front of my belly button. But when I pressed the Do with my thumb, the next two keys went down at the same time because, Maman said, "The piano has arthritis. It sat in this cold living room while we were away. Your father never rented the house."

So, after pressing the middle C, I had to sing Ré, and Mi, put my thumb under to play Fa, and the rest of the scale. And then I did the same in reverse. After four repetitions of playing the scale and singing Ré Mi at the top of my lungs and coming down the scale Mi Ré, Maman told me to read a book.

They soon joined me. Maman picked up the newspaper, the Larousse, and a pencil, and sat down to do her crossword puzzle. Suzanne, book in hand, read *Les Malheurs de Sophie,* and annoyed me with her giggles while I struggled to sound difficult words in mine. Distracted, I couldn't keep up with my story. I managed to read only two pages and then the phone rang.

"Suzanne, why don't you answer," said Maman

Suzanne ran to the kitchen. "It's Papa. He wants to

292

talk to you."

I didn't recall Papa ever calling before. I followed Maman.

"*Allo*... Yes, but...should we wait for you? ... You are coming tonight, aren't you? ... I will leave the back door unlocked... Yes, we will see you later."

Slowly, Maman hung up the receiver. Her hand clung to it. She frowned as if she had not understood what she had heard.

Suzanne and I stood waiting. Finally, Suzanne burst out, "Is Papa coming before we go to bed?"

Her hand still lingering on the phone box, Maman turned around and looked surprised to see us there.

"What did you say?" she asked.

"Is Papa on his way?"

"Yes, eventually. But we will eat now." I was hungry and pleased not to have to wait any longer. I would see Papa later anyway. We ate our dinner. Suzanne tried to interest Maman in the story of her book, but a few nods and sighs did not nourish the conversation. Except for short sentences to correct our table manners, "Suzanne, watch your elbows. Marcelle, please, cut smaller bites and don't eat so fast," the dinner hour was laden with uncertainty like a question mark at the bottom of an unwritten page.

Papa came back the following day while we were in church. He was a day late. His sheepish smile lingered on until our bedtime. I imagined it resembled the guilt on my face when I was caught lifting the lid of the candy jar. But unfamiliar to me was Maman's countenance; a pinched-mouth in a set face, moist dark eyes glittering with resentment, yet, no tears were falling.

The week started and the old routine resumed. In bed, early in the morning, I listened for the familiar rumble of Maman's activities. Maybe yesterday was a bad dream.

Maman, in the kitchen, however, did not try to soften the noise. The sounds were quick, loud, and sharp; there was no patience in them, and no caring. She rebuked Tellie for being in her way, sending her scampering to the hallway.

Papa did not whistle as he had done the morning he left for his vacation. Nevertheless, the gargling, the grunts; the mumbling I still could hear through the bathroom walls. But I did not hear Maman rush to Papa's aid to help him hitch his suspenders and button the back of his white starched shirt collar; nonetheless she served the breakfast he expected: a small bowl of bran cereal with milk and dates, two soft-boiled eggs, a bowl of applesauce, two pieces of Jewish rye toast and a cup of tea. As usual he kissed us, told us to be good girls and said, "Good-bye."

After he left, we sat at breakfast with Maman, but she stayed only a minute, she would eat later, she said. An atmosphere that lay like a damp blanket of haze after a downpour squashed the pleasure I usually found in food. We received our hugs at the front door. No amount of powder or rouge could conceal her sadness.

Nothing changed during the week. But on Friday after school, we noticed a change in our parents' bedroom. Twin beds replaced the large one we had seen for ever. That day, Maman's eyes would not meet ours. We asked no questions.

Before long, the hugs became more frequent, and, "Call me Maman Margot" was again a plea for our love.

Madame Thibodeau

CHAPTER THIRTY SEVEN

A VISIT TO THE CHATEAU

A visit to Maman's friend, Madame Thibodeau, boosted the level of my imagination to a higher sphere. I bristled with anticipation. What it meant to Maman and Suzanne I can only imagine.

My nine-year-old sister would find in Claudine, the eleven year-old daughter of Madame Thibodeau, a friend: gregarious, quick minded, generous, imaginative, and who had the good fortune to have a room three times as large as ours, and did not have to share it with a sister. It also housed a generous amount of books, dolls and toys.

As for Maman, Madame Thibodeau had been her first visitor when our parents arrived in Saint-Eustache. A friendship developed quickly, and soon, with Papa, they were invited to evenings where plays and informal concerts were a frequent part of the fare. Maman, who loved the theater and music, enjoyed participating in any production, and her new friend Gaby always encouraged her to sing. Sadly, it lasted a short time. Papa's jealousy made it impossible for her to be part of the group. The evening parties ended; however, the friendship blossomed.

Unlike Maman, Madame Thibodeau, with her parents, had traveled around the world, studied in Paris, and returned every summer with her husband who pursued advanced medical studies. She had an enlarged picture of life and a candor that was refreshing. Maman who had been raised in the buttoned-up restrictions of a left over Victorian era, and lived with a husband who had never left it, found her friend's candor, at times, startling.

We visited them not long after the large bed in our parents' bedroom had been replaced by twin beds. Since then, Maman's vivaciousness had frozen into an unmelting sadness and Papa had covered the sheepishness of the first days by an air of "all is well, nothing has changed." In our home silence hovered like a ghost-parent.

Before leaving the house, Maman skillfully hid the dark circles under her eyes with a double dabbing of powder, blotted her lipstick and reapplied it, and added rouge to her cheeks. As we walked she stared frontward and did not encourage conversation.

She uttered her first sentence as we approached l'Hôtel des Mille Iles. "Do not look at anyone." I supposed it had to do with inebriated unsure-footed men, or others who stood against a post leering at the occasional passersby.

I safely peeked across the street at a hotel that had been built in the late nineteenth century by the grandfather of our life-long friends, Francine and Lise. Monsieur Pesant recognized the attraction the rivers and the lake had on city dwellers, and promoted the village by having postcards of Saint-Eustache printed. Traveling salesmen, who had stayed at his hotel left Monsieur Pesant's postcards wherever they went, and became free publicity agents.

One card in particular shows his hotel, a lovely two-story wood building, painted a cream color with brown trim. A wide platform traversed the length of the façade showing oversized windows and shutters. A dozen carved columns delineated by the same color as the veranda's trim supported the second floor. The upper porch displayed more oversized shuttered windows and a

299

railing of perfectly lined curved posts, looking like a series of well-shaped legs.

Aged by scorching weather and then below-zero temperature, the hotel of my seventh year had faded and peeled. Its façade had an old western-cowboy-less-movie-look. Once in a while a horse tied to a post attracted my attention. I would have liked to see a real cowboy jumping on it and escaping in a swirl of dust. A closer examination of the horses would have given me a strong hint that anyone in the village could have outrun the poor beasts.

Once we had gone by the hotels I knew the longest part of the walk was over. The terrain, which had seemed flat until now, had already started to rise. Before the eye had noticed, one's calves gave warning.

October had burst with intoxicating splashes of color, as if a dozen Van Gogh had created a gigantic canvas. Two days of rain had swept away the summer dust, and the redolence of autumn's good housekeeping filled the air.

"Marcelle, your shoes!"

I sighed and stopped dragging my feet in the blanket of leaves. We were in sight of our destination; there was no point to grumble, and Maman's disposition did not fare well with grumblings of any kind, anyway.

We had reached the upper part of the hill where Doctor Thibodeau's office stood. At the right of the front door, a gold plaque told the visitor that the doctor had completed his internship in Paris. For professionals of every field, a stay in Paris gave a certain badge of distinction, a reassurance that the said honoree had studied in our mother country and had earned the respect of his peers.

The doctor's office sat on a narrow stretch of land perched thirty feet or more above the river. From his office window he could hear the rush of water over the small dam and see it play over the rocks of the shallow riverbed. I knew because I heard it myself when I lay on the operating table, before going to sleep to have my tonsils removed.

While I mused, Suzanne questioned Maman, who, looking tired, kept saying, "ask Madame Thibodeau," or "Madame Thibodeau will know."

At last we reached the entrance of the property. A wall of fieldstone encircled it and was surmounted by a wrought-iron fence decorated with a large *Fleur-de-Lys* pattern. Brilliantly white, the chateau, surrounded by a pure blue sky and a flurry of gold leaves, stood like a mausoleum to our past; however, for us, it was a home where friends lived and where laughter, music and love flourished.

Madame Thibodeau and Claudine were waiting for us at the balcony door to the entrance of the library sitting room.

After the usual embrace, Claudine, who had not seen us since our return from Montréal, took a good look at Suzanne and me, exclaiming, "You are so tall!" To me she was the same. The same joyful nature, the same rich laughter like a cascading of warm creamy chocolate fudge; when she spoke the same soft lisping, like an excuse for the easy flow of words. There was no angularity to her body or personality.

As usual when visiting, I felt awkward in the presence of the hosts. Yet the comfortable elegance of the surroundings and conversation attracted me, without, alas, endowing me with the skills or temerity to converse. Suzanne did not have the same problem.

In a few minutes, by asking Madame Thibodeau "Is your head feeling better," having remembered our hostess' headache during her visit to our house, she insured herself a place in our hostess' heart and a smile from our proud Maman. After Madame Thibodeau replied, Suzanne asked her, "Madame Thibodeau, I cannot understand why there is a flour mill across the street from your chateau?"

"Ah, ha, you don't think it fits the décor, do you?"

Suzanne tilted her head to one side, looking uncertain as to what a proper answer should be. She smiled, shrugged her shoulders, "I'm not sure," she said.

"First let's sit down," said Madame Thibodeau. "You had a long walk, and after I tell you the story of the mill, you will go play with Claudine while your Maman and I visit."

I was thrilled and scooted to the back of my seat ready to be entertained.

"A long time ago, the county was divided in seigneuries," said Madame Thibodeau, "each one given to a person who the French authorities thought had enough wherewithal and wealth to hire enough people to clear the land, run a farm and build houses. After some years, and more population moving in, among them doctors and notaries and merchants, it would become a village."

"Did you forget the story of the mill, Madame Thibodeau?" I dared ask.

Madame Thibodeau laughed. Maman's eyebrows came near one another, and for once Suzanne did not say a word.

"*Non ma chérie* I did not forget. Without it there would have been no one wanting to establish themselves in Saint-Eustache."

"You see," said Claudine, "People needed the mill to turn the wheat into flour to make bread, and the wood mill to prepare the wood for them to build houses."

"Yes that is correct. And what you call the chateau is actually a manor house where the Seigneur and his family lived, and all around were fields and orchards, and farm animals. The Seigneur built his house here, I assume, because it was the highest spot in the area. As for the mills, they are built near a river that has enough of a current to give them the power necessary to operate. And chère Suzanne, this is why we have a mill across the street."

As if a great light had entered her understanding Suzanne's head bobbed in response. "*Merci* for the story Madame Thibodeau," she said with a semi-smile that in a

304

way made me think she might have liked to ask more questions, but Maman being in a no-question mood, Suzanne simply said, "I found it very interesting."

"I'm glad you enjoyed it. And now, Claudine, why don't you take Suzanne and Marcelle to your room. In an hour or so, we will have tea together."

"Let's go," said Claudine.

I smiled at our hostess, and followed them.

They rushed toward the large staircase. I could not climb as fast as they did and when I arrived on the second floor they had disappeared.

Following the sound of their voices, I found Suzanne and Claudine already involved in a game. Claudine got up. "You can play with my dollhouse," she said. *"Merci."* I whispered. We did not have one at home and I enjoyed looking at all the rooms and tiny furniture. Soon I rearranged the décor. I played for a while, but after dropping a dish and a table, and hearing a couple of, "Don't break the dishes!" from my sister, I exited quietly and went down the staircase to the entry hall and sat on the bottom step.

There I sat, mesmerized by the play of light through

the towering beveled and iron glass door. I had never seen anything so beautiful. At Aunt Marianna and Uncle Jean's house, despite the Louis the XIV and Louis the XV furniture and the high ceilings, their home possessed a feeling of coziness because of its narrower walls, and did not overwhelm. I felt smaller sitting on this staircase than I would have at their house.

Nonetheless, the one element that lightened up the atmosphere of the Chateau, which had been bought and remodeled by Madame Thibodeau's father, was Maman's friend herself, and her three irreverent, voluble, and bright children. Madame Thibodeau was the light touch, the thoughtful, caring mother and friend. Laughter and good humor brightened the dark woodwork and rattled the Limoges dishes in the cupboards.

From my seat I could hear sniffling and the voice of Maman's friend. I rose and went to the library door. I stayed in the doorway, far away from their eyes, and listened.

"Margot, your story is nightmarish. But you have made the right choice," Madame Thibodeau was saying. "Now you have to make a life for yourself. Louis is gone all day five days a week. You have time to see your friends and play bridge. And please, join us when we go to Montréal to the theater. We have day time tickets."

"Louis will not want me to go."

"Tell him that Gabrielle is going, and invited you to join us. He trusts his sister, doesn't he?"

I did not hear Maman's reply.

"Margot, you have to use your wits for your sake and the girls'."

I heard Claudine and Suzanne laughing and I retreated to the bottom of the staircase.

"Let's go see if the tea is ready," Claudine said as she went by me. Though it was partially opened, she knocked at the library door and entered. "Maman, may I check and see if our tea is ready?"

"Yes, *chérie*, and please ask Madame Laviollette if you could eat in the kitchen; Madame Mignault and I will take our tea here."

This was the end of overhearing the tenth of the conversation, leaving me as usual with only bits and pieces of information. Knowing the intricacies of our parents' relationship would not have changed what happened outwardly in our household. I suppose our partial knowledge helped Suzanne and I enjoy the good moments of our lives, which outnumbered the sad ones.

A visit to the Thibodeau's fulfilled my expectations. And teatime, what a marvelous excuse for ingesting delicious gâteaux and sweets while enjoying the company of our hostess! This was as near to paradise as I could imagine.

Chateau Thibodeau

Entreè hall of the Chateau

CHAPTER THIRTY EIGHT

THE LOQUACITY OF SILENCE

We did not see Maman cry, yet, from time to time, like percolating coffee, a sob escaped through lips that dared not speak.

Suzanne and I witnessed no violence, shouting matches or crude language between our parents—only civil interchanges and cold, silent looks. The atmosphere, calm on the surface, reverberated underneath like an insidious undercurrent, fraying nerves. Thoughts lying deep in secret chambers were turned every which way and ruminated upon.

"Madame, you have a nervous stomach," the doctor said. "Take a little Bicarbonate of Soda."

"A lack of appetite," she complained.

"A glass of Porter beer with your meal may help."

Aware of Maman's marital problems, Doctor Thibodeau knew well that there were no remedies on his apothecary shelves with the power to cure what ailed her.

CHAPTER THIRTY NINE

ARE THE BUTTERNUTS READY TO SHELL?

At Christmas time, Maman, the magician, excised all gloom from the house and ensnared Papa into her magical sphere. Noël must be joyful and mysterious for the enjoyment of their daughters. We accepted the gift, seeing what we wanted to see and feel, joy, unmitigated joy.

Without protest, our father began his holiday chores at the end of autumn. He took some of his bounty, dozens of woodcocks and partridges, to Montréal to store in freezers. Taking advantage of the last days of hunting, he picked up butternuts and carried them in burlap bags to the awaiting cab of Monsieur Binette. Back home, he lugged his harvest to the attic. Spreading newspapers on the floor, he arranged the nuts in a single layer. Their coarse outer shells needed drying before we could use them.

In the meantime Maman checked the cupboards and bought the ingredients she needed to cook for thirteen guests for the *Réveillon de Noël,* an extensive meal served after Midnight Mass. Not long after, labeled jars of pickled beets, green tomato relish and cranberry sauce garnished the pantry shelves. On an upper level two plum puddings soaked happily in sherry.

Two weeks before Christmas, Maman prepared her sausages, ragout of pork and meatballs, and six *Tourtières,* pork meat pies. She kept the perishables frozen on the table of the enclosed porch.

At the beginning of December, Papa checked the readiness of his store of nuts. The day he came down from the attic with a bagful marked the beginning of a ritual.

He brought a log to the kitchen and installed it next to his kitchen chair. Armed with a hammer, he placed the pointed end of the butternut on the log, and hammered down. It was a long process. The small sweet nut protected by a thick, tough, blackish-green outer shell did not easily yield her fruit.

Sitting near the dining-room swinging door, and a few feet away from her master, Tellie watched with a wary eye. Luckily for Papa, he had a good eye and a sure hand. As soon as he took his flying debris, log and hammer, out of the kitchen, Maman removed the nuts from the opened shells and stored them, figuring quite accurately how many pies, pounds of chocolate fudge and pralines they would enrich.

For a month Suzanne and I had inhaled the spices and the sautéed onions, and with great interest watched Maman put her sausage mix in long casings. During most activities we were only fascinated onlookers. Nevertheless, at Maman's request, we cleaned away the dishes and cleared the table, which not only had nine lives, but also nine different functions and disguises.

And when the twenty-fourth day of December appeared under the golden door of our holiday calendar, we knew with certainty that at last Christmas Eve had arrived.

CHAPTER FORTY

A FRENCH-CANADIAN CHRISTMAS

The Christmases of my youth are a series of golden moments ready to be leafed through at the recall of a sound, a sight, a scent. Like a book opening naturally to a page read over and over, the select page in the album of my reminiscing opens up at Noël 1937 as the most perfect and magical of all.

It is seven o'clock on Christmas Eve. It is the first time that Suzanne and I will go to Midnight Mass with our parents. I am too excited to sleep.

"Suzanne, are you awake?"

"Yes."

"What are they doing?"

"I don't know."

"I'm getting up."

"Don't, we're not supposed to."

"I'll just peek in the hallway." I tiptoe to the door. "I can't see anything," I whisper. "The kitchen and the dining room doors are closed."

"Well then, go back to bed."

I hear the kitchen door opening to the porch, then a lot of back and forth tap-tapping of Maman's heels, and the grating and sliding of pots on the stove.

"I think Maman's bringing in all the frozen food."

"Go-to-bed. We won't be able to get up at eleven."

Suzanne's sentence is cut short by a change in the direction of Maman's heels and the dining-room door swinging and moaning.

"Maman's going to the living room.... She's speaking with Papa. Oh, they're opening the vestibule door."

The outside door groans.

"Suzanne, I think they're bringing in the Christmas tree!"

"Sh, sh, they'll hear you." Suzanne gets up, elbows

me to one side and puts her nose into the door opening.

"It must be huge," she says. "It sounds as if it's scratching the door frame."

The cold air reaches our toes and legs. We shiver. Suzanne jumps back into her bed and I in mine. My sheets and covers have the feel of the outdoors. "I'm freezing," I complain. "My teeth are clacking."

Suzanne walks over to my bed with her two pillows. "Move your back to the wall." She slides one of my pillows the length of my back, and jumps in with me.

"It feels good. *Merci.*"

"Let's go to sleep now."

"Suzanne, do you remember last year, the Christmas tree bouquet, when we were sick and Papa was not with us?"

"Yes, I do. But now we will have a real tree. We're not sick and Papa is here. That's enough. I want to sleep. *Bonne nuit.*"

"Bonne nuit."

She snuggles up to me and we fall asleep like two soupspoons in Maman's velvet-lined cutlery

319

compartment.

While we sleep, Papa and Maman bring in the Christmas tree and secure it in a corner between the left bookcase and fireplace. Papa decorates it.

Meanwhile, Maman opens the dining room table to its full length, covers it with a damask cloth and decorates it with our best silverware, dishes and crystal. From time to time she goes to the kitchen to make sure the oven is staying at an even temperature. When needed, she slides another piece of wood into the stove.

At nine thirty she checks the twenty-four pound turkey, bastes it, and closes the oven door. She sits at the kitchen table to peel a bucket of potatoes, repeating the process with carrots and rutabaga. She looks at the kitchen clock. It is ten forty-five. She changes her clothes, combs her hair, and adds powder and lipstick.

When done, she enters our bedroom. We are sound asleep. She puts a record on the turntable of the big phonograph that she and Papa hid in our closet, and we wake to the sound of Russian Cossacks singing folk songs, and the redolent odor of a feast slowly progressing toward its full potential.

Suzanne jumps out of bed immediately.

"Hurry, Marcelle," chides Maman. "If you want to go to church you better get up and get dressed."

She pulls the warm covers away from me. I shiver. Due to the swirling wind rushing across the river, our bedroom, despite its huge double-stormed windows, still suffers from constant drafts. Of course we have experienced this before, but never at eleven o'clock at night when sleep is so warm.

I watch Suzanne put on her cranberry-red velvet dress. She looks so beautiful that I resist no longer. In no time, with Maman's help, I am ready to slip on my own dark blue velvet dress.

As fast as we can, we pull knitted wool stockings over our cotton ones. Warm boots, coats, hats, scarves and mittens are pulled on, zipped, buttoned and tied.

From the living room our father's voice tries to hurry us. "We will be late, it's eleven thirty!"

"Coming Papa," we shout as we dart from our bedroom. Maman stops us at the dining room door.

"Not so fast girls. Promise me you will not look in the living room as you go by."

Reluctantly we agree, and make our way to join him

with our eyes fixed on the floor. For me, pure torture!

The excitement of going out at this time of night is tempered when Papa opens the door to the vestibule and cold air pours in, a prelude of more to come. And come it does, as we step out into the freezing air. It takes my breath away.

We spread out across the width of our quiet street between snow banks as tall as Papa. Shivering, I stay close to Maman, trying to absorb extra warmth.

Regardless of the festive occasion, Papa cannot help but recite his instructions about nature and health: "Smell the fresh air, girls! Put your shoulders back and breath in deeply. This cold air is good for your lungs!" Papa's words, like a prayer uttered too often, floats away with the white stream of frozen breath escaping from his lips.

We climb the small hill of our street and turn right onto rue Saint-Louis. We are no longer alone. Light filters through window sashes and doorsills; Saint-Eustache is awake. From both side of the street people come out of their houses and a few cars chug by on the newly plowed road, all going in the same direction—to the church.

"Listen!" Papa says. "I hear sleigh bells. Do you?"

We stop. Suddenly, church bells vibrate through the air, their heavy melodic voices floating over the village and surrounding farms. Underneath this majestic outpouring, the sleigh bells, like children's cascading giggles, scatter joy en route to church. In the eerie stillness of a winter's night, sounds and sights take on a different dimension. I feel lighter, skipping more than I walk, no longer concerned with the cold.

As we near our destination, a cacophony of sounds greets us: horses pulling sleighs, cars edging along, and pedestrians converging from each end of rue Saint-Louis and mingling with the gathering parishioners from rue Saint-Eustache.

Greetings, lifted hats, smiles and laughter, slow steps, hurried steps: a joyful unrehearsed dance unfurling on the church square! Over the babble only single words reach my ears: "*Joyeux!*" "*Froid!*" "*Bonsoir!*" "*Noël!*" "*Madame.*"

Finally, Papa opens the church door. From the darkness of the night, through the dimly lit vestibule, I enter into a paradise of light. I am unprepared for this magical sensation. To my seven years it is a miniature Versaille. The chandeliers radiate a flood of sparkling lights, picking up the colors of their surroundings from the gold and cream of vaulted ceilings and walls, to the multi-colors of stained glass windows.

Holding on to Maman's hand, I walk down the aisle, my eyes darting now here, now there, from the fairylike décor to the large somber manger with Mary and Joseph kneeling, and shepherds and sheep standing around an empty crib. Over the manger hangs a lonely star.

An usher directs us to a pew near the front. Suzanne and I barely have time to remove our mittens and scarves before the congregation stands. The priest, his assistants and altar boys come in. We all sit. There is a moment of quiet expectation. Softly, Aunt Gabrielle begins to play the introduction to *Minuit Chrétien* O Holy Night, the prelude to my first Christmas Midnight Mass.

For this special holiday the music is theatrical and romantic. Except for a Bach's fugue and a sprinkling of Gregorian chant, Bizet, Gounod, and Massenet resound. Tonight we are listening to throbbing organ music and full open-throat singing, and I delight in it.

Papa is especially satisfied with some of the singers and nods approvingly. "What a beautiful velvety sound!" I hear him whisper to Maman.

It is Monsieur Guilband, the miller, who is singing. He

provides us with the good buckwheat flour that Maman uses to make her delicious pancakes. And now, *le Père* Groulx, a tall older farmer, sings the solo. I turn around to look at him in the loft. Papa puts one firm hand on my shoulder I must face forward. But I had time to see him; he was still wrapped in his big raccoon coat.

Every time Papa hears him sing, his verdict is the same, "Monsieur Groulx's powerful bass has the edge of hard farming labor." Sadly, he always added, with a tease in his eyes, "His voice lacks the lushness of the fruits of his fields." But I like him. To me he sounds like the big bass Cossacks on our record.

During the sermon I draw close to Maman, lean my head on her upper arm, and slip into a welcome rest. I hear about Joseph, Mary, and the infant Jesus, a story I like. The sermon is short, shorter than usual. Maybe the Curé's housekeeper told him that if he speaks too long he could be held responsible for a series of overcooked turkey! After telling the story of Christmas, he carries the small statue of the infant Jesus to the manger.

The music starts again. With the kneeling, standing, genuflecting, I stay alert until the end of High Mass. At this point some parishioners leave, not waiting for the following low Masses. Maman goes out with them to put the last touches to our *Réveillon de Noël*. But Suzanne and I remain in our seats with Papa.

We listen to French carols sung by the choir. This will always be my favorite hour. The melodies are familiar and from time to time I join in the singing, shaming Suzanne. She elbows me. I glance at Papa; the corner of his mustache is up, an outline of his smile. I resume my singing, but softly, like walking on tiptoe. The hour goes by quickly.

Papa helps me secure my scarf and button my overcoat. He looks at Suzanne. She is ready. Along with the rest of the congregation, we walk out of the church to the sound of Aunt Gabrielle's last march.

Outside, a gentle snow falls. It is still cold, but it is not the biting, shivering cold of two hours ago. Suzanne and I make plans to play outdoors the next day.

"I am hungry," says Papa, "What do you say? Should we hurry home?"

"Yes!" Suzanne and I start running, and Papa with his long woodman's legs follows not far behind.

When we enter our street, I feel as if we are encircled in the bubble of a Christmas snowball. Three inches of feathery snow cushion our walk, and on each side of our path the banks look more and more like miniature mountain ranges. Up above, the sky is still raining snowflakes. We climb the little hill, and hand in hand walk the last few yards to our home. We shake our boots on the veranda and brush the snow off each other. I try to remove snowflakes from Papa's mustache, but he pinches my nose.

Maman hears our commotion. She opens the front door and invites us into her magical realm.

Walking into the living room, our senses are deliciously teased; tonight our home is a gift of smiles and embraces, of spices, pine and wood crackling, of scintillating gold and red, of silver and green. Suzanne and I are transported. But Papa claps his hands, startling us, and shatters the magic.

"Alright, girls, it's time to remove your coats and boots, our guests will soon be here. Hurry. Hurry! Go. Go!" We moan.

"I promise I will not return the tree."

We rush to our bedroom, put our over clothes away, Maman puffs up the bows on our heads, and we dash back to the living room. A small flame is already pushing through the logs. But tonight the Christmas tree takes predominance over the fire.

Suzanne and I are rooted next to the tree, a real tree, not a tree bouquet. I want to touch every ornament and make sure that none were left in Montréal: the yellow finches and red cardinals, the small houses in silver, red and amber are all here.

Again this year Maman made colorful paper cones that she hung throughout the tree. They are filled with red and yellow spicy candies made in the shape of fish. I look up. There at the very top is the five-pointed shaped gold lame remnant of Aunt Irène's dress. I elbow Suzanne; we smile at each other. Many small parcels are hidden in the branches; we wonder which ones are ours.

Our hands itch to touch, but we have to wait for our guests, eat Christmas dinner, go to sleep and wait for tomorrow to come.

The first guests to arrive are Uncle Charlie and Aunt Berthe. My Aunt joins Maman with the final preparation. I follow her. Suzanne stays behind listening, I suppose, to discussion of politics, road situations and weather.

I take post in the hallway where I can watch the goings-on in the kitchen. When I see Aunt Berthe ready to bring food to the table, I rush into the dining room to hold the swinging door open. Every time Aunt Berthe passes me, she says with an unfailing graciousness, "*Merci*, Marcelle," and returning to the kitchen, "you may let go of the door now."

Little by little, the table comes alive with color: pickled beets, cranberries, butter, cold-white celery with graceful blond and spring-green leafy tops; Maman cannot resist adding suppleness to rigid forms. Like her spring bouquet, the celery platter must delight the eyes. All the dishes, platters and bowls, and the breadbaskets covered with embroidered napkins, come in two's, and are evenly divided along the table.

From my post in the hallway I see the golden turkey sitting in back of the stove. In front, rivulets of steam surge out of large pots of potatoes and ragout of pork. How I love the tender morsels of pork and meatballs, spiced with cinnamon and cloves, floating in rich-brown gravy. No French-Canadian *Réveillon de Noël* would be complete without it.

Over sizzling sounds of the large iron frying pan, gurgling of boiling water, and sliding of pots and pans on the stove, I hear Maman tell Aunt Berthe, "We should be able to serve in about ten minutes."

Oh no! Ten more minutes, I may not survive!

329

My impatience is tempered when Aunt Gabrielle, Uncle Achille and our five cousins arrive. Maman pampers our dear organist and forbids her to come to the kitchen; she must rest after two hours of organ playing. But Jacqueline offers to help and, at last, I watch as steaming bowls, platters and gravy boats fill the table. I know because I am still the official swinging-door-holder. Cousin Jacqueline and Aunt Berthe carry thirteen entrées of stuffed Woodcocks, each decorated with a bouquet of parsley. They deposit one at every place setting.

Maman announces that dinner is served and Papa brings in the turkey.

For two hours, eating and conversation intertwine. I listen to hunting stories, teasing about the bird that got away, weather predictions, the last election, and happy sounds of compliments and gastronomical satisfaction: "Oh, this is so good!" "I shouldn't, but I can't resist." "Oh, my, that sausage will kill me but I just have to eat another one."

With great authority I explain to the table that my mother had made the sausage herself. "Really, I saw Maman make it," I insist.

After such a meal how any of us could eat dessert is

hard to fathom. At any rate, there must have been reasons enough, because the maple syrup *tartelettes* filled with butternuts and garnished with a rosette of whipped cream, the *beignets* rolled in powdered sugar, and the steamed pudding, are, after dinner, only a shadow of their original wholeness.

The kitchen is too small and too overwhelmed with the feast's debris to let the younger children help in the clean-up. I join Suzanne and our cousins Louise, Renée and Henri, to sit at the foot of the tree. The oldest, Jean-Pierre, joins Uncle Achille, Papa and Uncle Charlie. They are laughing. Uncle Achille is telling a new version of his tumble at church. We are quiet. Even Renée who told us the original version has lost her spark. But Henri reacts gleefully to his father's story with his usual hearty laugh, head thrown back, every feature of his face molded in an expression of pure joy.

I am ready for sleep, and eager for tomorrow to arrive when I can discover what is inside all those little parcels on the branches of the tree, and some larger presents hidden, though not quite well enough, at the back of Maman's closet.

For as long as I live I shall carry with me the memory of that 1937 Christmas, wrapped as a wondrous gift of sounds and smells, of sights and tastes, held together, despite their estrangement, by the love of our parents for us, their two daughters.

CHAPTER FORTY ONE

DIAGNOSIS UNKNOWN

Maman and I were alone; Papa somewhere vacationing, and Suzanne staying with Aunt Berthe and Uncle Charlie until the doctor could decide what ailed me.

Before Papa left I had been in bed a couple of days with what he called the overplaying syndrome. "She forgets she is a girl, I told you before you have to watch her." As usual, Maman took the blame and let it drop like an old letter not worth reading over. As for Papa, he convinced himself that in a couple of days my malaise would vanish. He proved to be wrong.

Maman was left with a sick child, and Doctor Thibodeau for all his knowledge and care could not attach a name to the illness. A week later, the fever kept on rising and Maman's worries increased. She called Uncle Georges. Many days he showed up after his office hours to listen to my chest and my heart. Days went by with no sign of progress. In despair Maman called Uncle Pagé, a brother-in-law of my father, also a physician. He had a consultation with Doctor Thibodeau, but neither could find a sure diagnosis. They thought of typhoid fever as a possibility, but no one else in Saint-Eustache suffered from the disease…maybe a growth spurt.

To bring the fever down, they recommended to Maman that she should wrap me in sheets dipped in cold water. How many times a day did Maman do this? I do not know. For a five-foot-four petite woman to practically carry me, a soon to be nine year old, and hold me up while she wrapped a cold-water-logged-sheet around me, exchanging it more than once, for a colder one, and then dry me, carry me back, dress me, and put me to bed must have been exhausting.

Every day, while the fever rose, and after my bath Maman moved me to Suzanne's freshly made bed. She washed sheets and more sheets and pillowcases, hung them on the clothesline, and hoped for sunshine. Did she still iron them? She always had in the past.

At night she slept in the available bed next to mine to listen to my breathing and pray. Sleep came in between Ave Marias and Pater Noster. In a month's time she

334

mouthed years of prayers and promises to God. The hardest one to keep would be that if he saved my life, she would not eat chocolate for a full two years: for Maman a deprivation of the first order.

Papa was not there to share her worries, no friend to sit with her or tell her to rest while she watched over the sick child. Though the house was not quarantined, doctor Thibodeau had told Maman to let no one in. Even Monsieur Binette left his deliveries at the back door. I can well imagine that every day after she finished her morning routine, she stood next to the phone and called Adrienne or Germaine, Gaby or Gabrielle or maybe Annette. She cherished her friends. With them she could be herself, exteriorize what at home she kept under lid, and now share her worries.

When my fever neared one hundred-five, Maman called Mademoiselle Dubois, a home nurse, to come shave my head; the belief being, that it would grow thicker if the patient survived. By then, despite every ones care, and doctor Thibodeau feeding me injections of liver, and even coming at night when his patients had kept him on the go all day, my chance of surviving looked thin. The good doctor decided that he must find my father.

Probably, under Maman's guidance, Doctor Thibodeau went to the taxi stand at the center of the village and asked if one of the drivers had taken my father to his vacation retreat. The three cab drivers looked at each other as if they had been sworn to secrecy, but once told that Monsieur Mignault's daughter was near death one of them drove away to pick him up.

Of that period I clearly remember the cold baths, the head shave, and at his return, seeing my father standing at the foot of my bed; however he does not reappear in my mind during the rest of my illness. The fever kept on climbing, and short of one hundred-six precipitately started falling soon to reach ninety-four. Five months of recuperation started, and my mind flashes images of happier portent.

I see a white chenille robe, a gift from Aunt Irène, games and new coloring books. But the present I recall, that made me smile the most, was seeing the freckled face of my friend Bernard looking at me through the window screen. A cautious Maman would not let any children near me until assured that the illness would not come back.

Eventually that special moment arrived. Bernard entered my bedroom holding a bouquet of field flowers and smiling a shy smile. Maman stayed with us for the short time of his visit to facilitate the conversation. We had to be reacquainted. My bony face showed its structure, my teeth looked larger and a scarf covered my baldhead. I guess my friend did not lose courage for a week later he made his entrance holding a present.

For a while Bernard had stopped his boat production and made a bed for my doll. Alas, the doll's legs hung over the end. "Could we cut her legs?" He asked Maman. She offered a less drastic solution. "Let's sit her up in the bed." It worked! A humongous smile pushed his cheeks up, propelling the brown freckles on his face to dance!

CHAPTER FORTY TWO

WORLDS' APART

When the war that brought so much misery started, I was nine years old and recuperating from whatever had ailed me. "When you can walk all the way to my office bring your father's flute." Doctor Thibodeau had told me. "I will give you a lesson and some exercises to practice."

Three months later, on a day ablaze with colors, warm sun and cool breezes, I left the house wearing my favorite fall dress, made of soft woolen, navy blue and white hound's tooth material and shaped in a princess line The hair on my shaved head had grown one inch. Uncle Charlie promised that it would keep on growing, and showed me how to make waves in the front. The dress and the waves gave me a boost. Yet, what gave my step its buoyancy was the pride of walking all the way from our street, through rue Saint-Louis, and all the way up the main street to Doctor Thibodeau's office perched above a cliff, a few yards from the mill, and across from *le chateau,* silvery flute in hand.

Even at that young age, instruments meant romance. Prints of the male violinist sweeping over a female pianist or Liszt sitting at the piano, coat tails flying, ladies swooning, decorated many a wall. I envied the violinist carrying his violin in a case of the same shape, and now I held a flute in my hand, Papa's flute, its beauty and its promise in my own hand igniting on my face a smile that bloomed with every step, and crossed over the threshold of Doctor Thibodeau's office.

While I romanced about musical instruments and musicians, young men over the world were taught to handle instruments of war. But none were as well equipped as the German soldier.

On the tenth of September 1939 Canada declared war. It decided against conscription using a softer approach the provinces could digest more easily, though the word mobilization still gave ulcerous attacks to Québec. One group would volunteer to go fight overseas, the other, defend Canada. Propaganda for or against joining the fight flourished. Youngsters, ready for adventure or so poor, that a set of warm clothes and three meals a day seemed a good bargain, joined.

Some villagers looked upon Monsieur Tremblay, a professor at Oka Agricultural College with suspicion. A reservist, he now recruited young men for the war. My father an isolationist opposed Canada's involvement, but, in character, did not demonstrate against it; railing privately was a safer avenue. Oh, how often the "I told you so," peppered the end of a sentence. We had become accustomed to this message portent of gloom, so we did not ask which prediction had come true.

In our classrooms we had no world map on which we could have watched the marching armies of Hitler invading the European countries. We studied our past history; its glory, its failure, its missionaries and martyrs. We learned about the kings of France, every Louis and Henri ever printed in the Larousse dictionary, and Jeanne d'Arc and Napoléon, but knew nothing of the history raging across the ocean. We did not see the newspapers. The nuns adhered to their strict curriculum and the pupils, most of them, most of the time, followed in lock steps.

Ration books appeared; butter, flour and sugar disappeared. Margarine looking like an unappetizing pound of lard made its debut. A store selling only horsemeat opened on rue Saint-Louis. Our friend Monsieur Pesant raised rabbits for the market.

Maman accommodated her cooking to the new restrictions. Rabbit became chicken a la king concealed in *béchamel* sauce and clothed in delicate pastry, the horse meat, a beef stew; softened margarine mixed half and half with butter, with a dash of yellow coloring and molded in a pan the size of a brick pretended to butterhood. The results of Maman's effort were at times delicious; however, bread spread with the butter/margarine amalgamation never reached the stage of delectability.

For some families in the village the war meant more than victual restrictions. Their sons were leaving for training camps and then for Africa, England, Holland, France or Italy.

I knew only three of them, our cousin Paul Sauvé and his brother in law, and Adrien the oldest son of doctor and Madame Thibodeau.

Canada's contribution was more than only its young men. In a short time, the country became a major supplier of munitions and war machinery for itself and for other nations of the Western Alliance.

The majority of the habitual transient poor, knocking at our backdoor for something to eat during the endless years of depression, now worked. The generations of women who had kept our houses clean for a pittance were now earning decent wages in war factories and would in time have sons and grandsons graduating from college: education and money narrowing the divide between classes.

At home, the routine of our family life stayed firmly in place; however, with the event of the war Papa found one more thing to oppose. The "I told you so" which we learned had germinated since 1936 with the visit of Georges VI and Queen Elisabeth now came to fruition. Maman explained to us that our father believed that there had been a nefarious reason behind the visit, and, "*mark my words*," he had predicted, "sooner or later we will pay for it."

As vexing as the doings of the government might have been to Papa, it did not erase his preoccupation with Sally and her Irish setter; moreover, he still found ample time to developed and nurture a new phobia.

Moulin Légaré

Dr. Thibodeau's office next to the mill

Marcelle after typhoid 1939

CHAPTER FORTY THREE

PAPA'S PERMANENT VACATION

"Your father has too much time on his hands."

Recently, Maman communicated with us in a one-sentence statement. Since Papa's retirement the voltage of the usual undercurrent existing in our household had increased. He could have worked longer..."

In high spirits Papa spent days imitating bird songs, watching the river flowing and changing color with the capricious weather, taking walks with his dogs or training a young one to retrieve without hurting the game. He did not have to rush in the morning, but did not change his habits; the sun would not wait. When we sat at breakfast we heard the familiar "You missed the most spectacular sunrise," for by then the sun had established residence for the day.

347

"Your father has too much time on his hands," Maman repeated.

With an anxious eye, Papa had watched the leaves clinging to their summer green; however, the day he spotted a yellowish tint, if only on one leaf, an inner smile grew in him. A few weeks later when a tentative red blush painted its autumn wardrobe and like a peacock displayed it to our small world, Papa's smile burst into the open.

With renewed energy he took long walks with Tellie or her son Castor. Their legs had to be exercised; their lungs emptied of that lingering dusty heat. He breathed deeply, walked faster. They needed to keep up with his long strides. It was not a sniffing walk.

Papa had already cleaned and oiled the barrels of his hunting gun, and like a musician putting his instrument away laid it with great care in its felt-lined case. From now on the hunting season would flow without the interruption of five-and-a-half days of work. For him this was heaven on earth; he could hunt as often as he wished. He chose to avoid the weekends, when too many amateurish hunters gallivant in the woods.

In a short time I would hear Monsieur Binette's taxi arrive in our driveway, brakes screeching, pebbles flying

348

stopping abruptly.

Now that Doctor Thibodeau had declared me healed and not contagious, Monsieur Binette delivered our groceries to the kitchen and I had the chance to see him many times. In a tease, he called me "P'tit Gas," little boy, a nickname I liked and that brought a smile to Maman's face but that soon she would discourage. My hair would grow and fat would start filling the sharp angles of my body; no more looking like a scrawny little boy, I would be all girl. Nevertheless, Monsieur Binette's teasing never stopped. I thought he was, with Uncle Charlie, the most fun person.

Though I dearly loved Papa, he was not in competition for the title of most fun person! At present, he kept his mind occupied with a project, which for him was of great importance. Maman had been right; Papa had too much time on his hands.

At least three times a week we heard a statement containing the word turtle. "Oh, I like turtles well enough but a house looking like one? Hm, what do you think girls?" It was not really a question as he always added promptly, "I love the French Canadian style house with its pointed roof." Like a pebble thrown on the water by an inexperienced hand his statement barely made a ripple.

Finally, when he saw we paid little attention to his turtle sentences, we heard him state "This house looks like a turtle. We'll raise the roof."

What a throw! What a ripple! It sounded like an exciting venture to me; however not to Maman. Not a sound came out of her mouth. Her jaw locked like a box of dynamite one must guard and not open until the right time and only under propitious circumstances.

To her relief the hunting season kept Papa, body and mind, occupied. The roof's uplift disappeared from his conversation. Maman hoped it would not raise its pointed head again.

CHAPTER FORTY FOUR

MONSIEUR BINETTE'S LAST HOPLA!

The leaves in full autumn garb were not willing to lay still and give winter the right-of-way. Like butterflies, they lifted with every breeze flitting over sidewalks and streets. But Papa knew; the hunting season had arrived.

Monsieur Binette exchanged his white butcher's apron for his chauffeur's hat, though, now and then, he still found time to work at Monsieur Trépanier's store and deliver our weekly meat and grocery provisions. Now that my legs were stronger, I could run to the back porch to greet him. One day seeing my plucked chicken look and taking pity on me, he asked Maman,

"Do you think that *P'tit Gas* here would enjoy a ride? She could come with me to pick up her father."

Maman could not resist my supplicating eyes. "I think

351

it's a good idea," she said.

I applauded and flashed a smile that lit the kitchen.

"Can you be ready at four o'clock?"

I bobbed my head, and Maman said, "She'll be waiting for you."

What a trip! I never had such a good time. On our way to Montagne Saint-Joseph we drove through countryside I had never seen before. Rounded in the center, the narrow highway left little space for meeting other cars. Monsieur Binette kept to the center. We seldom encountered anyone. And when we did, there came out of my driver a series of vociferous recommendations to the other driver, "Stay out of the way, we're coming! If you know what's good for you fellow, move to the side!" Fortunately they all did, each car tilting to its right. But the best was yet to come.

After a long climb on a straight road, we arrived at full speed at the crest of the hill, and for a second I was suspended in the air. At that moment Monsieur Binette threw both hands up and shouted, "Hop la!"

I laughed and laughed. And, down we went, my stomach feeling as if it left my body. The next hill arrived and I joined dear Monsieur Binette in the game of hands-up-in-the-air, and in duet with him produced a series of sonorous Hop las!

We arrived at our destination in one piece. Papa and Tellie were waiting for us at the edge of the wood.

Monsieur Binette stopped the car in his usual manner: wheels screeching their distress. The left side of the car lopped toward the ground. I could not open my door against gravity. Papa, who had yet to see me, opened the back door to let Tellie in.

"What are you doing here?"

"I came to pick you up. I wanted to make you a surprise."

Papa looked at me listing like a sapling planted on a hill.

"Wait I'll help you get out."

"Merci Papa." I gave him a kiss. "Can I sit in back with Tellie?"

"She won't be much company. She's exhausted."

I joined my dear old Tellie and patted her gently. She opened an eye, and as soon closed it going back to a

353

state of beneficial somnolence.

After trying to close his door, gravity working against him, Monsieur Binette gathered his strength and slammed it while uttering a couple of words new to me. Papa cleared his throat; a gentleman's reproachful utterance.

The car lurched from the side of the road and we recovered our equilibrium.

"Did you shoot a lot of birds Papa?"

"Enough for three meals."

As soon as the car had its four wheels on the pavement, Monsieur Binette cleared his throat ready for conversation.

"Well, M'sieu Mignault, are you ready to join the army and help *les Anglais*?"

I could not make out what Papa answered; Monsieur Binette cackled and kept on talking. Papa grunted a couple of times, and from then on, silence like a sulking child sat among us.

As soon as we arrived home, I said good-by and thank you to Monsieur Binette and rushed to the kitchen to tell

Maman about my trip and all the Hop las.

"I hope you did not tell your father."

I shook my head, "Oh no!"

I could imagine my father saying to Maman, "What were you thinking, sending Marcelle with that idiot, she could have been killed. Don't you care?"

I never told, but never again drove to Montagne Saint-Joseph with fun-loving Monsieur Binette.

Papa & Tellie

Montagne St. Joseph where Papa went hunting

CHAPTER FORTY FIVE

THE HOUSE LOOKS LIKE A TURTLE

The turtle looking house returned to Papa's menu of complaints. No amount of telling by Maman, that the house looked lovely could deter him from putting in motion his newly found project.

Maman's thinking could be fanciful, but practicality always surfaced and kept her in the straight and narrow. It was simple really, but difficult to live by; don't spend what you don't have. If you want it or need it badly, save money until you have the means to buy, or in this instance remodel.

My father had no such belief.

"But Louis, we don't have the means to pay for the work," I heard Maman repeat many times.

"It will be added to our mortgage and the increase will be minimal. I told you only yesterday."

"But Louis, your salary is not the same. Your pension…"

"It will be sufficient. Stop worrying."

Generously, the bank loaned him the money. The plans were drawn, and a crew of workers hired. At that point, Maman proposed that the present stairs leading to the attic be removed, and instead, build a new staircase starting in the large walk-in closet off the entrance vestibule.

"I don't see the point of it," Papa said, not happy with any suggestion.

"The point is," Maman replied, "the appearance of the house would not change from the outside. The renters would enter the house through the regular entrance into the vestibule, and go to their apartment by the staircase built in the large walk-in closet, and they would not invade our privacy."

"Of course they would, the door between the vestibule and the living room is all glass."

"That can be fixed by putting curtains or simply by

358

replacing it with a full wood door.

"It doesn't matter. I will not have strangers on my property"...

"But Louis, after a while the rent money would pay off the mortgage."

"I will not discuss it any longer."

In spring the construction started, and life continued.

Unlike Maman and Suzanne, I enjoyed every minute of the construction, and hurried home after school. I watched with great interest the activities taking place in back of the house. Since my head had been shaved during my illness, my hair had grown thick and a darker shade of blond, but was still short. I could not resist attaching those long curls of blond wood shavings to my hair and showing off my new hairdo.

By summer I had lost my golden locks and the house had lost its warmth and its charm. It stood taller, impersonal and with no particular distinction. The debt increased, and so did Maman's silent planning on how to reduce it.

CHAPTER FORTY SIX

SUMMER BLISS

Spring showers had scattered the peonies, and like the aftermath of a wedding, white, and pink petals littered the ground, their perfume still lingering in the soft, moist breeze. Lilacs, took their place in the sun, their conic heads, a montage of tiny individual flowers. In the hill next to the steps, laden with white and purple blooms, branches bent over offering a display of colors and spreading their fragrance over both terraces.

As long as they lasted, weekly, Maman offered a bouquet to the hostess of her bridge group, or to other friends. The vase at the center of the dining room table overflowed with their beauty. The sun peering through the sheer curtains of the French doors played shadows and light games with the flowers, and forbade the woodwork's darkness to interfere. I could not go by without smiling. Spring had bloomed into summer.

Already, one year had gone by since the beginning of my recuperation. At last, I could take part in all the regular summer activities, plus a new one, tennis. Uncle Arthur and Aunt Marie-Louise had given their tennis court to the church, for the benefit of the village's youth. That summer, on my tenth birthday, Uncle Charlie and Aunt Berthe gave me a tennis racket, and the mother of my school friend Suzanne, a membership fee; fifty-cents for a whole summer of enjoyment.

The fact that none of us knew how to play tennis did not stop us. Monsieur Pesant, the same dear Monsieur Pesant who took us skijoring, and whose rabbits we ate, had played tennis in his youth, and started to instruct his oldest daughter Francine, Suzanne's friend. Day after day, we watched, and learned and practiced.

While we exerted ourselves with sporting activities, Maman, with the opening of the summer porch, had eleven more square feet to wash and scrub. As usual, she did not wait for manna to fall from heaven to save money to help pay a debt, this time, the roof. She started saving by depriving herself of her once a week cleaning woman. She did not moan about her extra work but dreamed up more ideas about resolving the problem.

Her friends were a good sounding board. Since Papa

362

was home seven days a week and conversation on the phone with them, guarded; her weekly game of bridge became a door to the outside, and essential to her venting of ideas.

From early morning until she left, she choreographed all her chores to the smallest detail; the meals, the picking up, the cleaning, the time she would need to change her clothes, and refresh her hair and make-up, all she executed by the clock and flawlessly. The house was left in a welcoming state, as if guests might show up for supper. How could my father complain? The supper simply needed to be removed from the refrigerator, and warmed up on the stove.

In the meantime, Maman lost herself concentrating on the cards her hands held, and between games sharing some ideas on how she planned to pay off the debt accumulated by her husband's extravagance.

CHAPTER FORTY SEVEN

"HONG KONG!" HE SPUTTERED

"I told you so!" Papa brandished his newspaper. "Now you believe me! Canadian troops in Hong Kong! As if Europe is not big enough! Of all places for the Canadian army to be: Hong Kong, and Africa, and God knows where else. You tell me, why are we there?"

Papa paced up and down the living room, stopping briefly and resuming his pacing. We sat six feet away but he spoke to no one in particular, venting his frustration, expecting no answer. Finally, he grabbed his newspaper and plopped himself in his high back chair.

"I wish I knew," said Maman trying to be sympathetic. She glanced at him. He was adjusting his glasses and then disappeared behind the screen of his nationalistic newspaper *Le Devoir*. She returned to her knitting. Suzanne and I kept our eyes in our study books.

365

Except for Papa, we all wanted one thing, to listen to our favorite radio program *Un homme et son péché,* a man and his sin, at seven o'clock. It seemed a long time ago that the clock had sung the quarter of the hour. What would happen when it struck seven times? Would Papa's anger have diminished enough for Maman to suggest listening to their program?

Suzanne and I had yet to understand the seriousness of what was happening across the ocean, and the suffering that would ensue. We lived cushioned in our little world, but Papa could see further. He lit his pipe and blew a couple of perfectly formed smoke rings. Maman eyed him, and feeling that the pleasure of his pipe must have mellowed his mood, suggested: "Should we listen to our program?" Without waiting, she turned the radio on.

The following night we were not so lucky. He informed us as to what had happened in the world before we had a chance to come near the radio. Suzanne and I, at the dining room table, readied ourselves to start doing our homework; Maman sat in her comfortable chair with her knitting, and Papa, glasses on and newspaper in hand, started reading.

"Listen to this," he said. He had never read to us from

366

his newspaper.

We lifted our eyes from our homework. I draped myself across the back of my chair to face him, Suzanne dried her pen, and Maman put down the khaki scarf she was knitting.

"Listen to this," he repeated. "Our troops arrived on the hills of Hong Kong Island and the Kowloon Peninsula with *no transport at all.* Their vehicles had been put on the wrong ship." Papa dropped his newspaper, looked at each of us to make sure he had all our attention.

"Did you hear? Their vehicles had been put *on the wrong ship!*" Suzanne and I nodded. Maman said, "It's hard to believe."

"I don't know why you're so surprised," Papa continued. "No one seems to know what they're doing except the Japanese and the Germans." He pushed his glasses back to a comfortable spot on his nose and resumed his reading but *a mi-voix*, in a half tone, so only Maman could hear, forgetting that it would be a sure way to peek my interest. I turned myself around pretending not to listen, but sitting a few feet away from Papa, all my attention became riveted on the words he apparently did not want us to hear.

"It seems that out of two thousand Canadians, five hundred were killed or were taken prisoners."

"Where did the poor boys come from?"

"I'm not sure, wait…here it is. One regiment's name is the Winnipeg Grenadiers and the other The Royal Rifles. It's evident they were not French Canadians, thank God."

The little click of the needles stopped. Maman said, "Louis…they're just boys. Just think…one thousand fathers and mothers mourning their dead sons or waiting for news of those who had been taken prisoner; worrying every minute that if still alive, their son might be tortured…just think."

"Hm."

For a short time silence loomed over the room. I held on to my breath. It was eerie. I knew without being told, the radio would not be turned on. The clock struck seven times. No one moved. Then I heard the rustling of the newspaper. A section folded over by Papa's impatient hand, and following, the click of the needles in a mad rush: this long khaki scarf would be completed before the evening was over. Maman had many more scarves, socks, and gloves to finish, before winter came.

CHAPTER FORTY EIGHT

MAMAN TAKES CHARGE

Maman's heart might have been with the poor soldiers, but her mind focused on one thing; how to repay the debt. Ideas abounded. She asked her friends many questions, and received much advice, some such as, "don't do it," which she ignored. Nevertheless, she appreciated the sharing of ideas from an acquaintance that operated a bed and breakfast, an enterprise similar to what she had in mind to start. Once she had analyzed the feasibility of her plans, she presented them to Papa. He could not refuse. He would have none of the worries and do none of the work.

He offered a pretense resistance, while I can well imagine, an inner sunshine warmed his heart, and why not? Following Maman's plan, he would spend two months at Uncle Georges' summer chalet on the shore of the loveliest crystal clear lake where trout abounded. He would fish with one of his visiting brothers or sisters. He would be fed regally by Aunt Yvonne and her helper, and once in a while be asked to perform a chore or tell a story to a young visitor. Papa might spend the rest of the evening playing cards, or out on the screen porch rocking and smoking his pipe, conversing with family members he seldom saw during the year. This is how Papa would spend his summer.

During the time Maman planned and implemented her project, the war in Europe had become the subject of articles in the newspaper, of newsreels in the movie theater and the one news that permeated the radio. We heard many national anthems; our own, Oh Canada, the British, God Save Our Gracious King, and the French, La Marseillaise. It did not matter which one I happened to hear, it squeezed my chest in a little ball and tugged at my heart. A sorrowful feeling lingered until the routine of daily life displaced it.

Nonetheless, nothing could attenuate Papa's rage about our soldiers killed in Hong Kong. When the news came that Churchill had been against sending troops to protect their colony, as there was not the slightest chance of saving it, Papa lost his speech. He gestured a couple of times at the radio, got up, put his overcoat on and went out. We could hear him pace up and down the veranda. He came back in to kiss us good night. Before we fell asleep we could hear him tell Maman, what I assumed had been percolating in his mind during the hour he walked entertaining his discontentment.

The following day, Maman went ahead with her project: a summer pension. She would rent both bedrooms and serve three meals a day. Papa's new roomy attic would become our dormitory for the summer. Needing bedding for the two additional beds, she collected from the merchants, giant cotton bags that had contained flour or sugar. She opened their seams, washed and bleached them, ironed and sewed them and transformed them into two pairs of sheets and pillowcases.

While Papa went on long walks, we helped her carry bed frames up the steep staircase. The mattresses, Maman pulled up while Suzanne and I pushed or at least stopped them from sliding back down. I discovered that she had already covered six windowpanes with shades and curtains, and cleaned the wood dust and residues the workmen had left behind. We helped her make our

371

beds, the cotton sheets were a bit rough to the touch and a seam went right down the middle, but it went well with the primitive décor.

Maman had not yet shared her plans with us. When we asked why we were doing all this she simply said, "I thought you might enjoy sleeping in the attic during the summer."

It more than satisfied me. It sounded as if one could have a rollicking good time up there. We stood directly under treetops, at arm's length from the moon. What was not to like about sleeping up near sky and foliage and chirping birds and walking on moonbeams. I could see clearly that Papa's idea of raising the roof made complete sense. So from now on I would volunteer for any errands that took me from our ordinary first-floor-life to the new heights of our adventure-filled-summer residence.

CHAPTER FORTY NINE

FICTION AND FACT

Sometime in May, Maman informed us that from the last week of June to the end of August the bedrooms would be rented. The realization the attic had not been planned as a playroom and that strangers would surround us, sounded to me like a bad fairy tale.

"During their stay", she said, "Our guests will have the use of our home, except for the kitchen and back porch. They also will have the use of the outdoors and the rowboat. We will serve three meals a day in the dining room."

This scenario did not sit properly in my mind. "Will Papa sleep in the attic with us?" "No, during that time your father will vacation at your Uncle Georges' and Aunt Yvonne's chalet."

"But why?"

"Why what?"

I was not sure, thoughts ran into one another all mixed and stirred up like Aunt Berthe's India Relish. I spoke the first idea I could untangle, "Why do you want people all over our house and even in our row boat?"

"Because Marcelle, they will pay us. We need the money to pay for the expense of raising the roof."

"But I saw Papa paying the carpenters," said Suzanne.

"Yes, but this was money borrowed from the bank."

Suzanne looked surprisingly serene.

"Where will we stay?" She asked

"Right here. We have the kitchen, the back porch, the attic, and the whole backyard. And of course, I will need your help."

I recoiled. "People we don't know will be all over our house."

"Let me reassure you, our guests will be lovely. I have corresponded and exchanged phone calls with them. However, I cannot do all the work by myself and be successful."

"I will help you." Suzanne said.

"Merci chérie. I think you can serve the table, and do it very well. After every meal, you two will wash and dry the dishes, and as usual on Wednesdays and Saturdays, we will clean the house together. When your work is finished you still can go play or visit your friends."

I visualized myself buried under mountains of dishes or sitting on the floor dusting all the carved legs, and strangers telling me with a snarl on their faces, "Child, have you ever dusted before?" Without one more thought to offer, stubbornly I mumbled, "But we don't know them."

"You will soon," Maman said. "Please, now go play, I mean, go do your homework."

One month later Papa left for his summer vacation. From then on the tempo of our lives picked up. We emptied our closets and bureaus and carried our belongings to the attic. All this activity I found thrilling. I had no time to worry. I could not wait to sleep under the roof. And, this would be a perfect place to hide in case the good fairy did not pop-up into this new story.

375

Summer Chalet of Uncle George & Aunt Yvonne
Mignault at Lac Dore

CHAPTER FIFTY

NEAR THE MOON, OR THE WOOD STOVE

Maman's networking bore good results. Both rooms were rented for the months of July and August. She had scheduled only one guest for the last week of June; a rehearsal for the weeks to come.

A tall young man in his thirties showed up with a suitcase and a large portfolio filled with heavy drawing paper. He stayed only a week. He had hoped to eat *en famille* to extend his rudimentary French. Maman refused though we had no other guests that week. Maybe she found it improper in Papa's absence to have the young man sharing our table.

The following week two ladies, who also spoke only English, rang the door bell. Knowing the approximate time of their arrival I stayed as far away as possible from the living-room. I feared Maman saying, "Marcelle would you please open the door." While they lived with us I spent a great deal of time in the attic reading and listening to the only two records we had. To this day, Bizet's *L'Arlésienne* is like an old friend visiting through time via radio.

Bravely, Suzanne served their meals, said a couple of rehearsed sentences, asked necessary questions— would you like more tea or coffee—and smiled a lot. By the end of their visit, she could repeat some endearing sayings the ladies verbalized when speaking to her.

After a week, of tasting Maman's good cooking, one lady asked if she could invite her male friend for the mid-day dinner-he is Jewish, she added.

Maman had appreciated the gesture but I could not understand why the lady even had to mention the fact that he was Jewish. Maman answered that maybe the lady assumed we were catholic and that we may object. How isolated we were in our little world. It was 1941 and our most pressing concern was to pay the mortgage. Some years later, a book, *The Twenty Fifth Hour,* revealed to me a corner of a world of anti-Semitism I had not known. Leon Uris' *Exodus* continued to lift the veil to the horror: the gruesome canvas of Munch, *The Scream,* suddenly overshadowing the dream-like flowery

378

landscape of the Renoir's of our youth.

On the lists of guests who stayed with us I remember the Leduc's, a lovely older couple. The white haired gentleman made his own yogurt, but what particularly endeared him to Maman, was that he always emptied his ashtray.

Newlyweds spent a week and Maman taught the new bride how to press her husband's slacks—no more rounded knees.

Monsieur and Madame Lajoie stayed for a month, and would return the following year. He was broad shouldered, healthy; she pale, fragile. "I can't breathe if there is too much food on my plate," she told Maman. Suzanne brought her miniature portions; her husband appreciated the generous servings he received. On weekdays Maman sent him on time to his office.

So far, I had no need for the good fairy's help. Maman had been right. Our guests were lovely. A friend of Aunt Irène joined us on the weekends. Our two bedrooms were rented, but she insisted that she could sleep on the enclosed back porch on a cot. Maman slept there to avoid disturbing the guests, when at five o'clock in the morning she would have to come down the creaky

379

staircase. Nevertheless, to accommodate Aunt Irène's friend, Maman joined us on Friday and Saturday nights. I gave her my bed and squeezed in with Suzanne.

I still marvel at what Maman accomplished so successfully. How could she do it? The more I think, the more I realize that she had little to change in her routine. She had a remarkable work ethic and took pride in her work. She always got up to ready stove and breakfast. Papa's suits were pressed, his shirts washed, the collars starched—he shined his shoes—the table was set, his food served, his daughter's clothes ready for school; each was sent on time to her or his occupation, and came back to a clean orderly home, greeted warmly and fed great food served in appetizing fashion. Instead of waiting on three people, she now served seven or eight, and ran her business without worrying about Papa's criticism or displeasure.

September arrived. Maman deposited her profit at the bank. Papa came back on time to get his dogs ready for the hunt, and Grand-Maman joined us for her yearly two weeks of sewing.

The night after she left, Suzanne and I slept in our bedroom. I pined for the attic's spaciousness, the hours alone reading, the rain drumming on the roof. I did not miss the ear-splitting thunder and the lightening which despite window shades traveled from the front of the attic to the back. On those occasions my poetic feelings about living near treetops and sky briefly lost its romance.

Maman turned the radio back on to listen to our favorite programs, unless, overwhelmed by his frustration with the war, Papa read aloud articles from his newspaper. Maman resumed her work for the Red Cross, knitting and rolling yards and yards of gauze. Papa did not like the Red Cross. He was sure they would neglect our French-Canadian soldiers. Maman kept on with her work; a wounded soldier needed help, ethnicity did not change the pain or the need.

Music with friends in the Peasant's home. Early 1900

CHAPTER FIFTY ONE

DEBUTS

Despite the war, my father's new and old phobias, and Maman's new project, school continued at the same pace and Maman's attention to our studies remained unrelenting.

At school, my new schedule still included a thirty-minute piano practice during class time which delighted me, not because of my love of music, but because I often missed thirty minutes of math or grammar which I disliked equally. Now, I would have an added thirty minutes free of school subjects while rehearsing with the choir—what a bonus! My enthusiasm must have registered with *la directrice* of the choir, because she gave me a solo to perform at our yearly concert. Sadly, my enthusiasm did not carry the day, and my mind hid the memory of that disastrous debut for over sixty years. The memory of one is like a song without accompaniment. I found that accompaniment years later, when a dear friend brought it back to my memory; music and words alike.

It happened during a trip while visiting family members and friends in Saint-Eustache. Lise Pesant-Lethiec, the friend of my school days, invited me to stay with her and her husband Claude. They lived on a piece of land that had belonged to the family and given to Saint-Eustache by her father as a gift to be used by the residents of the street who did not have access to the river. At their return from years lived in many countries, Lise and her husband bought the land back from the town. Thanks to the beautiful design of our friend Laurent Calame, a friend from the days of gathering in the tennis club house and being entertained by him and Jean-Louis, on the piano, Claude and Lise now lived in a multi-leveled home above the river.

During my stay with them, Lise, the companion of my school's mischief days and I were walking in the street of my youth reminiscing about our past, and *a propos* she said, "Do you remember when at a chorus concert you forgot the words of your solo?"

"No, when was it? What was the song?"

"Oh, we must have been twelve or thirteen years old. The song was about the cicada and the ant."

Lise started singing it, and in two seconds, the melody and the words came rushing in my mind and out of my mouth. Fifty years after experiencing an embarrassing moment, there we were, two gray hair old school friends, singing with total disregard for any passerby *"La cigle ayant chanté tout l'été se trouva fort dépourvue quand la bise fut venue."* The cicada having sung all summer found itself without food when the cold breeze arrived." The solo and the chorus came forth reinforced by Lise's memory. How we laughed. As I write this, that refreshed memory has triggered another one about the day it happened.

I knew the words and the music of my solo which the nun had made me rehearse many times as had Maman. I was ready. After a couple of songs from the chorus, the time came for my special moment. The nun gave me the cue to start my solo. Instantly, the well-rehearsed words vanished. After a second try, she faced the same silent, blushing-brain-frozen-would-be-soloist. The weight of my silence crushed any hope of redemption; the nun in an enveloping gesture led the whole chorus into my solo. That was it.

Blocking one's memory may not be such a bad thing, for two years later I decided that I would become a great singer—never thinking it might be impossible. After all uncles and aunts played the organ and the piano or thought music or composed, and what about my grandfather's cousin Albani who had a great career in Europe, and now, my twelve year old cousin André played the cello and planned to play professionally. Yet, what inspired me most was Jacques' concert debut.

For the occasion Grand-maman, or was it Aunt Irène, had worked her magic and made Suzanne and I a similar soft pink dress to wear on that special night. I remember not only my lovely dress, but I also can see the family sitting in a row in the middle isle of the concert hall. A family, Jacques described gallantly, as the most handsome family in Montréal. Grand-maman at the edge, then Uncle Charlie and Aunt Berthe, Aunt Irène, Suzanne, Maman and me. The ladies in different stages of graying, well coifed and well dressed. Uncle Charlie as usual stood straight as an arrow, polished to a glow, pride raising his chest one inch higher. Jacques, his son, who could not hold a hammer and had showed no interest in hunting, a son he did not quite understand, tonight, would make him proud. As for Aunt Berthe, I am sure she felt a fear in her bones knowing the pitfall of a debut concert and the volatility of voice easily influenced by weather, health, or emotions.

How fortunate that at my last move I had taken my mementoes of Jacques' career and filed them, enabling me to find two newspaper write ups of the concert, that in themselves predicted what the scope of his career would become, and how as an artist he would be recognized locally and internationally.

From the critics of his concert debut I read in part, and I paraphrase "How wonderful it is to applaud without reserve the great success of one of our own singers. Jacques Labrecque sang the pages of Fauré, Debussy, or Duparc to perfection…" and, "may it be Handel, Fauré, or a folksong, the singer has a sure taste, his interpretations are varied and balanced." Another quality mentioned was his impeccable pronunciation in whatever language he sang.

The success of Jacques' concert may have alleviated, for a short while, the fear of Uncle Charlie and Aunt Berthe that their son might be called to the army. In print or over the radio they had learned what had happened with our army in Japan and now, the bloody disaster at Dieppe. I am sure that like parents all over Canada they must have spent many nights awake, and days inventing

387

nightmarish scenarios in their minds. Our family embraced Jacques' career. Grand-maman's very small family, now comprised only her sister in law, her four daughters, Berthe, Irène, Flore and Maman, and three grand children, Jacques, Suzanne and me. We were as close as beads in a rosary; love and music the unbreakable link.

Claude Lethiec

Lise Pesant

Cousin Jacques, The Singer at 20
years old

M. Jacques Labrecque se révèle véritable interprète du chant

Après la consécration récente de l'art vocal de Mlle Irène Moquin et de M. Gérald Desmarais, voilà que M. Jacques s'est révélé, hier soir, au Plateau, lui aussi, un intelligent et sensible interprète du chant.

Chanteur français, Jacques Labrecque considère la voix comme un instrument qui doit être mis également au service de la partition et du texte qui l'inspira. Ainsi lorsqu'il chante "L'Invitation au voyage" il fait goûter en même temps le génie de Duparc et celui de Beaudelaire. Avec l'idéale collaboration au piano de M. John Newmark, le jeune ténor a chanté ces pages célèbres avec perfection. Il n'y a pas d'autres mots.

Des trois Fauré inscrits au programme certains préférèrent "Au bord de l'eau" pour la finesse de la ligne mélodique et les nuances rendues au poème de Sully-Prud'homme. "La Fée aux chansons" fut remarquable de couleur et de caractère. Et même avec le souvenir dans la mémoire de Ninon Vallin. "Après un rêve" fut presque irréprochable. Très en place le "Noël" des enfants qui n'ont plus de maisons" et rempli de goût et de sobriété le Rêve de "Manon", donné en rappel.

Le groupe des chansons canadiennes mit en valeur les dons de diseur de M. Jacques Labrecque qui déploya là une vie intense un vigoureux humour et tout juste le centiment qu'il fallait, et "pas plus qu'il n'en fallait". Une vive impression fut créée par "Pique à la pointe" d'Hector Gratton, trois mélodies raffinées et courtantes jusque dans la mélancolie par Oscar O'Brien, une autre de Lionel Daunais.

Le chanteur rendit également avec art "I Love Thee" de Grieg et dans un style excellent un récit et un air du "Messie". En anglais et en italien la diction fut aussi nette qu'en français. Le seul reproche à faire au jeune ténor c'est d'oublier parfois de chanter. Certaines phrases courtes furent simplement suggérées par un murmure. Et encore cela ne se fit sentir qu'à deux ou trois reprises au cours du récital dont le succès fut remarquable et suscita dans la salle les plus élogieux commentaires.

Marcel Valois

Jacques Labrecque

Chaque fois qu'il s'agit de critiquer (au sens général du mot) l'un des nôtres, on voudrait n'avoir que des compliments à faire et le plus souvent on n'est ni sincère ni persuasif, ce qui est tout aussi désagréable pour l'artiste que pour le critique.

C'est pourquoi il est si plaisant aujourd'hui d'applaudir sans arrière-pensée au grand et légitime succès qu'a remporté Jacques Labrecque. Ce jeune ténor possède de grandes qualités: il est toujours intéressant — des plaisants prétendent que c'est parce qu'il aime la musique — et il a du charme à en revendre. Sa voix n'est pas d'une étendue et d'une puissance extrêmes, mais il sait s'en servir avec art. Son goût est fort sûr et son interprétation pleine de variété lui permet d'exprimer avec autant de facilité la ferveur de Handel que la délicatesse de Fauré, le romantisme de Grieg que l'humour du terroir.

Parmi plusieurs interprétations de premier ordre, il faut mettre à part *Au bord de l'eau* de Fauré, détaillé avec finesse, l'heureuse *Chanson roumaine* de Jongen et tout le groupe de mélodies canadiennes, auxquelles il a ajouté en rappel plusieurs chansons populaires. Jacques Labrecque, qui ne cache pas tout ce qu'il doit à Oscar O'Brien, ce dont il faut le féliciter, a chanté des mélodies originales de celui-ci, ainsi que d'Hector Gratton et de Lionel Daunais, et nous a prouvé que nos compositeurs ne sont pas exclusivement des harmonisateurs d'airs de folklore, ce dont nous commencions à douter. Il a montré de plus que ces mélodies peuvent tenir le coup contre la plupart des oeuvres que l'on chante d'habitude dans les récitals à l'exception près des grands chefs-d'oeuvre.

Puissent le succès qu'il a remporté l'inciter à recommencer et l'exemple qu'il a donné être suivi par d'autres.

Romain-Octave PELLETIER

CHAPTER FIFTY TWO

MAMAN'S PENNY THEATER

Suzanne and I greeted the second summer of Maman's venture, with less fear. We knew what to expect. Our roles remained the same, but to our dismay, every weekend the dishes reached a higher and higher level, Maman's cooking and her hospitality attracting family members of our guests.

Sunday, the dinner table vibrated with conversation and laughter, except one Sunday when a guest mentioned that a cousin had been killed in battle. Suddenly, silence hovered over the table like an evening fog, an uncomfortable quietness we even felt into the kitchen, until Maman sent Suzanne to announce the choice of dessert. One by one, voices pierced through the gloom. Soon conversation resumed; however laughter did not.

That second season, our guests felt more like family members, and treated us as such. Maman, confident and in control, gave us more free time, permitting us to include tennis with other activities .

During the last week of August, we celebrated the end of summer and a lovely relationship, by offering our guests a home-made musical play.

During the month, most afternoons, Suzanne, Maman and I sat at the porch table. Maman had dreamed up a scenario using loosely knitted stories from Perrault's *La Mère L'oie,* Mother Goose and within this frame we wrote rhyming verses to popular melodies or folk songs. For the first time Maman included us in the writing. She always composed rhyming verses to celebrate the birthday of each lady of her bridge group. She read them to us, usually at nighttime when inspiration kept her awake. "Girls, are you asleep?" she whispered. Maman always found *le mot juste,* the appropriate tone to highlight the strong points or weaknesses of each personality, never in a hurtful manner, always humorously.

The night of our production the living room became the stage, and in the dining room we placed two rows of chairs for our audience. Guests and a few of their family members assisted. One guest, Monsieur Lajoie had joined our threesome; the props were in place; everyone ready.

Laughter greeted dear hefty Monsieur Lajoie, as Blue Beard, making his appearance riding on a tricycle and Suzanne, in her tower, for the occasion the top of one of the bookcases, head adorned with wood shaving long blond hair, crying her sorrow. Maman and I, the chorus, told the story while our two actors mimed their parts. Our audience laughter gave us the encouragement to enjoy, as much as they did our singing-story-telling. Once the play was over, Maman, wearing one of Aunt Irène's evening gown, a cushion adding heft to her bust line, gave, to everyone's surprise and delight, her singing impersonation of an opera singer.

This had been the best part of the summer, and a great ending to Maman's project which erased the debt of Papa's costly remodeling.

Marcelle age 12 in white dress
With summer boarding guests

Summer boarding guest 1942

CHAPTER FIFTY THREE

THE AMBULANCE AND THE TEA KETTLE COZY

While Papa had been away and our guests occupied most of the house, the radio had not been turned on and we had not seen the newspaper which usually was brought home from Montréal by Papa.

Occasionally, at the table, Monsieur Lajoie had made comments about some invasion in France, but he never went into any details not to worry his fragile wife. However, now the guests were gone, Papa had returned, and with him his after dinner habit of reading his newspaper. Again, from time to time, we missed our program, *Un homme et son péché,* Papa lecturing us instead, about an invasion in France by our troops, and telling us about the dire consequences.

Maman reorganized the house, resumed her knitting

for the soldiers, rejoined her bridge group, and supervised our studies.

Overly tired by all the extra work of her summer enterprise, she caught a cold that would not heal. Doctor Thibodeau diagnosed pneumonia and told us to call an ambulance. I do not see Papa in this picture. Despite the seriousness of the situation, a moment of levity shook away the gloom. After the doctor left, Suzanne and I dressed Maman warmly. From the front door to the ambulance she would be exposed to the biting cold. But, what to do about her head—a hat would not do. She refused to wear a warm headscarf; she could not suffer making a grand entrance in the hospital with such a head- gear. I had an idea…

During one of his hunting trips, Papa had stayed with a farming family. The lady of the house knitted with unrefined wool—thick and rough. Papa thought that it would be wonderful to own some socks and a head covering made out of that warm wool. The lady obliged and made him what he wanted.

The white wool stockings were not sufficient; he purchased a pair of felt boots that laced up to mid-calf and had the distinctive look of back woods countrymen about them. Most gentleman of the period dressed in shoes with shoe coverings that fitted tightly, more like a glove than a boot. That is what sat in Papa's closet. The new boots I ignored, because his pant legs covered them, but…the head covering was another story.

It is one thing to admire other children's parents who do not fit the mold, and are thought of as being unique. I did, but when it came to my father's eccentricities, my convictions were shaken. Just think; I had to walk to church with him! Well, I slowed down trying to disassociate myself from the one parent I resembled the most, as if the whole village did not know I was Mademoiselle Mignault, the daughter of the man with the white head covering, walking three steps ahead of her.

Indeed Papa had achieved his goal, warmth. "If the others want to freeze, it's their problem." That unfashionable *thing* covered the head, and the forehead, and half the cheeks, and the throat, and worst of all, it did not fit smoothly on top. I think the dear lady did not know what to do with the excess yarn, and the white cap ended up looking like a tea cozy, the dome ready to let steam out at anytime.

We were still waiting for the ambulance and Maman's head was still uncovered. I had an inspiration! I put on my father's wool cap and showed only my head around the corner of Maman's bedroom door, and said, "Wouldn't this be just darling!" Instantaneously, the three of us burst out laughing. At the same time the doorbell rang, the ambulance had arrived. Cackling all the way, Suzanne ran to open the door. Maman and I could not stop laughing. She kept on saying, "We have to stop, we have to stop, no one will believe I am sick."

Dear Maman Margot, she had to play the right part at the right time; this was the time to be sick in a dignified manner, even with an unfashionable wool scarf on her head.

CHAPTER FIFTY FOUR

CHOCOLATE AND PÂTÉ DE FOIE GRAS

At breakfast we ate toast spread with pâté de foie gras, and chocolate cake after lunch and after dinner, and at snack time chocolate fudge. Suzanne had taken Maman's place, and the menu changed drastically.

Even Papa relaxed his grip and while enjoying the pâté in the morning, a conspiratorial smile floated on his lips. The house director was in the hospital. Suzanne was in charge.

Other than having pâté for breakfast and chocolate cake as a regular diet, I do not recall what else Suzanne fed us, but I do remember her inviting a friend after class.

That in itself was an event out of the ordinary, however most extraordinary was her friend's name: June Scofield, the only English-protestant girl in the whole school. Papa welcomed her graciously. Suzanne introduced me, I said, *"Bonjour."* She said, "Bon-ne-jour," we smiled, and that was that. Our vocabulary in each other's language was equal—nil.

Suzanne invited June to join her in the kitchen and whipped up a recipe of chocolate fudge. If Maman had been home, Suzanne and her new friend would have been sitting at the dining room table doing school homework or in the living room where Maman would have served them a snack on a tray. Like two proper young ladies they would have sit, napkins on their laps or in hand, delicately sponging off a crumb or a drop of milk from the corners of their mouths.

Our dear Maman stayed in the hospital for ten days and afterward recuperated for a week at Aunt Berthe's home, and another week at Aunt Irène's. She came back to us looking rested and ready to take over the running of her home, and alas, making sure I was doing my homework.

Suzanne must have regretted her short-lived chocolate bounty. Yet, to play the part of housekeeper and cook and still try to retain her high grades at school had taken its toll. She looked drawn. Of her natural spontaneity and gaiety only a deceptive coat hid the weariness she felt. She did not complain, but the week before Maman's arrival she asked me to help more often and would not indulge my short spurt of good will. She held me to the job at hand though it probably robbed her of more energy than if she had done the chore herself.

Maman returned on time to relieve Suzanne and let her prepare herself for her final school exams. Despite the additional work Suzanne had taken upon her shoulders, and the presence of our father, she had felt a certain amount of freedom. In a month's time she had become an adult in charge of a household, without the presence of a mother telling her what to do, when to do it, and how to do it.

Maman and her rules were back. The ingestion of chocolate and pâté de foie gras would return to a special treat status. Suzanne could live with that rule but she would miss having a friend visiting once in a while. She had experienced the joy of friendship outside of school without the hermetic rules of behavior prescribed by Maman.

Through her life Suzanne developed many friendships;

she was faithful, relaxed and generous. She corresponded with friends or family members who had moved away and needed news of home and the reassurance they were not forgotten.

The coming summer would be different, no paying guests would people our living room, dining room, and bedrooms, and to my delight Maman would agree to let me sleep in the attic. Suzanne in her last year of schooling looked forward to have quietness and a place to study away from my chatting or Papa reading aloud news of the war. Of course in his quiet way Papa's presence would be felt all around the house. We would have both parents watching our every move. A depressing thought, though it probably did not cross my mind. I was too busy dreaming; I could always concoct my own scenario.

CHAPTER FIFTY FIVE

OUR UNCLE JOSEPH, *le curé*

Like an anchorite out of seclusion, Uncle Joseph walked soundlessly into our lives. Straight-shouldered and long necked, he gave the impression of being a tall man. A large forehead, high cheekbones, and a square jaw were softened by the transparency of deep set blue eyes--his mother's eyes; *un regard that had an intensity* projecting strength as well as the luminosity of an ascetic. I had seen him only a few times in my life, and to me he looked like a soul in black robes, the flesh thinned and adhering to the bone where not an ounce of indulgence could have insinuated itself.

Not long after his arrival, my parents planned a visit with us in tow. Maman told us that, as *a curé*, Uncle Joseph had insisted that his female parishioners dress modestly for mass, even refusing to give communion to a lady wearing an outfit with short sleeves. He must be very severe I thought. I did not look forward to visiting him. I liked priests like l'abbé Joli who had a tease ready to escape at the corner of his lips. Nonetheless, Maman said, "Your Uncle is sick and old; he needs company, and that includes you." That was that: end of conversation.

A few days later, we found ourselves on his doorstep, Papa dressed in his dark suit looking as serious as a funeral director, and Maman, Suzanne and I in our most virtuous Sunday clothes from neck to wrist.

Papa rang the doorbell. We heard a muffled sound and Uncle Joseph's helper opened the door.

"Bonjour, Mademoiselle," said Papa and Maman. Suzanne and I echoed the greeting: a quartet expressing a diverging scale of enthusiasm.

"Bonjour, *M'sieu l'curé* is expecting you, he is in the living room," said Mademoiselle greeting us with the self-effacing look of a long time clergy's employee.

There was a family name attached to the Mademoiselle, but like her face it was erased from my memory. A woman, part old maid, part nun, who like thousands of others working in presbyteries for men of the cloth, labored in their shadows. Never wives, they performed the same duties less one, and unlike nuns attained a lesser degree of respectability.

406

She led us to Uncle Joseph's living room. I tried to shrink myself, though by then it was more out of habit; I could not hide, being taller than Maman and almost as tall as Suzanne. Standing behind my sister or not, I still had to do the inevitable go and give a kiss to Uncle Joseph a chore I accomplished promptly if not gracefully. Later on, I became aware that a smile, like a fine tablecloth over a stained table, would help to camouflage an inelegant moment.

For many years, Uncle Joseph taught Zoology at the seminary of Sainte-Thérèse, a college serving the young men from the villages around Saint-Eustache and Montréal. That is where Papa and his four brothers had pursued their college education, and where our cousins Jean-Pierre and Henri presently studied.

Papa and Uncle sat in two rocking chairs, while Maman, Suzanne and I, like three dandelions in a jar, sat stiffly on seats not propitious to long thoughtful deliberation. Nevertheless, now and then, Maman injected a word in the conversation, and Suzanne attentively nodded, or produced little sounds of acquiescence. This was not my cup of tea. I turned my mind to a more important function; I inspected the surroundings.

The living room looked more like a large studio where the piano lid had been closed and music scores hidden in drawers for years; where vibrations on walls had ceased, and melodies no longer lingered on shelves and cornices. A bay window lacked draperies, and the wood floors a carpet.

After fourteen years of teaching, and twenty as a parish priest, he had garnered few possessions. Mountains of books had not yet found their place in bookcases, however, frames of birds and butterflies, part of an extensive collection he had worked on for many years, already decorated a long white wall. Through the years, Papa had saved the best specimens of snipe, woodcock, and grouse and gave them to Uncle Joseph. Nephews and nieces furnished the butterflies. The bird or butterfly frames had landscaped backgrounds, and at their edges grasses where they would have foraged. The bottom center of the frame contained a tag with the Latin and the common name.

I was abruptly brought back to the family circle by soft shoed Mademoiselle coming into the room with a dish of chocolate fudge. She offered us each a piece. As quietly, she left with the dish. Dismayed, I gawked at my one-half inch square of fudge and glanced at Maman's and Suzanne's; theirs looked exactly the same size.

Maman gave me a look that said *appreciate what you received*, her eyes like a neon sign flashing *don't you dare say a word.*

Uncle Joseph, having been operated on for colon cancer many years before moving to Saint-Eustache, could eat only small bites of food. It seemed, dear Mademoiselle could not think outside of that measure.

I would have loved to walk around and inspect the rest of the apartment, but, "no, stay on your chair unless invited." I never received an invitation, but Maman told me that Uncle Joseph had an altar in his bedroom where he said mass every morning.

Mademoiselle knew more about Uncle than all his family. Was he kind, patient, exigent, short-tempered? Did he provide for her old age?

I knew Uncle Joseph only superficially. Visiting always with my parents, the conversation did not involve the young people. Nevertheless, I had a feeling that he possessed a generous nature. When pursuing his education in Europe, he bought a violin for Uncle Georges and a flute for Papa. At that time, both of them studied those instruments in college. I assumed that the other brothers received similar presents. He also had purchased cameos to distribute among his sisters and nieces. At one of our visits Suzanne and I each received one.

How could he afford to buy anything? Most often, his dear father, the Doctor, received in exchange for his services products from his patients' farms. By the time Joseph went abroad, two more brothers would be entering college to be followed by two more. Not supported financially by his father, Uncle Joseph, probably on scholarship, must have deprived himself to afford gifts for his family.

Half a century later, away from the daily life of a professor or the religious and human ritual of a parish priest, he remained faithful to his calling of saving souls. One came to him in the form of a thoughtful young woman making sure that her new renter, the old sick priest, had the care he needed. She stopped by often and a friendship ensued. A few years later, she embraced his beliefs and converted to his faith.

Uncle Joseph had come full circle to the simplicity of the aspiration of his youth.

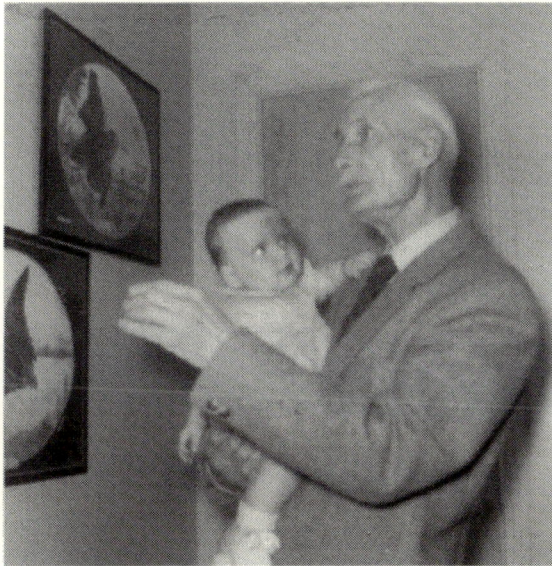

1956 Papa showing Grandson Bruce
picture frames Uncle Joseph made

M. l'abbé Joseph Mignault

CHAPTER FIFTY SIX

UNCLE ARTHUR LEFT US

No longer would I see him sitting in the doorway of Monsieur Lapierre's shoe repair shop, or half turned toward the back of the church greeting his constituents with a glance, a smile, or a small nod of his head, and for me alone, I was sure, a wink if our eyes made contact.

The sixth of February, Maman received a phone call from her friend, cousin Mercédès, with the sad news that her father had died. They would bring the body back to Saint-Eustache for a four-day viewing. Would Maman be kind enough to see that the house was ready to receive hundreds of people and also, that there would be enough food to feed the family, and guests who because of distances might stay for meals.

Maman was happy to help. She dearly loved Aunt Marie-Louise and Uncle Arthur. She would surprise the

413

family and prepare dinner, and a few dishes they could refrigerate and use later.

Maman called Aunt Marie-Louise's two indispensable helpers, Madame Lanthier and Lucienne Mondou, the same women who always helped her when she gave a large reception or received the family for the yearly dinner on the First of January.

While the two women cleaned and arranged furniture for an easy flow of people coming in and going out, Maman looked in the ice box and the kitchen cupboards to see what was already there. She then went down to the cellar and brought back root vegetables and a bag of mackintosh apples. After preparing a list she called Monsieur Trépanier, the owner of her grocery and meat store, who immediately filled the large order.

Monsieur Binette, anxious to know why Maman was putting in an order, *and what could she be doing at the Sauvé,* delivered it at a most unusual speed. "On my way, I stopped at the bakery and got you two fresh breads, the kind you like." He said. Maman thanked him, and knowing his propensity for long conversation, led him toward the door.

I can imagine dear Maman Margot preparing a large pot of soup. "They will be tired, and it is freezing cold outdoor," she thinks. She makes multiple recipes of piecrusts. A large ham boils on top of the stove, three meat pies bake in the oven—they can freeze a couple. She has enough dough left to make a couple of apple pies. On the counter top, peeled potatoes, carrots and a quartered cabbage, soak in cold water.

Hours later, two apple pies sit on the stove shelf and the three meat pies are on trivets on the cooler back burners. The women are gone. Maman goes to every room for a last look and leaves a light in the rooms facing the river. As the returning family crosses the small bridge, she wants them to see their home lit and welcoming.

She goes back to the kitchen and leaves a note. "I will see you tomorrow. My thoughts are with you. Affectionately, Margot."

The family will arrive at dusk, and enter a home where the kitchen aromas will momentarily restore them to a sense of the familiar, the everyday life where death had not yet entered to disturb its rhythm.

Alice Mignault and Dr. Joseph Page

Arthur & Marie-Louise

Alice Mignault and Dr. Joseph Page´

Arthur & Marie-Louise in Cairo

Arthur Suavé

CHAPTER FIFTY SEVEN

THE BELLS TOLLED

We closed our books and in silence left our class rooms. Wrapped in our winter accoutrement, we walked a short distance to the front of the church, and two by two we climbed the circular staircase to the second loft. We saw little of the congregation, and only the upper bodies of the priests as the ceremony took place in the sanctuary.

Somewhere in the center aisle stood Uncle Arthur's casket surrounded by a community who had come to pay their respect. Regardless of politics he was well regarded by people of every station in life who recognized him as a genuine man, a good man, a simple man.

Two days before the funeral my class had prayed at his casket in Aunt Marie-Louise's large parlor filled with flowers. But I did not look at him. I wanted to remember Uncle Arthur as I knew him; smiling and laughing at the head of the table when we celebrated New Years *en famille.*

Sometime before his death, when speaking to cousin Pierrette, his granddaughter, Suzanne had mentioned how lucky she was to have such a nice and joyful Grandfather. She agreed; however, she told Suzanne that during the depression there were days when he became short tempered. So many people came to ask for his help, and he had no job to give. He felt so frustrated, so powerless. As for myself, I knew that for a long time to come I would still see him at mass, sitting somewhere among his fellow parishioners, and at a propitious moment wink at a niece who like him spends too much time looking back.

Unable to see the ceremony perched all the way back in the loft, and not wanting to attract the attention of our guardian, I furtively glanced at the singers until Monsieur Groulx stuck out his tongue at me. I blushed, and turned my head an eighth-of-an-inch to the left to watch Aunt Gabrielle playing the organ. Her feet moved as fast as her hands, the latter reaching up and down the four claviers and pulling and pushing side buttons. Suddenly flute or violin, clarinet, oboe or French horn played their solo or joined in, and then the organ sounded like a powerful orchestra. That I did not like. To my ears it

422

sounded like a musical bombardment; sounds hitting the ceiling, the crystal chandeliers, the stained glass windows, sounds that unlike the repercussion of the piano, clean, detached, felt to me as if notes melted into one another; to my ears a cacophony.

Liking it or not I still felt great pride in Aunt Gabrielle's talent. How could she do all that? How could her fingers and her feet know where to go?

The choir started singing and my glance moved away from Aunt Gabrielle. I rested my head using a straight look forward; however, the beautiful sound of a bass baritone jerked my head a full quarter of an inch toward the man with the golden voice. But his song was so sad that soon tears filled my eyes. I had heard this poem by Victor Hugo before, but not at the funeral of someone I loved.

In time, I would meet the singer, Marcel Prudhomme and his sister Margot, a pianist. Both would become friends, selflessly promoting my singing.

At home during dinner, the conversation was all about the funeral and Aunt-Marie-Louise's sorrow. Little by little, as stories are apt to do, Aunt-Marie-Louise's life opened up under my eyes like a book whose pages I had never seen before.

"They had been married forty-five years," Papa said "Hmm, Arthur didn't even know if Paul would ever come back from the war."

"Poor Marie-Louise," Maman said. "What a hole it makes in her life, and now, she worries a lot about Paul. I heard that he is in France."

"It doesn't look good over there," said Papa, "there is talk of a big invasion."

"I hope she knows nothing about it. *Dieu merci,* she has three children left to bring her some comfort...she has had quite a life despite all her losses."

"That she had." Papa said. "Well ladies, you will have to excuse me. I need a little exercise."

"May I go and practice?" asked Suzanne. Both were excused. They folded their napkins, put them through their holders, and left the table.

Maman and I sat content to be alone. I got up, brought the teakettle to the table, and sat on Suzanne's chair nearer to Maman. "Would you like more tea?"

While I poured, Maman served us a second piece of custard pie. Though, this time, only a sliver. She looked tired. It had been a long week. So much walking in the snow back and forth to visit with Aunt Marie-Louise and her family; so many emotions, and today the funeral and a walk to the cemetery in the freezing cold.

"You said that Aunt Marie-Louise had many losses. What did you mean?"

I was not sure that I would ever hear that story. Maman looked as if she might sit on her chair, her back to the stove and stay there until bedtime, yielding her will to the warmth, and the knowledge that tomorrow would be a plain, ordinary day.

"It's a long story," she said.

"I will do the dishes with Suzanne, I promise." I warmed up her tea. She sat straighter. I removed the pie and our plates from the table. Now, we could freely leave our elbows on the table. I was ready to hear a slice of family history.

"You know that Aunt-Marie-Louise is your father's first cousin, don't you?" I nodded. "Her mother, Mercédès-- Sophie died a few days after her birth. The father was left with three young children and a baby."

"What did he do?"

425

"The grandparents Mignault offered to raise and care for the baby. The father accepted and brought little Marie-Louise to them."

"The poor father must have cried."

"I am sure he must have been very sad, after all he had just lost his wife."

"Were Marie-Louise's grandparents Suzanne's and mine?"

"No, the old Doctor Mignault and his wife were your great grandparents. Don't forget, that was in 1876, between you and Marie-Louise there is over fifty years. Anyway, your great-grandmother died three months later."

My mouth dropped. "What happened to the baby?" Maman's face showed me that too many questions were not welcome. I would have to save them for a more propitious time. I swallowed the next two questions that had begged to escape from my lips. Was she very old? What did the old doctor do?

"I am not too sure what happened next," said Maman. "Nevertheless, I assume that your grandfather and grandmother Mignault who already had a couple of children, may have taken care of the baby. Anyhow, what I know is that the old Doctor Mignault remarried two years later and that he and his new wife, Malvina Filiatrault, raised little Marie-Louise."

"Oh, I hope she was a good woman." I could not help myself.

"She was strict, but she must have been loving, because Marie-Louise grew up to be a kind and joyful person."

"Did you know the new wife, Malvina?"

"Yes. She was a cousin of your Grand-maman Rhéaume. We called her the old Aunt Mignault...Oh, please don't!" I had come to the edge of my chair, ready to ask more questions.

"You asked me what I meant by Aunt Marie-Louise's sorrow. Let me tell you now, and some other time I will tell you more about Malvina."

I had no choice but to sit back and wait for the rest later. I could not help but be intrigued. Two families unrelated by blood, called the same person; on one side, The Old Aunt Mignault and on the other Old grandmother Mignault.

Maman paid no attention to my knit brow and continued.

"So after the old doctor married Malvina, little Marie-Louise had a permanent home.

When Marie Louise was in her early twenties, your Uncle, Doctor Pagé married to your Aunt Alice Mignault introduced a young journalist to her."

"It was Uncle Arthur?"

"Yes indeed. The young couple fell in love, married, and started raising their family. In those days, immunization did not exist, and in the late 19th century epidemics abounded. After about ten years of marriage, they lost three children in the space of six months. When the Old Grandmother Mignault found out, she begged them to send her their little baby. So, in her early seventies, Malvina took the little baby, Mercédè. And took care of her until the epidemic ran its course."

"She was a very good lady."

"Yes, indeed. Not long afterward, Marie-Louise and Arthur moved to a home where Malvina could watch a new family being born. Now that her three brothers had died, Baby Mercédès became the oldest of two new brothers and a sister."

428

"I know them, Paul, Gustave and Pauline." I said it so fast; Maman had no time to stop me. "And I know cousin Mercédès too."

Maman smiled. "Yes," she said. "And did you know that Mercédès has been a good friend of mine since we were about ten years old?" I shook my head. "You will know this story when we talk some more about the Old Aunt Mignault. This is it for tonight. It is getting late; you and Suzanne have homework to do. Please go tell her to stop practicing, and *please,* no chatter."

I looked at the pile of dishes. Homework sounded a bit more appealing. "I promised that I would help you," I said in a less than convincing tone.

"I know, however, you have homework left to do. I feel better. It will take me no time. *Merci, mon chou.*" Maman gave me a peck on the cheek, and once more, I left the kitchen enriched with one more family story.

As revealed to me by their 94 year old daughter, Mireille Pagé Dufresne, it was Aunt Marie-Louise and Uncle Arthur who introduced Alice Mignault to the young doctor Joseph Pagé.

Gabrielle Mignault at 16

CHAPTER FIFTY EIGHT

PERCEPTION ASKEW

I cannot recall which year or under what circumstance Uncle Joseph walked to his bookcase and handed me a book saying, "I think this will interest you." Had he heard from Papa that I liked singing or that I had sung a solo at church? It does not matter. Sometime around my fourteenth year, I read *The Life of a French-Canadian Prima Donna* on one breath. I found out she had been a first cousin of my grandfather Mignault; what a thrill!

Her theatrical name had been Albani, and she had sung in every major operatic house in Europe and England. My eyes grew larger when I read that crowned heads showered her with jewelry. I could not believe my eyes reading that she spent many private tea hours with Queen Victoria, at whose funeral she sang.

I overlooked Albani's cruel apprenticeship with a harsh

father, her years of study, and her exploitation as both a child pianist and singer. All I could see were images of bowing deeply to acknowledge a standing ovation or being feted by royalty: an enthralling scenario for this dreamer.

My desire had found its mooring. I had concrete proof that even in my family a woman could achieve such a goal. So far, I had heard excellent female soloists on the radio, but they were not crossing to Europe. The female pianists usually accompanied other artists, or became organists out of view in church lofts. After seven years of piano studies and more to come, I knew this would not be the career I would choose. Yet, something more fundamental than glory alone spurred me toward a career.

Observing Maman and her female friends, I was well aware of their lack of freedom, and of their titles: "*ménagère.*" The Larousse dictionary defining the word, *ménagère*: woman who cleans and occupies herself with the administration of the home. On the other hand, a cleaning woman was also a servant, who until the mid nineteen hundreds, cleaned one's house for a pittance and had no social standing. So, who were they, our mothers? How could their title *ménagère* ever enhance their status?

And what of the manipulations women learned from their mothers: a necessary compass to navigate a world steered by a patriarchal society? I detected a thread of understanding between the women of Maman's bridge group, the unfinished sentence that needed no ending. I overheard the giggles when they talked about their husbands and how they circumvented their demands all the while accepting their subservient role and lying to boost their husbands' egos. In our case, prevaricating so often to avoid recriminations from our father, we still straddled the truth when not necessary.

This is now *une histoire passé,* yet I was living at the edge of it, a story I promised myself I would not enlarge by adding another character.

Singer would be my title. I would be appreciated not because I kept the house clean. I would be recognized for my talent. I would escape the restrictions of established old edicts. I would visit the world. No longer would I sit on the terrace gazing toward the bridge, seeing cars traveling back and forth going somewhere, while I sat and watched with a heart filled with the desire to escape a life circumscribed by what my village could offer, and bearded social rules.

Albani

CHAPTER FIFTY NINE

MADAME MALENFANT

"Could I take voice lessons?" I asked Maman. Suzanne had already started. Every day I heard her practicing scales and songs called *Bergerettes.* I was sure I could do the same.

"I cannot promise you just yet," said Maman. "First, let's go see Suzanne's voice teacher. I will ask her to hear you sing, and then we will follow her advice."

"Albani was already giving concerts at my age."

Maman said nothing.

"Find a song you would like to sing for Madame Malenfant."

"When can we go?"

"We will go after your birthday. It will give you enough

time to practice a song."

That was it! I stood at the edge of a career. I was on my way to fame.

I was nine years old, when for the first time, I heard Jeannette McDonald sing in a movie. I could not forget her. Five years later when I lay in bed in the dark, my memory, a giant screen, recreated her coming down a long set of stairs: Hollywood relished staircases coming from heaven with the singing-dancing star coming down to earth with as much feather as an angel. My Jeannette McDonald did not come down one of those heavenly show-your-long-legs-staircases. No, singing, she walked down a path of stairs in the center of a small amphitheater emptied of people, but each side filled with millions of tulips: all in Technicolor. The very first movie I had ever seen in color. I thought I would never see anything so beautiful again. I trembled so, Maman had to cover my shoulders with her arm...and the whole time Jeannette sang and smiled.

Now the day that would propel my career had arrived. I had learned Maman's song. The one melody I had heard many times when, at a party, someone asked her to sing. I had performed for the occasion of Papa and Maman's twenty fifth wedding anniversary. But that song, *L'anneau d'argent,* was a bit solemn and full of nostalgia. I liked the lyrics of Maman's melody better, the poet saying: if my poem had wings, day and night it would fly toward your garden. That song had élan, I felt, and a smiling future.

Once, sitting on the train, waves of uncertainty or hope flooded my thinking. Maman patted my hand. She always felt anxious before singing so, without me saying a word, she understood.

How did we find ourselves in front of Suzanne's teacher's door so quickly? There she was, as tall as a monument to the métis nation, imposing, beautiful.

Madame Malenfant ushered us in. She looked seven feet tall. My new five foot eight frame shrunk. Her black hair was loosely gathered into a low bun. Her dark eyes were warm, but a sense of power emanated from her, contrasting with her quiet sensuality. She offered us a seat. Madame Malenfant's speaking voice, like the voice I had heard over the radio when she sang, had the sound of a cello: at times vibrant and powerful, then mellow and velvety.

I sat stiffly at the edge of my seat while my heart pounded its pre-performance solo. After a few moments of polite chatting with my mother, Madame Malenfant asked me what I would sing for her.

"*Si mes vers avaient des ailes, de* Renaldo Hahn." I answered in a voice I did not recognized.

"Wonderful, this is one of my favorite melodies."

I stood near the piano my knees doing their solo shake; the pounding of my heart blocking my ears giving my voice an uninvited tremolo. At last, the one high note on the treacherous word "*rit*" had gone by; I felt safe and indulging myself I chested the low note in the last sentence, which I believed would duly impress her, a contralto. She smiled at me.

"How old are you?"

"I am fifteen years old, Madame."

"My dear girl you have a voice, a big voice." Looking at Maman, she added, "The best thing for your daughter, Madame, is to finish her studies, and then come and see me."

My face must have dropped and my smile vanished for she said, "Ma chère, your voice will not go away; it is yours for keeps, but you must care for it."

She turned to Maman and added, "Madame Mignault, make sure Marcelle stays away from chorale singing."

Maman must have understood because she agreed without discussion.

We left.

We were on our way back home, and I could not decide if I should be happy or disconsolate.

Silence traveled with us to the train. Once comfortably seated in the familiar musty scent of old, upholstered, high back seats peppered by whiffs of steam, my spine swooshed as if sponges had replaced bones and cartilages.

Maman again patted my knee. "It went well, don't you think?" she said.

"Why can't I sing in the choir?"

"Probably because you will get carried away by the powerful sound, and to hear yourself, you will try to sing louder, and this is hard on the voice."

I knew this was true, but I argued, "It will be three whole years without singing. What will the sisters say?"

"It will not matter; you will not return to the same school in the fall."

My spine regained some stiffness. I sat straighter. Yet, everything else in me plunged into a state of bewilderment and mild panic. This news came as a total surprise and Maman left me no time to say a word.

"Your father and I have discussed your future and have decided to enroll you into a boarding school"

My future! Now everyone was interested in my future and had a different idea about it. If they all kept adding more ideas, I would be dead before I could have a future.

"Albani made her debut at Covent Garden in La Sonnambula at age twenty." I managed to say before Maman uttered another word, "and I won't be able to sing for another three years, and why do I have to go to a different school?" My spine had regained its full height.

Maman put her hand up: a familiar gesture to stop me from crossing the line, and calmly, said, "Your father is concerned that Suzanne's social life will interfere with your studies, now that she finished her schooling." Bending over toward me she whispered, as if the rumbling of the train would not cover up the shame she would convey in her words. "You know you are a poor student. Your father fears that you will not get a proper education if you stay home."

I was dumfounded and finally speechless.

We settled in our respective seats facing one another, but looking away through a dusty window: trees, houses, clouds, fields, birds, cows, horses, more houses and farms, dogs and more cows; a scenery running away from the train. Everything was moving, vibrating, pulsating; screeching wheels and gong sounding bells advertising an arrival, another foretelling of danger. Sitting there I was caught like an album in mid air, photos dispersed by a tornado, time and people out of sequence, lives pulled away from their roots.

I looked away from the window. I glanced at Maman. She hurried a smile I did not return. "Where will I go to school?" I asked.

"I am not sure yet," she said.

CHAPTER SIXTY

WHILE MAMAN MAKES PHONE CALLS

Papa was preoccupied otherwise. He had spent only a couple of weeks at Uncle George's lake, and now he would have to wait two more months at home before hunting.

Last summer he had devised some entertainment for himself. While sitting on the upper terrace and contemplating the river, his eyes lingered on a large expanse of grass on the lower terrace. Before our births, Maman had made a large flower garden along the cement wall, but now all was uniformly green. A tall, well shaped pine tree stood on the right corner and in front of it a cement bench. The left corner of the terrace had been planned with the same décor in mind, but two successive pine trees refused to grow, and the cement bench stood forlorn.

Papa had stopped talking about the turtle roof. He had

taken care of that. During meals he studied his carrots and celery, and pinched his lips and nose at the sight of globs of canned spinach.

"How wonderful it would be to have fresh vegetables," he said, while pushing aside the post mortem looking greens.

This time he faced less opposition from Maman. His daydreaming started taking shape: a gardener appeared. And now, a year later, Papa, sitting on the upper terrace, looked at his agricultural enterprise. Planted in straight rows, he admired healthy leaves of radishes, carrots, leeks, beets, lettuce, aromatic celery, bouquets of summer savory enough to flavor a whole year of yellow pea soup and near the cement wall facing the river, vines of yellow string beans. Maman's plants of Bijou tomatoes looked with an air of superiority over the lower growing vegetables; after all they produced fruits.

Papa had imagined, and a gardener had appeared, and reluctantly his two daughters did the picking. Once in a while, in a pinch, Maman went down the crooked cement sidewalk to pick an ingredient for a meal, but her legs suffered from those trips.

The year of the planting, the dogs, no respecter of gardens, had been the force that propelled my father away from his observatory position into one of action. He took wood boards, nails, hammer, and went to work. In amazement Suzanne and I soon contemplated a perfect white picket fence. A miracle had taken place under our eyes; never before had we seen our father hold a hammer except when shelling butternuts.

It was all lovely, but now Papa, proud as a peacock, had ample time to sit and contemplate his work of art while Suzanne and I were relegated to the less glamorous task of picking the forever growing and multiplying vegetables.

Fortunately, Uncle Charlie added one more feature to the lower terrace, by giving me and installing a gym set anchored, on one side on the largest elm tree, and on the other on steel posts. For many summers I hung upside down from a bar, or again, feet straight up in the air and head toward the ground, hands holding firmly on rings; all this earthy view not altering my lofty dreams.

While I reluctantly picked the fruits of Papa's imagination, Maman made decisions for my future, and Papa's mind, always prolific, flashed new ideas. How many he rejected, we will never know. One, however, tempted him greatly. The summer was hot and this idea when implemented would be most beneficial.

Maman had found a boarding school that met her criteria: good education, reasonable price and near enough that once in a while she could visit me. She went on her own to see the school and meet the superior. Grand-maman was on her way. I would need a different uniform because my new school belonged to a different congregation.

As for Papa, his imagination contemplated other matters.

CHAPTER SIXTY ONE

SAINTE-GENEVIÈVE DE PIERREFONDS

The name of my new boarding school pleased me. The preposition *de* giving it, I thought, an air of noblesse. When I read that the first Canadian Mignault, from whom we descended, called himself Jean Mignot de Chatillon, I gained a few inches in pride and promptly added de Chatillon to my name on the first page of each of my school books. I did not know then that many French settlers added to their family name the name of the town from where they came. Chatillon was the city where his christening certificate is registered and is signed by his father in 1620.

I also knew little about the new curriculum of the school I was about to enter; however, I fell in love with the school itself from its distinguished name, and from a description Maman gave me of the dormitory. There were dormers along its length. What more could I ask.

I saw myself at night lying flat on my stomach, facing a window looking at the stars and the moon or watching the rain fall. How stupendous it would be to see a new snow covering roof tops against a dark night's backdrop. Regardless of the season, I could see clearly a pot of red geraniums sitting on the windowsill. The child who wanted to jump from Aunt Irène's dormer window and ride on clouds was still alive and well.

In the meantime Grand-Maman had joined the family providing a touch of reality to my wandering mind. The dormer windows were not in her agenda, the making of two uniforms was.

At the end of spring, in summer and early fall the sewing machine, like the family, vacationed on the porch There we ate all our meals and watched the weather going every which way, and felt the river breezes through the opened windows. Between meals the table served as a top for spreading material, cutting and pinning. I had been promoted to removing basting, or with a razor blade cleaning seams from clothing being transformed into new shapes.

Early mornings Papa walked and groomed his dogs which gave him ample time to contemplate nature sitting in the shade of the elm and basked with pride at the sight of the vegetable garden. By eleven o'clock, Maman sent me to pick yellow beans or anything else needed for our noon dinner. The sun performed its job with great energy, while my blond-self reddened and perspired.

While everyone else bended toward the job at hand, Papa's mind remained alert, a new project flourishing in its recesses. From the porch we saw him surveying the hill, and from different angles one specific tree. After a few trips up and down, and putting his hand on the bark, serious, and looking satisfied like a doctor sounding the chest of a healed patient, he went to the garage and came out with wood boards. Hammer, saw, and a box of nails soon lay on the grass next to his chair.

"Oh dear," Maman said, "What's next?"

Grand-maman did not move. She concentrated in making the pleats of a skirt the exact same width. As for me, I was already contemplating the sky from the dormitory dormer window.

CHAPTER SIXTY TWO

BATHING UNDER THE NEIGHBORS' EYES

Although less quaint than the picket fence, I marveled at how straight and sturdy the structure stood. The plumbing was minimal requiring no permit. On a long hook nailed to the tree hung the garden hose; my father had created an outdoor shower.

I feared it would be visible from our neighbors' every window. By now, not only did I worry about Sally on our right, but also the Brochu on the left. The lovely young couple had built a house in the field of my youth.

The shower's unattractive structure worried me the least. My father's disrobing in the early morning and showing himself to the neighbors in his late 1930's bathing suit I found appalling. At least, I hoped, only the early birds, watched him. The robins, no doubt ignored him; they were too busy around the platform on the grassy hill where the water from the hose softened the ground and brought their morning meals wriggling to the surface.

The mid afternoon shower worried me most, when all was still but for the strident call of the cicadas. The sun reflected on my father's white body like a beam of light from a screen projector for all to see: the shoulders, missing their pads; the chest peppered by grayish hair calling for a white starched shirt; the legs, long and so white, ill at ease without the flair of the trousers. How vulnerable, to my eye, was the sight of my father, as if the aristocratic head had hooked on to the wrong body, the body of a mere mortal. My annoyance with my father seemed so puerile when considering the overwhelming tragedies still happening in Europe and the part our own country played.

My father had successfully sold Victory Bonds, Maman still kept up with her knitting or rolling yards and yards of gauze into individual tight rolls. I shed a tear hearing patriotic songs, and seeing movie reels about the war. Like a bad conscience it replayed in my mind until replaced by the teenager's preoccupations about what the neighbors would think of her father's embarrassing uniqueness.

The bloody battle of Normandie had taken place.

452

Thanks to the ultimate sacrifice of lives from our troops at Dieppe, the Allies had learned what they needed to successfully attack a similar front, though the attack still resulted with the death of thousands and more wounded.

Cousin Paul who had joined since the beginning of the war, commanded the regiment Les Fusilliers Mont-Royal in Normandie. He came back to Saint-Eustache to take over his old post of député, congressman, won during his absence, in his name, by his brother Gustave, and his wife Luce. His brother in law and his squadron les Alouettes came back to Montréal, and were celebrated with a ticker tape parade.

Alas, for many others, the end of the war meant shattered hopes. The Thibodeau's son, Adrien was missing in action. Madame Thibodeau like thousands of other women read and reread the letter; nowhere did it say he had died. She refused to believe that her son would not return. No, her red haired son, a dare devil, at some point, at some time, from God knows where, would reappear.

Maman's good friend never wore mourning clothes, but her son never fulfilled her hopes. Sixty- three-years later, long after the parents passing, my dear friend Claudine, their daughter received the news that her brother's plane and his remains had been found in Holland. Wars do end on papers, but the wounds of wars remain in the heart of the living.

After the war, as in so many places, Saint-Eustache started a long transition to modernity; some of it painful for the citizens who appreciated nature and their heritage. Though the greater Saint-Eustache is now a town, the center of the village is now known as the old Saint-Eustache, all spruced up and charming.

CHAPTER SIXTY THREE
SUZANNE'S BURGEONNING

Suzanne may have had her own dreams; nonetheless, she had inherited a practical mindset from Maman. She planned. She dispersed small white envelopes among her clothes. One envelope contained a dollar bill, enough to buy two hot fudge sundaes a week. During her afternoon break she left the bank and crossed the street to the drug store.

The druggist, Monsieur Migneron, a man of few words and gestures, if not busy filling brown glass jars with not-too-pleasant-to-the-taste medicine, stood, immaculately, dressed in a white jacket behind the soda fountain and methodically filled a cup with the ingredients necessary to rejoice Suzanne's palate. Despite Monsieur Migneron's aloof personality, I like to imagine that he still enjoyed this interruption; few could resist Suzanne's outgoing personality and verve.

Beside the Hot Fudge-Sunday-money-cache there

were more envelopes. Another contained the amount for a thirty-minute voice lesson and her bus ticket to Montréal, another one for clothing, and if some money remained from her meager check, again she stored it away until it increased enough to buy something grand, or go into the bank.

Papa insisted that Maman accompanied Suzanne to her voice lessons. Dance, not singing, was Suzanne's first choice. "Only bad women danced and showed their legs." Papa had spoken.

My dear sister had the misfortune of being the oldest and the first to try to initiate some independence from the family. During the summer and winter months, she practiced every sport she could in Saint-Eustache. She invited friends at home to play cards and enticed Papa and Maman to join in. With the two of them involved, criticism of her friends or activities became minimal.

Nevertheless, as often as she could, she also escaped the house's four walls, and Papa's restrictions, by taking sewing night classes in Montréal He could not disapprove of this worthwhile knowledge, a must for a future *ménagère.* She took advantage of her stay in the city, away from his supervision, to join classes at the YMCA, an inappropriate place for a young lady, he would have argued.

Through the years, Suzanne developed a strong dislike for our father. She found him unjust, unreasonable, and at times phobic. Sadly, she also felt a growing resentment toward Maman for not standing up to him.

Neither of us knew the terrible toll that Papa's threat had on the way Maman led her life. In my young years, listening at a door, I had heard Uncle Georges telling Maman to stop crying because Louis threatened to take the girls away from her, there was more to the sentence but Cousin Jean had called me and I had to hurry away from where I should not have been. Yet, once the family moved back to Saint-Eustache, my fear abated: comfort, routine, and the familiar covered its memory.

I would know the full extent of my father's threat to Maman only a few months before her death. Even then, it took me some years to come to the realization of how much Maman must have disciplined herself and how much it affected the way she raised us. She kept us in the mold that would ensure her a home and a standing in society.

Suzanne would have loved to confront Papa; Maman would not let her. The permission to do this or that came from Maman interceding on our behalf.

A year before her marriage, Suzanne's long range saving's envelope must have burst out of its flap. Its small denominator bills surely had found their way to the bank, for in the third year of her work as a bank teller she invited Maman on a weekend cruise to Tadoussac. I marvel at how much she had saved from her pitiful salary and how generous she was; at eighteen years of age she could have bought so many things for herself.

Suz, Tillie's puppy

Suzanne & Francine

Suzanne & Francine at bank where they worked at 18

Suzanne and cousin Henrí

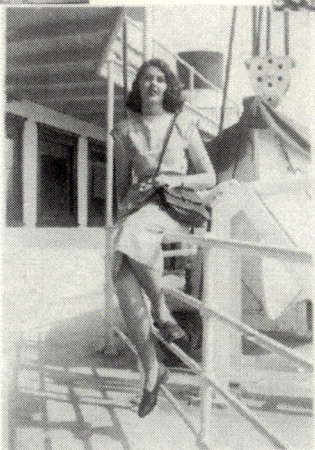

Tadoussac Cruise 1946
Suzanne & Maman

CHAPTER SIXTY FOUR

DEPARTURE

We stood at the bottom of the stairs saying goodnight, a last goodnight before I left home. We embraced. I knew I was taller than Maman, but suddenly her five-foot-four height seemed disproportionate to the authority she had as a mother and her need to protect me. We held each other closely.

She cried. "I will miss you."

I shed a tear. "I will miss you." I repeated.

She expected the same concern from me, needed to hear my words expressing sorrow at leaving home, especially at leaving her. Finally we said a last good night.

I climbed the stairs slowly, weighted down by a rush of contrasting feelings. I knew then that my sadness was only a visceral reaction to hers. I did not mind leaving.

Through the years, this detachment at leaving behind the known, the friendships, and family members I loved, puzzled me. Each time I wondered about my capacity for love and permanence. From the perspective of seasoned age and a cold honesty, I have little doubt that my need to move away came from a need to escape who I was—a person I did not like.

Moving distracted me, until I settled into a new environment. When all quieted down, I was still left with the same person.

At fifteen years of age, and on the eve of my first step into a different world, the thought of being lonely did not enter my mind; it was too filled with fantasies. Tomorrow I would move away from home toward a sliver of freedom.

In the morning, I said good-bye to Papa, and then Maman and I were on our way to Sainte-Geneviève de Pierrefonds. Monsieur Binette drove us to the train station, and in less than an hour we arrived at Roxboro. The train stopped in front of a shack in a field. I did not know what Roxboro itself looked like? Was it a village, or just a convenient place for the train to stop?

We walked on the side of the tracks to the road and waited for a bus. In the next three years I would become familiar with that area, traveling alone before and after holidays.

One memory, however, stands out.

It is nighttime, freezing cold; the snow like popping popcorn crackles under foot; the sky is steel blue, the stars bright, the white moon a disk of ice; Maman and I shiver.

She had come to see me in a Christmas play, a take on the story of the birth of Jesus, the general scene augmented by new personages taken from the Perrault's stories. I am the feared Blue Beard, and try to frighten the whole ménagerie. After lots of puffing and chest pumping, my heart softens. Angel like, I kneel down in adoration.

After the play, we wait for our train:,white breath escaping from our benumbed lips.

"Let's go into the shack," Maman says. "There is a stove." Indeed, a stove stands in a corner, but not a piece of wood can be found.

"Oh well," says Maman, "the train, should be here soon."

We stamp our feet on the frozen wood boards trying to force a rush of warm blood through our veins with no effect. Maman opens her handbag, takes out a large pill bottle, unscrews it and offers me a swallow of brandy. We laugh, feeling deliciously naughty.

Once in a while we peek outdoors hoping to see and hear a train moving toward us. After fifteen minutes a fox crosses the tracks, unconcerned. I can visualize its luxuriant tail around someone's neck, its little pinched mouth holding onto one of its legs like a huge hook closing a lady's collar. The poor dear is lying limp and so dead on the unfamiliar landscape of her bosom.

Fortunately, on the first day of my new life, September had spread its luxurious warmth. We walked along the tracks, crossed the street and waited for a bus to take us to the school. At the entrance to the village proper, a canopy of giant trees greeted us, a reassuring sight. The view of the church, presbytery, and school, all dressed in their severe gray stone and proper white trimming, was a staple of French Canadian landscapes going back to the beginning of the colony when the Seigneur, after building a mill and attracting a population, gave land to the clergy for building a school, a priest house and a place of worship. This catholic trio became the heart of each village.

The bus stopped in front of the convent: lawn, gravel, a

statue of Mary centered in a round of flowers; the outside accoutrement of a convent. We climbed the long staircase. A nun answered the doorbell. We walked into the century old building. I was familiar with the scent of old wood floors, stairs, and banisters, well scrubbed and worn into new shapes. I recognized the same statues; the same muffled sound of religious life.

A nun met us to direct Maman toward the office, and me to the dormitory. We embraced and said good-bye. She was on her way to drop a check for the first month of my schooling, and a ration book that would deprive her of my sugar, flour and butter provision. This was not the only sacrifice Maman would make to allow me a better education and the luxury of piano lessons and trips with my piano teacher to the Montréal symphony. I would learn about it later.

Unburdened by any worries, I followed the nun up three flights of stairs, and with a flight of rosy expectations.

At the last landing, I noticed an old piano.

We entered a large room, well lit, well scrubbed, and as white as an infirmary waiting for its first patient. A design in symmetrical form: a row of dormer windows, a row of cots, a walkway and a row of *cellules*, in this case

467

a French appellation for a one-person bedroom in a religious institution varying in degrees of human comfort. My room had a wall as background, two wood partitions, and serving as the fourth side, a curtain hanging from a rod. This would be my night domain for the next three years.

Not a geranium in sight, no stuffed animal or doll resting on a pillow, not a picture. It was bare and efficient. The dormitory served exclusively as a place for dressing, undressing, washing, sleeping and prayers before bedtime and early morning when knees came in contact with a cold floor. Though my *cellule* was small and sparse, I came to appreciate its privacy.

How would the girls sleeping in the row of un-curtained cots wash, dress, undress, and not expose themselves to their neighbors or to the fortunate *cellule* inhabitants across the walkway? The dear girls learned quickly to undress under their nightgowns—a task full of contortion; washing, not a happy procedure!

In the future, at nighttime or early morning, if on my way to the bathroom I happened to glance at the row of exposed boarders, I would see nightgowns swaying, a few heads and elbows pushing out the limits of a white garment's width; a row of little ghosts gingerly moving in a modesty dance.

The nun left me at my four-by-seven foot *cellule*. I unpacked my suitcase. One small bureau with three shelves contained my wardrobe. My good uniform would hang in a closet somewhere. A large porcelain washbowl and a pitcher sat on a cotton doily on top of the bureau. In 1945 it already looked like a relic from the past. Our weekly bathing in the claw foot bath tub would be a Saturday night affair, washing to be done also under a nightgown. As no one inspected the bath ritual I felt free to shed the virginal garment.

After arranging my toiletry and clothing in a way my mother would have praised, I took my music out, closed the suitcase and slid it under the bed. The nun had suggested that after I put my things away, I go to the recreation hall or outdoors in the yard: instead, music in hand, I made my way to the landing.

A piano had become, in our home, as necessary as a kitchen table: two pieces of furniture that for me spelled warmth, family and friendship. I secured my music on the stand and chose the last piece I had learned. The title escapes me, but I recall that the piece had rain as a motif; four pages of broken octaves; raindrops falling one at a time. After sixty-five years, I remember that by the end of the piece my right wrist needed rest. As for what was happening with the left hand, I have no mental picture of its travail.

In´the middle of the musical shower, I heard footsteps on the stairs, the familiar felt-like sounding steps of a nun burdened by layers of heavy skirts: rosary beads swaying in and out of the folds whispering their Ave Marias. After studying for eight years in a convent, my ears could discern the sound even through the patter of raindrops.

I kept playing, until I saw her from the corner of my right eye. She smiled at me. I smiled back at a face, not pretty, not young, but kind; two blue eyes looking through thick glasses.

"I am Sister Euphrasie," she said. "May I ask who you are?"

I introduced myself.

"Well, Marcelle," she said, "you are the first pupil I ever heard play when not obliged to practice."

This conversation was the beginning of a three-year relationship. There was another piano teacher, she told me, "but please ask for me."

Sister Euphrasie left, and I continued playing until I

470

exhausted my short repertoire. I returned to the dormitory, stored my music in my suitcase and went downstairs. After walking down many corridors and stopping to acknowledge a passing nun, I found my way to a door opening to the backyard.

The look of the yard, to my eyes, seemed to have been designed by the same person as the dormitory: a row of dormer windows, a row of beds, a walkway, and a row of cellule. And here in front of me stood a row of gravel, a row of grass, and the straight flow of the river, all clearly delineated. It is not surprising that the dear river flowed as fast as she could and had no time to form inlets where reeds, cattails and water lilies spread their beauty, their large leaves a landing pad for damselflies in distress.

I may have belittled the river that went by our recreation area. However, seven months later, on a day when spring refused to release its warmth, I remember being in a procession of forty warmly wrapped bodies, heads disappearing under felt hats and wool scarves, and eighty black stocking-covered legs, with as many feet buried in wool-lined-boots, all walking toward a bridge. Forty girls followed by one freezing nun who unsuccessfully fought a relentless wind billowing her long black skirt.

We spread across the bridge railing, like forty crows too frozen to caw, and watched a river of snow and ice slowly waking up to spring. A subterranean rumbling preceded the rupture of ice. The river woke up in a roar. Her freed waters gushed through crevasses. Her current celebrated its freedom, giving us the vertiginous impression of standing on the bow of a moving ship struggling against her unleashed power. Weakened ice floes, like ill fitting jigsaw puzzles, buckled against the undercurrents pressure; pieces climbed over one another, some upright like menacing icebergs; white walls of ice coming toward us, hurled themselves against the pillars in a deafening crash.

Unbeknown to me, fifteen years later, Maman would also follow the course of this river, La Rivière des Prairies; it would be the last river upon which her eyes would rest.

Marcelle15, at
boarding school

My school friends from
St-Eustache visiting at my
boarding school 1945

CHAPTER SIXTY FIVE

MAMAN ALONE

So many years have gone by since Maman left me at the boarding school. What was in her mind while I quickly forgot home, practiced on the landing, met my future piano teacher and afterward went outdoors to look at the playground, and the river. Knowing Maman, I believe that she felt more as if she had been the one left behind.

I imagine her alone waiting for the bus. It arrives. She enters and sits in front; she is barely ten minutes away from her next stop. She watches through the window; autumn is slow coming this year, only a few leaves have turned yellow, and the rest look tired, dusty, in need of a shower, a little bit like her she thinks. She is bone-tired. She has had too many loads to carry. She dragged her youngest girl through eight years of schooling, trying to keep that frolicking mind of hers focused long enough on a subject to master it, alas, with mediocre success.

Her mind skips to Suzanne, the studious one. She has not worried about her, maybe not enough, she regrets, she is already working, and will have little time to spend alone with me. Suzanne, the convivial, will invite friends, and boyfriends, while Louis quietly watches, criticizing.

The bus screeches to a stop. She steps down and walks along the tracks to the little shack.

On the train she looks inside her handbag, she finds her return ticket and leaves it in its safe compartment. She closes her handbag, and opens it immediately. Of course, the ration books are gone. She wonders how long the rationing will last. The war is over.

The train stops. Maman looks out, it is not her stop. The conductor goes by and picks up her ticket. She sits back and closes her eyes. She feels such emptiness. Slowly tears roll down her cheeks. She searches in her handbag for her handkerchief. "Marcelle will be back at the end of October for a weekend," she hears herself murmur, as if by speaking the thought out loud her child's presence is more palpable.

She sits straighter. She cannot let sorrow overcome

her.

She smiles. She sees the child her husband called P'tit Blond, and that silly Monsieur Binette called P'tit Gas when her head was shaved, the child who was so shy, and yet so mischievous. Another image presents itself. Six years old, Marcelle walks into the kitchen playing a concertina she picked-out of a trash can. She muffles a giggle in her handkerchief. The child is so thrilled with her find, that she fails to notice that every time she pulls and squeezes the concertina, pieces of lettuce and other salad components fall on her skirt and shoes. In that sad apartment there were still moments of levity, she likes to think.

Her mind cannot be duped so easily. It brings forward another picture frame of their lives cruelly reminding her that sadness had more of a hold in that dismal place than joy. She sees Marcelle cuddling with her trying to console her, she, the mother with the absent philandering husband, and with her oldest daughter away at boarding school. Her mind will not let her go easily, she now sees the child near death. She is alone with her twenty-four hours a day except for the doctors' visits. Suzanne is away at Berthe and Charlie's. She remembers the promise she made to God not to eat chocolate for two

477

years if he saved her child. Oh dear, how she yearned for chocolates, especially when two years in a row she filled her girls' Easter baskets. But, she kept her promise.

Her face lit up. That is what I have to do. Yes. If I can get enough sugar I will start a small business. First, I must serve chocolates to my friends when we play bridge, then maybe they will want some, and recommend me to their friends. I have been able to pay for Louis' silly roof. I will be able to pay for Marcelle's boarding school.

She feels lighter. She walks out of the train, finds a taxi and arrives home determined to make her first batch of chocolates first thing in the morning.

Maman does, and many more afterward, but that would not be enough to cover the complete cost of the boarding school. However, an offer she could not refuse comes her way. The husband of a niece has taken over a restaurant and remembered tasting her delicious pies.

"Aunt Margot, would you make the pies for the restaurant?" He asked her.

Louis could not stop her from doing that. After all, it is for a family member. She accepts.

At one of my visits, I saw Maman's pie production. What I did not know then, was that her labor helped pay the expenses of my boarding school. Many years later Suzanne told me how much she resented bringing those pies to the restaurant on her way to work. In summer, she piled them up in her bicycle basket, sheets of cardboard between each. In winter she carried them watching for treacherous patches of ice. In turn, she carried chocolate cream pies, lemon meringue pies, custard pies, raisin pies, apple pies, and multi fruit pies.

Not long ago, remembering that period, a cousin said, "Poor Aunt Margot, how humiliating it must have been for her."

Yes, women of our class were not supposed to work. Did Maman feel humiliated or was she proud that she could give her daughter a better education. And when Suzanne said to me, I resented delivering those pies, did she feel embarrassed? Why not, we were raised that way. If you belong to a certain class you were expected to behave in accordance with the standards of that class. In Saint-Eustache our cousins did not work, nor Maman's friends' daughters.

Papa could object to his daughters working; however, to act as if we were privilege did not pay the bills.

Maman's pride resided in her desire to be debt free and the caring of her family all the while never letting go of her lady-like demeanor.

Maman and Tellie

CHAPTER SIXTY-SIX

UNDER THE MOON

My first year at boarding school ended. Suitcase in hand I came back home ready to enjoy hours of tennis and swimming and Maman's good cooking. All those desires were fulfilled, but something unexpected was added to my summer schedule, and not for my enjoyment. The eight grades I had finished in Saint- Eustache did not include Latin and Algebra, so upon my arrival at the boarding school, I was put back in the same grade. After a month during which time I must have shown an unusual amount of scholarship I was promoted to the ninth grade with the understanding that I must pass the algebra test before entering the tenth grade.

Of course I had a whole school year to forget about it. Nevertheless, not only did my dear Maman remember it, but she had already hired a college student to give me instructions.

The young man was not attractive; Maman's intention was that I had no distraction, and learned so well that in the fall I would pass my exam with flying colors, proving that with some unattractive person at my elbow and nothing to distract me, my little brain could be quite efficient, and she was right. At my return I passed the exam with high marks.

Already a whole month of vacation had gone by. July had reached midway before my birthday—my sixteenth birthday, and the usual "sixteen never been kissed" or has she been, or will she be floated in the air like a subliminal propaganda slogan.

Maman circled the last day of the month in red, but so far, I could not imagine myself drawing a happy face in that circle.

Suzanne and I had no boyfriends—unless my sister kept hers a secret. Our only avenues to meet someone were the post office or the tennis club; nothing had appeared on the horizon and cousins were forbidden. Yet, my heart beat for cousin Jacques, and Suzanne's for cousin Henri. Maman and Aunt Gabrielle kept a vigilant eye on them, and Jacques kept me at arms' length.

Before the end of the month fate had a surprise for me; it offered me a dance under the auspices of the tennis club. Though I had a solid amateur's grip on most sport and should have been nimble on my feet, dancing remained a stranger. To release the control of myself to anyone, when I had no idea where the next step would take me, reinforced by the certainty I would look like a fool, kept me glued to my chair.

Of that evening my mind draws three tableaux. The outline of the first is barely sketched. How I found myself in the arms of a grayish, attractive stranger skips my mind. Who was he? An artist who lived on the lake, near the club, he told me. Stiff like a board, held so tightly that the imprint of my dress buttons probably stayed tattooed on his look-at-me torso, we stepped our way through the slow dance measure by measure of misery and ended up not far from the exit door. He seemed too interested in pursuing me. I needed a flight strategy. The benevolent god of oppressed dancers came along disguised as a young man standing alone. In an unusual bold move I asked him if he could walk out of the place with me. He agreed. We made our exit into the fresh air.

The next tableau I see clearly in my mind. Though the young man lives in the opposite direction he walks with me toward my home. Maman hurries ahead, far away enough to let us speak without being overheard.

"Let's join her, your mother should not be walking by herself." says Monsieur gallant. We do. Graciously, Maman returns the favor when we arrive home. She says good night, goes in the house, and we walk down the steps to the lower terrace.

You already know the décor of the third tableau: green lawn, giant elms, cement wall, benches, bird bath, pine tree, the river and yes, the obligatory moon sliding over the rippled water and embracing us. In all my years of dreaming of Prince Charming's entrance into my life with the appropriate décor, here it was a Hollywood Technicolor entrance. The rest, sweetly innocent: a kiss with more teeth than lips, but still, a kiss on the eve of my sixteenth birthday.

That such a little innocent kiss produced such an earthquake stunned me. My sixteen year-old body experienced a jolt that no convent-virginal-nightgown could contain. What would I do with those new feelings, that new knowledge? This must be the forbidden fruit, from which I could not take one more bite. And what did Maman say... *that boys always tell...*

All night long, the rattling in my poor mind went on and on. Sleep certainly came, for when I awoke, the moon had vanished, and a cruel sun shone on my confusion. My reflection in the mirror looked the same as before, and the moon glow I had seen on my face the night before had vanished in the harsh reality of daylight. Worse than the moon's disappearance, and the sun's disregard for my feelings, I feared that the church and my mothers' belief that good women do not experience such earthquake moments, meant I was a bad woman; someone abnormal. *Would he tell?*

Heavy hearted, I accomplished my chores, the day walking with me at a slow pace that despite the bicycling, and swimming, and lunch hour with dish washing took every minute to its full value, as if one second missed would alter what had happened or what was about to happen. Suzanne's return from work restored some normalcy as she always had some tale to tell. This time, she and her friend Francine, Francine annoyed at having men grabbing their hands at the bank window where they clerked, kept a ruler at hand. A little smile, a gentle *non, non, non*, and a ruler tap on the fingers never lost a customer. I marveled at how Suzanne could handle any situation.

Supper finished, dishes put away, white shorts on, and white skirts over, Suzanne and I were on our way to the tennis club. Will he be there? What will I do?

He was there. Shyness like a child's protective blanket clung to me. The boldness I experienced the night before, now foreign, left me with the familiarity of my true self, insecure and fearful. I could not imagine that he walked me home and kissed me because he found me attractive. No, he must think I am a fool. Maman must have been right, preaching to Suzanne and me that boys only want to kiss, they are not interested in *you* girls.

For the first time, and alas not the last I flew from the unknown of a new experience, a budding relationship. I walked away before being left behind. I would not look at him. I would ignore him. Against my heart, that is what I did, never thinking how hurtful it must have been to him.

In a few weeks I would go back to school: one year older, still immature in the affairs of the heart, yet, having had my first kiss, and by my own doing, losing sweet Monsieur gallant.

Manufactured by Amazon.ca
Bolton, ON